Ellen —

In recognition of
your outstanding efforts as
a Maverick Scholar, Fall 2000.
Good luck in the Spring!

Janette Kern
Coord. of Student
Success Programs

Transitions:

A Centennial History of
The University of Texas at Arlington

1895 - 1995

Transitions:

A Centennial History of
The University of Texas at Arlington

1895 - 1995

BY
GERALD D. SAXON

The UTA Press 1995

Library of Congress Catalog Card Number: 95-06113

ISBN 0-932408-19-2

For my family, Janis, Jared, and Jeffrey

Contents

Foreword

This history of The University of Texas at Arlington chronicles the evolution of an academic institution from its inception as Arlington College in 1895 to what we know today as UTA. It is a history written in terms of vision and values, individuals and events, social and economic forces, the politics of Texas, a few failures and many more successes. It is a history seen through the eyes of Gerald Saxon, an insightful historian and skilled writer.

A common thread runs through this history, and it is personified in a succession of strong-minded, determined believers in the value of education and in the importance of access to education. For nearly 100 years, generations of teachers, students, staff and friends of education have constituted academic communities that have endured, prospered and withstood the test of time.

In September 1895, Arlington College first opened its doors on a site near UTA's current Student Center. The impetus for the opening was Emmett Rankin, a merchant, and the first in a long line of citizens concerned about the quality of education, who would shape UTA's future. In 1902, James M. Carlisle took over Arlington College's facilities and began Carlisle Military Academy, an institution dedicated to "the literary, military and manual training of boys."

In 1917, the school evolved into Grubbs Vocational College, a branch of Texas A&M. The evolution continued with Grubbs Vocational College becoming North Texas Agricultural College in 1923 and Arlington State (ASC) in 1949.

During its eighteen years as Arlington State College, a series of fundamental changes occurred that laid the groundwork for modernday UTA. ASC went from junior to senior college status, became the first Texas A&M school to admit African Americans, added graduate level courses, and in 1965 moved from the Texas A&M System to The University of Texas System.

In 1974, Wendell Nedderman became president of The University of Texas at Arlington. During his twenty years as president, he had a profound influence on values, aspirations and programs of the university. He had the wisdom to know that one of the most important responsibilities of a university president is to listen. No individual has made a greater contribution to UTA than Wendell Nedderman. President Nedderman was succeeded by Ryan Amacher in 1992.

Ryan Amacher's tenure as president was a difficult time for him and for the university. The UTA academic community was unwilling to accept or support the vision of President Amacher and his Provost Dalmas Taylor. A management audit requested by UT System Chancellor William Cunningham revealed questionable administrative practices and financial decisions. This divisive period in UTA's history ended in the spring of 1995 with President Amacher's resignation and the removal of Provost Dalmas Taylor. On June 1, 1995, I became Interim President of UT Arlington, charged with the responsibility of restoring calm in the UTA academic community and helping the university return to its 100 year quest for excellence in teaching, research and service.

Robert E. Witt
August 14, 1995

Acknowledgments

The researching and writing of a book is often a collaborative process, and this one was no different. I am indebted to scores of people who helped in one way or another with this book. I was most fortunate during the four years I worked on this project to have the capable assistance of two bright and energetic graduate research assistants. Korin Schultz, from 1992-1994, conducted the research for chapters 1-6 before graduating with an M.A. in history and moving to Germany. Chris Ohan, a doctoral student in humanities, followed her on the project, compiling the research for chapters 7-8 and conducting the photograph/illustration research for the book. Without their dedication and commitment to the project, this book would not have been possible—at least by the 1995 deadline! I also want to thank Tom Wilding, director of libraries at UTA, for allowing me the flexibility to spend part of my work week in 1994-1995 writing at home. Tom was always understanding and supportive of the book project.

The staff members of the Special Collections Division of the UTA Libraries deserve special mention because it was they who had to compensate for my absences from the office while I worked on the book. They handled increased responsibilities and more reference desk assignments with seeming ease and no complaints. Each staff member—Maritza Arrigunaga, Jane Boley, Katherine Goodwin, Sally Gross, Betsey Hudon, Marcelle Hull, Bonnie Lindly, Shirley Rodnitzky, Jerry Stafford, Holly Wells, and Betty Wood—has my gratitude and admiration. In addition, I want to single out Jane Boley, university archivist, for working diligently with her students collecting and processing the school's archival records and cheerfully answering any questions that I or the graduate research assistants asked. Betty Wood, the division's senior secretary, deserves special recognition for the way she competently transformed my less than neat handwritten drafts into an electronic format and then making what must have seemed like endless revisions to the electronic version. I am also grateful to Sally Gross, the department head in the division, for keeping the division functioning smoothly and professionally during my absences.

Students in my graduate public history class on oral history methods and techniques, held in the spring of 1994, increased through their hard work the number of oral history interviews available in the university archives. Each student successfully researched, conducted, and transcribed an interview focusing on the university, and these oral accounts have been vital in helping me understand the university and its past. The oral history students were Rebekah Bandy, Elizabeth Bigham, Mike Brown, Richard Culbertson, June Dalrymple, Dan Griffith, Chandler Jackson, John Konzal, Allen Langford, Diana Mays, Donald Mitchell, Wayne Nichols, Eric Oglesby, Neil Simmons, Susan Smith, Jerry Stafford, and Oren Truitt. Though I never had the pleasure of knowing Duncan Robinson, I am deeply indebted to him for the research and interviews he conducted on the school's history in the early 1970s.

A number of people read various drafts of this book and offered suggestions, clarifications, and revisions. Among these were Ryan Amacher, Jane Boley, Jenkins Garrett, Frank Harrison, Wendell Nedderman, Elwood Preiss, Dalmas Taylor, and Jack Woolf. Mike Hazel, a friend and colleague in Dallas, read the initial drafts for style and grammar, and the book is the better for it. Of course, any mistakes in interpretation and fact are mine alone.

The beauty and eye-catching layout of the book is directly attributable to Carol (Milliren) Lehman of the Media Services' staff. Carol's sensitivity to and talent for design are apparent on every page and, in many ways, the book is as much hers as mine. Several of Carol's colleagues in Media Services also played significant roles in producing the book, including Anna Lou Busboom, who digitized the illustrations used in the book; Robert Crosby and Joel Quintans, who took a number of the color photographs and worked diligently in the darkroom; and Bob Cook, who supported the project by lending it his staff's considerable talents and expertise. Reggie Moon of Campus Printing provided valuable assistance in facilitating the book's printing.

Finally, I want to recognize and give heartfelt thanks to a group of people who rarely receive recognition—my family. It is my wife, Janis, and my sons, Jared and Jeffrey, who through their love, support, and understanding make projects like this centennial history possible.

Preface

I came to The University of Texas at Arlington (UTA) in October 1986 to serve as assistant director for special collections in the university libraries and teach history on an adjunct basis. Not long after I arrived on campus, Jane Boley, university archivist and a staff member in the Special Collections Division, told—perhaps warned—me that UTA would be one hundred years old in the fall of 1995. Frankly, I knew nothing of UTA's history and was surprised by this news. Could UTA *really* be one hundred so soon, I asked myself? Boley went on to suggest that with the school's centennial only nine years away, the university *should* begin planning for the research and writing of a school history. She also suggested that an industrious history graduate student looking for a thesis topic might make an ideal author. New to campus and unable to see beyond next week, much less nine years in the future, I listened politely to her, but did nothing.

For the next few years, Boley periodically reminded me of the upcoming anniversary. Still, burdened with administrative and teaching responsibilities, I took no action. By 1990, however, Boley's comments had convinced me to talk with then director of libraries Charles B. Lowry about the centennial and the need of the university to begin planning for the occasion. In Lowry's office, he and I agreed to volunteer—yes, volunteer!—to write UTA's history. Thinking back now, some five years later, it must have been a weak moment for both of us. We believed that a book on the university's first one hundred years would be "fun" to do in a masochistic sort of way. We were both library administrators, historians, and friends, and a project like this one would give us a chance to work together, sharpen our skills as researchers and writers, and, most importantly, learn more about UTA and make a real contribution to the institution. And since we were both relative newcomers to campus (Lowry having come the year before me), we thought we could be objective in our research and writing. In short, we had no axes to grind.

Buoyed by the sense of excitement that one gets after deciding to do a project not due for five years, Lowry and I enthusiastically wrote a memo in March 1990 to Peter Van't Slot, vice president for development and university relations, urging him and President Wendell Nedderman to appoint a committee to plan centennial activities. We also volunteered to do the centennial history, provided the university fund a graduate research assistant for the project. A year later, President Nedderman appointed the committee, and planning for a centennial celebration began in earnest. As part of its planning, the centennial committee recommended that a history be written, and it accepted Lowry's and my offer to write it. The committee also proposed that the administration provide us a research assistant and the funds necessary to publish the book. From the beginning, President Nedderman was an enthusiastic supporter of the project, as was his successors, Ryan C. Amacher and Robert E. Witt. They provided the support and funds necessary to complete this book.

Unfortunately for me, however, Lowry left UTA in 1992 for Carnegie Mellon University in Pittsburg, Pennsylvania. Not having the guts to back out and still intrigued with the notion of writing the university's history, I decided to tackle the book without him. During the book project, I was fortunate to have the opportunity to work with two of UTA's talented graduate students, Korin Schultz and Chris Ohan. Both served as graduate research assistants on the project. Without them this book would have been impossible. They conducted the basic research, chased after hard-to-find facts and illustrations, challenged my conclusions, proofread the text, and prodded me to complete the volume.

The research for this book was guided by four underlying assumptions. First, I wanted to write a *history* of the university, not a public relations piece. My intention was to cover what happened in the past and try to explain, based on the surviving sources, why it happened. During the research and writing process, no one at any time tried to influence or change my interpretation of past events. And since this is a history, I decided to include the scholarly conventions of end notes and a complete bibliography for anyone wanting to verify my sources.

Second, my intent has been to concentrate on university-wide events and trends—the forest rather than the individual trees. Consequently, this is not a history of a particular college or department on campus, but a chronicle of the life of the institution as a whole. Third, I wanted the book to be read and enjoyed, so I decided early on that it should be heavily illustrated, with photographs, maps, and side bar information included to complement the text and, at times, introduce topics not covered in the narrative. Last, I planned to organize the book around the eight different name changes the university had undergone because each change represented a significant transition in the school's history.

The book includes eight chapters. Chapter one, "Good Schools Make Good Towns," covers 1895-1902, the Arlington College years. These years were difficult ones for the struggling private academy that would eventually evolve into the university we know today. The second chapter, "A High-Grade Preparatory School for Manly Boys," focuses on James McCoy Carlisle and his efforts to operate the Carlisle Military Academy from 1902-1913. The next chapter, "One of the Best and Safest Places in Texas for Boys," covers the years 1913-1917, when the school was known first as Arlington Training School and then Arlington Military Academy. Chapter four is entitled "A Hard Road to Travel" and deals with Vincent W. Grubbs' successful efforts to establish a state-supported agricultural and mechanical junior college called Grubbs Vocational College, an affiliate of Texas A&M. "Northaggieland," chapter five, focuses on 1923-1949, the period the school was named North Texas Agricultural College and its students were the "junior aggies." Chapter six, "We Are at the Crossroads," examines the momentous changes that occurred at Arlington State College from 1949-1967, a period which saw the school evolve from a junior college to a graduate-level institution and leave the A&M system for the University of Texas system. The last two chapters, "A Positive Slope Institution" and "Change Is Hard," cover the UTA years, bringing the narrative up to 1995.

In working on a book like this one, an author gains a greater appreciation for archivists and librarians and the work that they do. Working behind the scenes to collect, preserve, describe, catalog, and provide access to vast amounts of information, these individuals make research possible and even pleasurable. The first three chapters of the book are noticeably shorter than the rest because relatively few sources are extant for the years the school operated as a private academy. Unfortunately for researchers interested in the school's history, the academies did not have a librarian or archivist on staff, and, as a result, there was no one to systematically collect the records and publications of the institution. This changed when the school became state-supported in 1917. Today, the university's archives are professionally cared for and located in the library's Special Collections Division. These archives now include an impressive and diverse range of sources, from student newspapers and publications to the office files of university officials, and from oral history interviews to university reports, self-studies, and budgets. All of these sources—and many located outside of the university—were examined for this history.

As the title *Transitions: A Centennial History of The University of Texas at Arlington, 1895-1995* implies, the focus of the book is on the many changes the university has experienced. Some of these changes have been embraced by the university community, others not. Some have been perceived as good, others not so good. My goal has been to describe these transitions objectively and honestly. As anyone who has studied history knows, the historian's craft blends the scientist's search for verifiable "facts" with the literary writer's use of the imagination to interpret these "facts." Since the historian cannot replicate the past in a laboratory, he will never *really* know what happened in the past and why. Instead, he will—or at least should—examine all of the available evidence and render an interpretation based on it. That is what I have done in this book. In this process, I have tried to keep these words of historian Walter Prescott Webb firmly in mind: "The historian whose work is to stand the test must deal with facts as if they were remote, with people as if they were no longer living, with conditions as they are or were and not as they should have been." That has been my intent with this book, but only the reader can decide whether I have succeeded.

FORT WORTH

ARLINGTON COLLEGE.

ARLINGTON, TEXAS.

This Certifies that _____ is the owner of _____ Shares of the Capital Stock of

ARLINGTON COLLEGE,

transferable only on the books of the Corporation by the holder hereof in person or by Attorney upon surrender of this Certificate properly endorsed

In Witness Whereof, the said Corporation has caused this Certificate to be signed by its duly authorized officers and to be sealed with the Seal of the Corporation this _____ day of _____ A.D. 190__

Shares $50.00 Each.

CHAPTER ONE

Good Schools Make Good Towns

Arlington in 1895 was a small North Texas town with a population of approximately 1,000. Located between the rapidly growing cities of Dallas and Fort Worth in eastern Tarrant County, Arlington was rural and relaxed, possessing an identity of its own. At the time, it had no hard surface streets, only three churches, and a number of businesses clustered on and around Main Street. According to an 1894 Arlington business directory, the town's residents were "enterprising" and "conservative." They were also primarily young married couples with children to raise. In fact, the residents' median age was a youthful twenty, and one-third of the population was under ten. Like many towns its size just before the turn of the twentieth century, Arlington desired growth and viability. In the eyes of many of its town leaders, one important component to foster this growth was adequate schools, something Arlington lacked at the time. It was the push to provide quality education for the town's school children that led to the founding of Arlington College, the school from which the University of Texas at Arlington (UTA) traces its beginning.[1]

Relatively little is known about Arlington College. It was a private school which opened in September 1895 on a site near the present UTA student center, approximately one mile southwest of the town at the time. In today's terms it was not a college at all, but rather a school for children in primary, intermediate, and secondary grades. The impetus for building and opening the school came from Edward Emmett Rankin, a prominent Arlington merchant. In the spring of 1895, Rankin urged the two co-principals of the Arlington Public School, Lee Morgan Hammond and William M. Trimble, to start a private school in the town. Rankin was convinced that such a school would offer Arlington parents a welcome alternative to the ill-equipped and underfunded public school, then located on South Street in the eastern part of the town. At the time, the public school in Arlington comprised District 48 of the county school system and had an enrollment of 365 pupils and a staff of 6 teachers.[2]

Rankin was the father of five children, one of whom, Rebecca, his oldest, taught in the public school. He knew the problems of the school firsthand, and he wanted another option for his school-age children. In addition, Rankin was a respected Arlington business leader, the first justice-of-the-peace in the town, and a civic booster who, among other things, donated money and land to build the

1.1 John W. Ditto not only helped put the city of Arlington on the map, but he was also an important community supporter of Arlington College which, on this 1895 map of Tarrant County, is symbolized by a rendering of its main building and the label "college." Although the school grew under the direction of citizens like Ditto, Arlington College faced financial trouble in early 1900 when college trustees were forced to sell stock to help maintain the school.

First Christian Church. Rankin convinced Hammond and Trimble to start the private school and to invest $500 apiece in the venture. To raise additional money for the school, the two educators sold fifteen $100 scholarships to parents of students and to community leaders. Rankin probably helped the two men raise money for the school as well because the early contributors to Arlington College reads like a local "who's who": Brent and Horace Copeland, John Bowman, John Barden, John Watson, Woods and Art Collins, J. D. Cooper, James Ditto, and M. H. Cravens. The Ditto and A. W. Collins families provided the land for the college, and the two-and-a-half story wood school building was built by a local firm owned by C. F. Thomas at a cost of $5,000. Rankin, Thomas Spruance, and W. C. Weeks sold the hardware, lumber, and other building supplies for construction at cost. The frame structure had four classrooms on the ground floor and two on the second floor along with an assembly room. There was no indoor plumbing.[3]

Hammond and Trimble seemed the ideal team to start the private school. Hammond was born in Alabama in 1869, the second child of James Knox Polk Hammond and Malinda Youngblood Hammond. In 1876, the Hammonds moved from Randolph County, Alabama, to North Texas, eventually buying an eighty-acre farm in Tarrant County, about two miles west of Euless.

Hammond spent his early years on the farm, starting school at Bedford in 1878. Three years later, he attended the newly opened Bedford College, where W. H. Kimbrough, a teacher, took special interest in him. In 1888, Kimbrough convinced Hammond's father to allow his son to attend school in Arlington, where Kimbrough was now teaching. So that he could go to school in Arlington in the fall, Hammond offered a pony to a young man to work in his place on the family farm. To raise the money to board in Arlington, Hammond went door-to-door in town and the surrounding rural communities selling sermons. After attending school in Arlington for two years and two summer normal schools, Hammond passed a teacher's examination and received a teaching certificate.[4]

Hammond began his teaching career in 1890 at the age of twenty-one, teaching

1.2 Little more than a railway stop between Dallas and Fort Worth, Arlington had a population of nearly 1,000 in 1895. The town was known for its mineral well located at the intersection of Main and Center streets.

for six months at Forest Hill in Tarrant County. During the remainder of the year, Hammond helped his father on the farm. The next fall he taught at a one-room school near Grapevine and, in 1892, at Marine Common School Number 20 in North Fort Worth. Despite having a contract to return to the Marine School in 1893, Hammond decided to join a number of his old schoolmates from Bedford College who were going to Sam Houston Normal Institute in Huntsville, Texas, to continue their education. One of his friends going to Huntsville was Trimble.

Trimble had been born on June 11, 1868, in Tarrant County, Texas. The son of Green B. Trimble and Annie Morrow Trimble, young William spent his childhood on the family's farm some twelve miles east of Fort Worth. Trimble attended the public schools in eastern Tarrant County and then Bedford College after it opened in 1881. In 1893, he accompanied Hammond and other friends to Huntsville for teacher training.

Trimble and Hammond returned to Tarrant County in the fall of 1894 and became co-principals of the Arlington Public School. They made up the school's faculty along with Bena Kelly, who had been valedictorian of their class at Sam Houston Normal Institute. At the public school, Hammond and Trimble attracted the attention of Rankin, who convinced them to invest time, money, and expertise to start a private school for students of all ages.[5]

1.3 Known as the father of Arlington College, Edward Emmett Rankin, pictured with hat and cigar at center, also ran a grocery and hardware store on East Main Street.

Arlington College offered classes from the first grade through high school. At this time, the tenth grade was the last grade in high school. Being a private school, the college charged tuition on a sliding scale based on a student's grade level, from $1.50 per month for a child in the lower grades to $3.50 per month for a secondary school student. The school's faculty included six teachers. Hammond, Trimble, and H. L. Graham taught academic subjects, such as Latin, history, algebra, geometry, grammar, reading, literature, and government, and Molly McDonald, Sally Hayter, and Frue Lanier taught courses in art, music, elocution, and penmanship. Hammond and Trimble also served as the college's co-principals.[6]

Approximately seventy-five students attended Arlington College during its first year and, based on photographic evidence, it appears that the student body grew to 120 in 1896-1897 and 150 in 1897-1898. The college's first commencement exercises were held May 25-27, 1898, with the first night devoted to the class completing grammar school, the second night to an "elocutionary contest," and the third to the awarding of diplomas to two graduating high school students. The salutatorian of the high school class was Lillie McKinley, who spoke on the topic "Women of History and Women of Today." William P. McGinnis delivered the valedictory address entitled "Education." The *Arlington Journal*, the town's weekly newspaper, covered the college's graduation and annual closing ceremo-

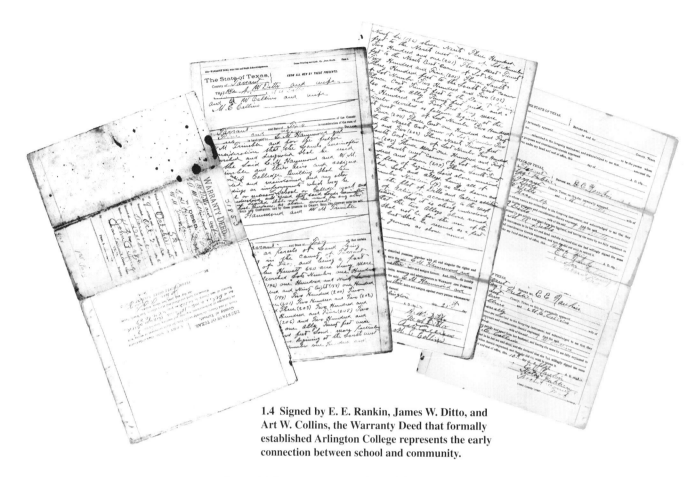

1.4 Signed by E. E. Rankin, James W. Ditto, and Art W. Collins, the Warranty Deed that formally established Arlington College represents the early connection between school and community.

nies, which were open to the public and generally well attended. In May 1900, four students comprised the college's high school graduating class.[7]

Not everyone supported the college, as the following children's rhyme, which pitted the college with another local private school, indicates:

> *Pocket full of rocks,*
> *Head full of knowledge.*
> *I'd rather go to Miss Patty's school,*
> *Than anybody's college.*

Arlington College had a rocky seven-year existence, as its fate became intertwined with the volatile debate over the need to adequately fund public education in the town. During Arlington College's second year of operation, Hammond and Trimble, feeling more and more community pressure, agreed to provide space for public school students in the college for five months and then charge those who stayed after that tuition for the balance of the school year. Hammond, along with the principal of the Arlington Public School, W. W. Witt, called on the parents of each student in the district to explain the options and help them to reach a decision for their children. To compensate Arlington College and its backers for adding public students for part of the school year, the college received two-thirds of the town's public education funds. Arlington College and the town continued this system through 1900. This accommodation to public education must have proven unsatisfactory to Hammond and Trimble because in 1898 Trimble sold his interest in the school to W. M. Glass for $1,000 and, two years later, both Hammond and Glass sold theirs to the "citizens of Arlington" for a like amount.[8]

At the time of the sale in 1900, the Arlington College Corporation was estab-

1.5 Lee Morgan Hammond, cofounder of Arlington College, c. 1898.

lished to administer, fund, and help run the college, with W. W. Franklin appointed president and C. A. Wright his assistant. Franklin came to Arlington from Dallas, where he had operated the Lone Star School of Oratory. Among the trustees of the corporation were A. J. Rogers, president; M. H. Cravens, vice-president; W. C. Weeks, secretary; A. W. Collins; and R. W. McKnight. Stock in the corporation was sold in an attempt to save the college. Advertisements for the college listed twenty-five stockholders for the corporation. These same ads emphasized the college as "financially solid" and "not a cheap institution," and appealed to students of "both sexes" to attend. *The Arlington College Exponent* in 1901 described the college as being divided into four departments: primary, preparatory, academic, and collegiate. It also listed faculty members and their responsibilities as being Emma S. Culbertson, principal of the Primary Department; Franklin, president and professor of literature, rhetoric, and oratory; L. J. Hancock, professor of Greek, higher mathematics, and teacher of bookkeeping; and Wright, professor of Latin and modern languages. Room and board was only $10 a month, and tuition—and the advertisements were a bit vague here—was "as low as in any first-class college in the South."9

While Arlington College struggled to make a go of it under Franklin's leadership, debate on public education and the adequacy of the Arlington Public School continued to rage. In June 1901, Arlington voters defeated a proposition which would have removed the administration of the school from a board of trustees and placed it with the city. Just before this vote, the school's three trustees declared the school building "unsafe and wholly unfit" and refused to hire teachers for the coming fall until something could be done about it.10

This problem was solved—temporarily at least—in August when Arlington mayor Weeks called a "mass meeting" to discuss the education question and arrive at a solution to the school building problem. Mayor W. C. Weeks did not mince words in his call for the meeting, saying, "The public school building is inadequate and unfit for school purposes, and the present condition of affairs as regards the city schools is a burning shame and a disgrace to the place. All persons who have the welfare of the town and schools at heart and who are not too weak-kneed to get up and speak out . . . are respectfully invited to be present. . . ." Harry O. Johnston, owner of the *Arlington Journal* at the time, also called for community action. The solution, which was approved by the school trustees, called for the rental of the Arlington College building for public school purposes for a sum of $350. The college did retain one room and one teacher, J. E. Rogers, while the remainder of the building was used for the school year which began on September 16.11

1.6 William M. Trimble, co-founder of Arlington College.

1.7 Shortly after the land for Arlington College was donated in May 1895, work began on the school's first building. The structure, later known as Fish Hall, was ready when classes began the following fall.

This was, at best, a temporary solution to a nagging problem. Johnston's *Arlington Journal* editorialized that renting the college and preventing it from offering a full schedule of classes would essentially be the college's death knell. The newspaper wrote, "Of course we must have a free school, but we think the private school is an essential adjunct to the public school. . . ." The paper also came out strongly in favor of an independent school district with the capacity to tax and issue bonds to finance the construction of a new brick building. Throughout the 1901-1902 school year, the *Arlington Journal* pressured for school reform, arguing, "Good schools make good towns; no schools, no town. Which will you take? Let's have the good school."[12]

The newspaper's editorials mirrored the sentiments of the town, as was evidenced by the outcome of an election held on April 5, 1902, to decide whether to create an independent school district for Arlington. Voters passed the proposition by a three-to-one margin, recommending the creation of an incorporated district and electing seven trustees in the process. The trustees elected were: B. F. Bridges, J. I. Carter, J. H. Watson, Joseph Finger, M. R. Collins, R. W. McKnight, and Thomas Spruance. As a result of the election, the Texas legislature, a year later, validated the election creating the Arlington Independent School District. Later in the spring of 1902, Arlington voters approved a $12,000 bond issue for school construction recommended by the new school board. The foundation upon which quality public education could be offered to Arlington school children had finally been laid.[13]

As was the case with public education, progress towards revitalizing private education in Arlington was also made in 1902. This progress, however, came only after Arlington College's demise. The *Arlington Journal* had correctly predicted the end of the college, when its facilities were used to accommodate the public school for the 1901-1902 year. Indeed, on July 3, 1902, the Arlington College Corporation, with Cravens now its president, deeded its property to W. M. Dugan, Ditto, and Watson. Simultaneous with the close of the college came the news that these and other town leaders had reached an agreement with James M. Carlisle to open a military school in the fall on the grounds of Arlington College. For the first time in the town's short history, Arlington residents could now look forward to adequately funded public and private schools.[14]

1.8 Opening in 1895 with only seventy-five students, Arlington College had grown to approximately one hundred fifty by 1898.

Edward Emmett Rankin

1.9 Edward Emmett Rankin.

In some ways, Edward Emmett Rankin can rightfully be called the "father of Arlington College," for it was he who convinced Lee Morgan Hammond and William M. Trimble to start the private school in 1895. Rankin was a southerner by birth, having been born on October 23, 1840, on a farm in Davidson County, Tennessee, near Andrew Jackson's homestead, the Hermitage. Rankin was the son of King and Rebecca Rankin. In October 1862, Rankin enlisted in the Confederate Army for three years, serving as a private in Company B in the Fourth Regiment of Tennessee Cavalry under General Nathan Bedford Forrest. In July 1864, he was taken as a prisoner of war near Atlanta, Georgia, and sent to Camp Chase in Ohio, where he remained a prisoner until the war's end.

Rankin married Edna Jerusha Broiles and they reared a family of five children: Rebecca, Wilson, Emmett Edward, Wallace, and Sue. Rankin moved to the Arlington area in 1874, settling southeast of town on what is now Arkansas Lane. Eight years later, he moved into town and opened the Rankin Hardware Company, which stocked everything from farm implements, stoves, tinware, glassware, guns, sewing machines, and fishing tackle to "staple and fancy groceries." Rankin was the first justice-of-the-peace in Arlington and was called "Squire" Rankin by many residents.

Rankin was civic-minded and strived to make Arlington a better place to live. He donated two lots at the southeast corner of Mesquite and South streets for a site for the First Christian Church. Rankin was also a Mason and a strong supporter of quality education. His oldest daughter, Rebecca, attended Sam Houston Normal Institute in Huntsville, Texas, from 1885-1887 and returned to Arlington and taught at the public school for four years. Rankin realized that the Arlington Public School was underfunded, poorly equipped, and not likely to be improved anytime soon. Because of this belief, Rankin wanted to see a school open in Arlington modelled after the Webb School, a private academy in Bell Buckle, Tennessee, with which he was familiar. Such a school, he believed, could offer Arlington parents a quality alternative to the public school.

In 1894, Rankin recruited Hammond and Trimble to start such a school in the town. The school, Arlington College, opened in the fall of 1895 and operated for seven years. Rankin supported the school financially and sent his two youngest children, Wallace and Sue, to school there. In about 1899, Rankin left Arlington to start an apple orchard near Canyon, Colorado, and, a few years later, moved to West Orange, California, where he spent the rest of his life. He died in June 1911.

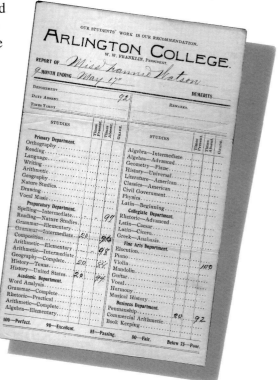

1.10 Whether or not Miss Fannie Watson represented the typical student at Arlington College, this undated report card does reveal the different school-age groups that attended the school: primary, preparatory, and collegiate, or ninth and tenth grade level.

CHAPTER TWO

A High-Grade Preparatory School for Manly Boys

When James McCoy Carlisle arrived in Arlington in 1902 to revive what was once Arlington College, he brought with him impeccable credentials as an educator and a consuming ambition to build a private military academy in North Texas. Born on May 11, 1851, in Coffee County, Tennessee, Carlisle was reared and educated in the Deep South. He received his A.B. in 1875 from Beech Grove College in Tennessee; an honorary A.M. three years later from Emory College in Oxford, Georgia; and an LL.D. degree from the University of Nashville. Before coming to Texas in 1880, Carlisle had headed the Mathematics Department at Beech Grove for a year and served as the college's president for slightly more than two years. It was in Texas, however, where Carlisle established his reputation as a noted educator.[1]

Once in Texas, Carlisle held a number of high profile positions before the turn of the century, including superintendent of public schools in Whitesboro, Corsicana, and Fort Worth; state superintendent of public instruction; president of the Texas State Teachers Association; and founder of private schools in Whitesboro and Hillsboro. As a result of his professional record, when Carlisle announced his intention to take over the old Arlington College grounds and facilities to open a private military academy, there was much enthusiasm and excitement in town. Indeed, Carlisle, by 1902, had established himself as one of the leading educators in the state, and he was bringing his statewide reputation and considerable expertise to Arlington. The school that he opened, Carlisle Military Academy, operated from fall 1902 through the spring of 1913 and developed into one of the state's better known military schools.[2]

The school opened on September 16, 1902, and, for the first year, was called Carlisle's School for Boys, a misnomer since the school accepted girls. Prior to opening the school, Carlisle had received a tentative deed to the school's land from the citizens of Arlington as well as a commitment by the townspeople to build a dormitory on the school grounds. The dormitory, officially called Arlington Hall but popularly known as the South Barracks, was completed just before opening day. The new dorm was located about where Preston Hall now stands, and provided space for thirty cadets, a dining hall, and a residence for the superintendent. Carlisle and his staff greeted forty-eight students on the school's inaugural day, a number which increased to seventy-one by the close of the school term

2.1 Attending Carlisle Military Academy was more than a dream for many young women. While the academy "officially" accepted only boys, there were at least eight female graduates during the school's eleven-year existence.

in May 1903. Of these students, twenty-five boarded on campus, while forty-six were "local" students who lived at home or with relatives in the Arlington area.[3]

During the fall of 1903, Carlisle secured a charter from the State of Texas incorporating the school as the Carlisle Military Academy. According to the charter, the school existed for the "purpose of conducting an educational institution for the literary, military, and manual training of boys. . . ." The charter also empowered Carlisle to accept "a limited number of girls" under rules and regulations adopted by the school's superintendent. The charter listed three directors: Rev. W. B. Fitzhugh, Carlisle's wife, and his daughter, Mary. Carlisle himself served as the school's superintendent and essentially ran the academy. Initially no capital stock was issued, but the corporation did have the authority to secure land and property to "properly operate the school."[4]

The school reflected Carlisle's educational philosophy, which emphasized balancing intellectual work with military training to produce well-rounded, disciplined students. The school's announcements stressed that the academic training the students received would prepare them for entrance into the finest colleges in the country, while the military regimen would instill in them "order, patience, punctuality, cheerful obedience, respect for one's superiors, and a sense of duty, honor, and manliness." These last traits presumably were not meant for the female students. Carlisle stressed the differences between public schools and military academies, saying, "In the public school, left to himself to regulate his course of study, and exposed to the innumerable temptations of society and good fellowship, the pupil unconsciously or needlessly loses valuable time. In a military school, life is as regular as clockwork. Not only recitation and drill, but also recreation, study, and even sleep have their allotted hours."[5]

2.2 After moving from Hillsboro to Arlington, James M. Carlisle erected this wood-frame structure, the second building on campus. The different age groups and genders reveal the diversity of the 1902-1903 student body.

The school accepted students ten to eighteen years old and placed them into grades roughly equivalent to today's fifth through tenth grades. The first two grades, fifth and sixth, were considered preparatory for the high school work to follow. The students in these grades took courses in arithmetic, geography, English, spelling, letter writing, and penmanship. By the time students reached the seventh grade—what the school labelled the "first academic year"—they were taking a mix of required courses, such as English, grammar, composition, algebra, and geography, and electives, such as Latin, modern language, and elementary science. In the eighth grade, or "second academic year," the requirements were English literature, English readings, the history of English writers, composition, plane geometry, and ancient history. Electives included modern language, civil government, commercial arithmetic, and "Julius Caesar books I and II." In the ninth grade, students were required to take solid geometry and trigonometry, English literature, composition, and English history. Latin, Greek, modern language, and "commercial branches" (bookkeeping, shorthand, typing, commercial law) were the only electives offered. During the "fourth academic year," or tenth grade, all students took physics, English literature, composition, and U.S. history, and, for an elective, could choose either higher algebra, modern language, commercial law, or political economy. Classes in military science and tactics were taught, and military drill was a daily affair for the boys. The curriculum did evolve and change over the school's eleven year history, but mostly for the high school students. Gradually, subjects such as chemistry, geology, and botany were added as required courses and more electives, especially foreign languages, were offered.[6]

Tuition for the year was $245.00 (later raised to $300.00), plus an additional $30.05 for uniforms, and could be paid in quarterly installments. Cadets were required to be in uniform at all times. The uniform most often worn was an army regulation khaki for field drill. For academic class and parades, cadets wore their "blues and grays," consisting of a blue shirt and cap, gray trousers, and black dress shoes. On formal occasions an all-white uniform was worn. In addition to a uniform fee, an application fee of $25.00 was added beginning in the fall 1906. With payment of the fees, Carlisle insisted that parents give his staff "complete authority" over the students while they were in school. In the school's promotional literature, the commandant, as Carlisle was called by the cadets, encouraged parents to write the staff with suggestions and ideas, but to leave decisions regarding the students to the faculty because "we are in a better position than you can possibly be to determine the details of our work." Carlisle encouraged parents to send their children $.50 a week in spending money, but the money was to be dispensed by the school. Moreover, the school warned parents not to send boxes of "rich edibles" or other "deleterious articles of food," such as cookies, candies, and cakes, to the students. Tobacco was strictly prohibited for students and staff because Carlisle found it "injurious," "loathsome," and "repulsive." Carlisle made it clear that the school was not a reformatory for "evil boys." Enrollment was limited to twenty-eight students per teacher. Carlisle's advertisements assured parents that Arlington was a "Christian community" with no saloons and a populace which was "intelligent, progressive, and refined." The promotional literature also promised buildings that were well lighted and ventilated, desks for each

2.3 Although Carlisle Military Academy accepted some female students, the academy's *Announcement* for 1911-1912 billed the school as a "A High-Grade Preparatory School for Manly Boys."

2.4 Explaining required military training at the academy, Carlisle wrote, "There is no other system by which are instilled so thoroughly, order, patience, punctuality, cheerful obedience, respect for one's superiors, and a sense of duty, honor, and manliness." Pictured here are the Carlisle Military Academy commissioned officers for 1905-1906.

2.5 While Colonel Carlisle was described as a strict disciplinarian, his wife was called the social leader of the academy. Mrs. Carlisle was responsible for organizing dances and other festivities during each term. Here Colonel and Mrs. Carlisle are pictured in the garden in front of their home, which also served as the school's mess hall.

student, "hyloplate blackboards," and athletic fields.[7]

The school's teachers were another selling point. Carlisle always seemed able to attract capable teachers. Early on, the Carlisle family was primarily responsible for running the academy and teaching many of the classes. Carlisle himself served as superintendent, his wife as principal and teacher, and his daughter, Mary, taught English and history. Other teachers were added as needed, with the school maintaining at least four fulltime teachers. Most of the teachers stayed on staff for only a year or two before moving on. Perhaps the most notable exception to this trend was Preston Weatherred, who was one of the academy's first graduates in May 1904 and later joined the faculty in fall 1906. Weatherred remained on the faculty until 1912.[8]

Arlington and the surrounding communities quickly embraced Carlisle Military Academy, leading to dramatic increases in enrollment in its first few years of operation. The school attracted students primarily from Arlington and north and central Texas. The academy ended its first year in May 1903 with 71 students, its second year in 1904 with 97, and its third year in 1905 with 150. Because of these increases and the strain they were placing on the facilities and staff, the academy closed its doors to female students in September 1905 and pulled back on its promotional efforts. Mary Carlisle and Maggie Smith, both former teachers at the academy, responded by opening a private school in Arlington called the Carlisle-Smith School for Girls. The school, located in a house on Abram Street at stop fourteen on the interurban line, accommodated girls from first through the tenth grades and billed itself as a "high grade prep school." The Carlisle-Smith School existed for only a couple of years.[9]

Carlisle Military Academy responded to the growth in student enrollment by acquiring more land and constructing more buildings. In fall 1904 the school built the East Barracks to house more cadets. The sixteen rooms in this new brick barracks were furnished with two folding iron beds, small study tables, chairs, and closets. Each room had electric lights and running water. The following summer the

2.6 Regarding faculty, Carlisle believed "that the best results are obtained through specialists, and that our boys are entitled to the best." Carlisle Military Academy's early faculty was composed of (from left to right) Preston A. Weatherred, Sydney Rowland, James M. Carlisle, L.T. Cook, and Garland Morton.

campus was modernized by adding running water and indoor plumbing to all buildings. A year later, the trustees of defunct Arlington College deeded the school's land to Carlisle and the superintendent moved quickly to purchase adjoining property. When the 1906-1907 school year began, the military academy campus encompassed four city blocks, bordered on the north by First Street, on the east by West Street, on the south by Third Street, and on the west by Yates. The expansion did not stop here. In spring 1907, the school constructed a track for athletic events and the following year built additional barracks on the west side of the campus. In 1910-1911, the school opened a new gymnasium and an indoor swimming pool.[10]

Hoping to continue the school's rapid growth, Carlisle and his staff worked hard to offer students a range of activities in which they would be interested and to incorporate these activities into the fabric of the town. To this end, the academy fielded teams for baseball (begun spring 1904), basketball (begun spring 1908), football (begun fall 1904), and track (begun spring 1907), as well as organizing military units which participated in sham battles, drills, and parades. The school also sponsored lectures, music recitals, plays, socials, recitations, band concerts, and other special events throughout the year. All school activities were open to the public, and Carlisle even made it a point to invite residents to visit the school at any time and sit in on classes. A reporter for the *Arlington Journal* took Carlisle up on his offer and sat in on the school's final exams and reported that "to listen to the examination of classes and watch the faces of the cadets, one was inevitably driven to the conclusion that the brain exercise had been intense. One could hardly help feeling that the strain had been even too great. Some faces showed such traces of mental strain as to be almost pathetic." [11]

2.7 In an attempt to create a girls-only school, Mary Carlisle, Colonel Carlisle's daughter, opened the Carlisle-Smith School for Girls on West Abram Street. Pictured here is the school's first class in 1905.

One of the Arlington community's favorite activities at the school was the graduation and advancement ceremonies held each year in May. The school saw its first students graduate in May 1904, when Sallie McKee and Preston Weatherred received their certificates. In addition to recognizing graduates, the academy presented its medals and awards to deserving students and honored those students advancing to different grade levels. Oftentimes speeches, recitals, musical performances, and recitations were made at these ceremonies by the students, and a noted speaker, recruited by Carlisle, would deliver the commencement address. The number of graduates leaving Carlisle fluctuated from a low of two in 1904 to a high of eleven in 1909. The local newspaper gave detailed reports of these ceremonies.[12]

Carlisle also moved to strengthen the academy's military affiliation, convinced that strict discipline and rigid structure were hallmarks of quality education. In March 1907, Lieutenant Harry King of the United States Army made an unannounced visit to campus and came away convinced that the Arlington academy was one of the best of its class in the country! In a letter to Carlisle, he lauded the teachers, the cadets and their discipline, the physical plant, the campus's Arlington location, and even the food. In the summer of 1907, the War Department, after a similar type of inspection, assigned an active duty army officer, Lieutenant Kelton L. Pepper, to the school as instructor of military science. Carlisle Military Academy became only the second school in the Southwest to have an active duty officer assigned to it. Each year after this, the United

2.8 Described as a fireproof, modern brick building with concrete floors, the East Barracks, pictured on this post card, served as the men's dormitory. Having designed the dormitory's folding iron beds himself, Carlisle called them "the best student beds in use, being free from bugs, and convenient."

States Army War College dispatched an officer to the school for inspection, generally late in the spring. The army replaced Pepper with a retired army officer in 1908 when enrollment dipped below one hundred.[13]

Despite the school's encouraging growth in its early years and its acceptance by the local community, problems soon began to plague it and superintendent Carlisle. In October 1905, a fire destroyed a barracks while the cadets were at breakfast. Luckily no one was injured. The structure, however, was not insured. More threatening to the wellbeing of the school was a significant drop in enrollment for the 1908-1909 academic year. In fact, the fall 1908 enrollment was only eighty-eight, the fewest number of students the school had seen since its first year. While the newspaper blamed the decline on the so-called "Panic of 1907" combined with a drought in the area, this did little to reassure Carlisle as he struggled to meet his financial obligations. Carlisle made two significant changes in an attempt to raise revenue for the school. First, he again opened his academy to female students and, second, in a desperate move, he converted the school's four city blocks of real estate to capital stock, which he sold for $100 a share. The stock offering had a value of $40,000, so he could have potentially sold 400 shares. Despite his efforts to increase his cashflow, Carlisle realized that he and his school were doomed if enrollment stayed low.[14]

2.9 Carlisle prided himself on the school's campus, calling it a beautiful sloping prairie of ten acres. This 1911 rendering shows Carlisle Military Academy from the corner of, what are today, South West and West Third streets.

To make matters worse—at least in the public's mind—the academy suspended its football program in November 1908 because the parents of four first teamers took their sons off the squad for fear of injury. CMA, not having enough players to field a team, canceled its remaining games. Adding to a declining public image, in January 1909, six cadets and a "captain instructor," who was also the football and baseball coach for the school, were arrested for fighting. A year later, Carlisle suspended half of the school for rules violation, and this during a period of falling enrollments![15]

Because of the amount of bad news, it is not surprising that the local newspaper began to report rumors that Carlisle was planning to leave Arlington to start a school elsewhere. These rumors became more believable when, in May 1911, Carlisle's financial problems forced the school into receivership. The news reports at the time stated that the school's stockholders and creditors had the academy placed under the direction of the county's district court (Seventeenth Judicial District), which appointed General R. H. Beckham as receiver. Beckham had been a former adjutant general for Texas.[16]

2.10 Carlisle was a firm believer in the healthy body, healthy mind principle. The 1907 football team, pictured here, is just one example of the many athletic teams at Carlisle Military Academy.

As receiver, Beckham faced a host of financial problems resulting from Carlisle's rapid expansion and the school's declining enrollment. A number of companies, vendors, and individuals were clamoring to be paid for services rendered or products sold to the school. Carlisle was simply unable to meet these obligations, and a number of suits were filed against the school in district court and in justice of the peace courts as a result. Beckham's orders from the district court were explicit. He was to "manage and control" all affairs of the academy and to make sure the physical plant was insured against "loss or damage by fire." In addition, he was to continue the employ of the teaching and support staff of the school and, if possible, pay them out of the "cash on hand." The court also ordered him to compile a complete inventory of all school property and a list of all liabilities of the corporation. Beckham went about his work in a businesslike manner, settling the suits with creditors whenever possible.[17]

Not all went smoothly, however. In October 1911, the lienholders of the mortgages on the school's property filed suit against the academy to force it to sell its land. The lienholders hoped to find a buyer who would maintain the land and physical plant as a "military school or college." The lienholders in this case were Citizens National Bank of Arlington and W. M. Dugan, Thomas Spruance, W. C. Weeks, M. H. Cravens, Frank McKnight, A. W. Collins, J. H. Watson, Joe W. Burney, and W. B. Fitzhugh, most of whom had been on the academy's advisory board of directors since 1907. They were convinced that the academy did not have the money to make improvements, advertise, recruit students, and operate efficiently. They were also fearful that if the land were sold and put to different use other than a school, they would not recover a reasonable portion of their financial obligations.[18]

The school operated for two more years before the suit was finally settled. In a lengthy judgment in August 1913, the court ordered the Carlisle Military Academy to sell its property to satisfy the promissory note it had with the bank and the lienholders. The school's indebtedness to the mortgage holders was set at $20,728.50. Spruance, a bank officer and a party mentioned in the suit, purchased the school's land and some of its personal property for $15,610 in a public sale. Because this amount was insufficient to satisfy the entire debt, the academy was ordered to pay as much of the balance as possible with money received from the sale of other school property. Moreover, B. R. Merrifield, a former teacher and purchasing agent at the school who also owned interest in the academy, was ordered to be paid $3,800 from the estate of Mrs. Carlisle, a sum which would increase eight percent per annum until it was paid off. The academy owed a few other debts as well as court costs. Finally, the court faced reality and ordered the Carlisle Military Academy Corporation dissolved and its "old record books, papers, etc., that are worthless" destroyed.[19]

For the eleven years the military academy operated in Arlington, Carlisle proved

2.11 Carlisle Military Academy's 1910-1911 baseball team.

himself a popular and capable educator, but a flawed administrator. The school suffered from ineffective management, "no accurate set of books," inefficiency on the part of its administrative officials, and philosophical disagreements among the staff—or at least so charged its critics. Whatever the reality, Carlisle found himself and his school squeezed by mounting debts caused by an overly optimistic expansion plan and declining enrollments. This combination, plus the court cases it sparked, served to drive Carlisle out of Arlington in 1913. Just after the close of the spring term in May, Carlisle and his wife left Arlington for Whitewright, Texas, where he once again opened a school, this one lasting for only a year. There is no doubt that Carlisle left the area a humbled and dejected man.[20]

Despite his ultimate failure to sustain the school, Carlisle did make significant improvements and additions to the school's physical plant and curriculum. He also skillfully wove the school's activities into the day-to-day life of Arlington and, for a short period of time, improved the school's

2.12 After the construction of two barracks and a mess hall, Carlisle Military Academy built an indoor pool and gymnasium in 1910. The cost of this project, however, added to the school's increasing indebtedness, which eventually forced it into bankruptcy. The structure, which was described as being cracked and in an unusable condition by the early 1920s, was torn down by 1927.

reputation throughout north and central Texas. It comes as no surprise then that the school was reopened in September 1913 under a new administration which had high hopes for the future—hopes, in large measure, built on the legacy Carlisle had left behind.[21]

In March 1907, Lieutenant Harry King of the United States Army paid a surprise visit to Carlisle Military Academy and came away impressed with the school, its staff, and students. A week after his visit, King wrote Carlisle of his observations, and the text of his letter follows. Everyone associated with the academy was flattered by King's comments, and Carlisle used them at times for promotional purposes. The letter provides an outsider's view of the school in 1907.

Fort Worth, Texas, March 28, 1907

Dear Colonel [Carlisle]:

I was so favorably impressed while visiting your school last week that I deem it proper to inform you of my impressions in regard to the school.

To tell the truth, I did not believe, at the time of my arrival at Arlington, that I would see much, but after spending the day there I went away with the impression deeply fixed that *there is not a better school or academy of its class in the country.* I do not mean Texas alone; I cover the whole of the United States.

In the recitation rooms I found able instructors—so able that they would do credit to any school, academy, college or university in the land. They showed a companionship and personal interest in the cadets which is lacking in so many of our halls of learning. I have found that a pupil takes interest in his studies very much in proportion to the interest taken in him by the teachers. I saw this condition in your school and it pleased me.

The mess was orderly, the food plentiful and well cooked and I was specially pleased to see the faculty at mess with the cadets. The new barracks is a model in arrangement, embodying comfort, perfect light, ventilation and heat and adaptability to the handling of the cadets quartered in it.

When the cadets were drilling I watched them closely and discovered no faults, though it is easy for me to find them in this exercise when they exist. The discipline of your school is excellent and the conduct of the individual cadets gentlemanly.

There are great advantages to a boy educated in a military school. His carriage is better, his figure good, or at least much improved, he learns to obey promptly and to be obedient to those in authority over him. The habits formed through military exercises are greatly to the advantage of the boy all through life. Your military department is a credit to the school. The cadet officers are a bright and interesting set of young men and the same might

2.13 Shown here in dress uniform, Morris Frazar, from Henrietta, Texas, represented the model cadet. Graduating in 1911, Frazar's daughter would later marry Arlington State College President Jack Woolf.

2.14 Inspections were a regular part of a cadet's life at Carlisle Military Academy. Here, a major from the U.S. Army is conducting a shelter tent drill.

be said of the whole corps. Your commandant, Lieutenant P. A. Weatherred, though having seen no service in the army, has had splendid advantages in the National Guard and in the maneuvers conducted by the war department and in which both the regular soldiers and the National Guard participate. Your military department is in good hands.

I must say that I do not see why parents send their sons to other states for the very advantages offered by your school as well and in many cases better than in these schools out of the state of Texas. I am not a Texan, but I would be glad to see every worthy Texas school like yours prosper. And they would have unprecedented prosperity if your own people but understood the superior work you are doing. The Carlisle Military Academy will give a boy as good education and exert as good influences over him as any of the outside schools.

From personal observation, and I have had much, and especially with military schools, *I find the Carlisle Military school is equal to the best.* I do not say this because of the courteous treatment extended me by the faculty of your school, but I am giving you an unbiased, true opinion as it impressed me.

I commend your school to all who have boys to educate. It is a credit to the State of Texas and to you. In talking with the cadets they indicated that they have a great respect for you, and this is no mean condition. In fact, it is one of the strongest points in favor of your school. When I went to Arlington I had never met you, nor any member of your faculty, nor any cadet in the school, but I came away with a feeling "kin to all."

I will close by saying that your location is an ideal one. You are free from the objections to the city as a location for a school, yet for all the real advantages of the city you have them, located as you are between the prosperous towns of Fort Worth and Dallas, both of which are railroad centers, giving you close connection with all sections of the country. Besides, the health conditions seem to be the very best.

Thanking you and your faculty and cadets for courtesies extended to me and wishing your school the continued success it so richly deserves, I am, respectfully,

Harry King
Lieutenant, United States Army

CHAPTER THREE

One of the Best and Safest Places in Texas for Boys

E ven before Carlisle left Arlington, the local newspaper reported that a new school, Arlington Training School, would open on the old Carlisle Military Academy campus on September 10, 1913. Coming to Arlington to run the new school was H. K. Taylor, who was moving to town from Missouri. Like Carlisle before him, Taylor brought with him an impressive background in educational administration. Born on August 10, 1858, in Vanceburg, Kentucky, Taylor was raised and educated in the "blue grass" state, earning both his A.B. and A.M. from Kentucky Wesleyan College by the early 1880s. Later the college bestowed on him the LL.D. degree. After a couple of years teaching chemistry at his alma mater, Taylor held a succession of administrative positions at schools in his home state, including president of Logan Female College in Russellville from 1883-1889; organizer and superintendent of Louisville Training School for Boys, 1889-1906; and president of Kentucky Wesleyan College, 1906-1909. He left Kentucky to assume the presidency of Northwest State Teachers' College in Marysville, Missouri, a position he held until coming to Arlington in 1913. Taylor had the reputation of being a capable administrator who paid close attention to the bottom line and an effective school builder and promoter. The *Arlington Journal* reported that he was leaving Missouri voluntarily "because of his preference for training school work and a desire to change climate for the benefit of his family."[1]

Taylor was not coming to Arlington unaware of the fate of Carlisle and his academy. In fact, Taylor's son-in-law, J. J. Godbey, had been the headmaster at Carlisle Military Academy during 1911-1913, and he obviously played a major role in convincing Taylor to start Arlington Training School. Taylor moved quickly to reach an agreement with property owners Collins, Spruance, Cravens, Dugan, Weeks, Watson, Fitzhugh, McKnight, and Burney. Taylor signed a one-year contract with them in the summer of 1913, in which he agreed to make the necessary repairs and improvements to the physical plant, organize and implement a promotional campaign to attract students, insure the buildings, pay the interest on the property loans, and employ a competent staff to conduct the school. For his efforts, Taylor would keep any profits generated by the school and be given an option to purchase the school and its grounds for $18,000 which, after a $5,000 down payment, could be paid out over a ten-year period at a 7 percent interest rate. The contract stipulated that Taylor had until January 1, 1914, to exercise his

3.1 In addition to regular military training, the young men at Arlington Training School engaged in supervised wrestling. Physical activities, according to the school's 1915-1916 *Announcement*, "give the boy ease and grace of movement, erect carriage, and a strong, robust body."

option to buy the school.[2]

Buoyant about the school's prospects, Taylor recruited a staff for opening day. Godbey was appointed principal with responsibility for history and some science classes. V. I. Moore, another of Taylor's sons-in-law, became athletic director as well as a Latin and English teacher. Major Attilla C. Grant taught mathematics and science and was commandant at the school, while O. W. McMillen assisted with English and taught modern languages. The school's social and domestic activities were directed by Mrs. Taylor and the Taylors' two daughters, Mrs. Godbey and Mrs. Moore. The local newspaper reassured the community that "these people are Southern people, thoroughly in sympathy with the cordiality and the spirit of sociability that characterizes the Southern people."[3]

3.2 After the close of Carlisle Military Academy, H. K. Taylor was encouraged to come to Arlington and start Arlington Training School, which opened in the fall of 1913.

Thirty-two students greeted Taylor and his staff on opening day, a number Taylor must have found disappointing. The *Arlington Journal* attributed the low enrollment to the continuation of a drought in the area and to Taylor's insistence that the school adhere to its advertised tuition fees at a time when, according to the newspaper, "cheap schools" were "taking pupils at cut rates." Nevertheless, Taylor and others actively recruited students in Arlington and the surrounding area, eventually boosting enrollment to sixty-six by the end of the 1913-1914 school year. Taylor promised these students personal attention, military training for the boys, "splendid moral influences," an attractive campus, "thorough and practical courses of

3.3 Believing that literary societies were an efficient means of "stimulating public speaking, composition work, debate and the study of parliamentary law and usages," the school organized the Martha Washington Society for young women.

study," and a student-teacher ratio of fifteen to one. The school's aims were to teach students to be "morally clean, considerate of each other's rights, careful of their health and physical exercise, punctual in the discharge of duty," and useful, productive citizens. The school did accept young women as day students.[4]

Like Carlisle Military Academy before it, Arlington Training School was not a reformatory for "vicious boys." Rather, the school's promotional material characterized the institution as a place for "gentlemen's sons," boys "who are willing to work heartily during study time, and play heartily during play time." Taylor and the faculty expected students to be "cheerful, considerate of others, [and] not given to complaining. . . ." The school's rules of conduct advised students to be "polite and respectful, especially to older people, those in authority, and ladies. . . ." On Sundays all boarding students were required to attend the church and Sunday school of their choice and to spend an hour writing to their families.[5]

Students could enroll in the school at any time during the year provided there was a vacancy. Additionally, the school required students to be, at a minimum, at the fourth grade level, this being the school's lowest class. According to Taylor, the minimum skills a student should have to attend the school were "to read fluently such matter as is found in Fourth Readers, spell correctly words thus found, write legibly, answer such questions as are usually found in primary geographies and perform simple mathematical problems in fractions."[6]

Taylor organized the school into two separate units, with grades four through six comprising the intermediate unit, while grades seven through ten comprised the secondary unit. The school did not offer elementary education of any kind. To graduate, a student had to successfully complete seventeen units of work above the intermediate level, a standard which met the entrance requirements of the University of Texas in Austin.[7]

3.4 The Jolly Junior Literary Society (pictured) was organized for the younger boys, while the Robert E. Lee Literary Society served the older boys.

At the secondary or high school level, the school offered a comprehensive curriculum. In math, Arlington Training School had classes in basic mathematics, college algebra, and plane and solid geometry, while its history offerings included medieval and modern history, English history, and U.S. history and civics. Classes in physical geography, physiology and hygiene, biology, physics, and chemistry made up the science courses. The languages offered were Latin, four years; French, two years; German, two years; and Spanish, two years. A full complement of English courses was offered, from classes in rhetoric and grammar to those in English literature. Vocational subjects included bookkeeping, business law, and agriculture for the school's first two years, and in 1915-1916 domestic science, domestic art, and household hygiene and economy were added. Physical education and band were also offered. The school did list "post-secondary courses" in its catalogs, but there is no evidence that any high school graduates enrolled in these.[8]

The school had a fairly elaborate tuition and fee schedule for its students. It included:

Board and tuition for boys over fourteen	$ 300.00
Board and tuition for boys under fourteen	250.00
Laundry fee	32.00
Medical fee	5.00
Athletic and library fee	10.00
Domestic Science fee, per term	10.00
Indemnity fee/deposit (to be returned if no damage is done)	5.00
Uniforms	42.00
Tuition for day pupils in secondary unit	75.00
Tuition for day pupils in intermediate unit	60.00

In addition to the above fees, the school charged students a $5.00 per month fee for piano lessons and a monthly fee of $4.00 for band. The school also encouraged parents to send their children $.50-1.00 per week in spending money. The school required that one-half of all fees be paid upon a student's entrance and the balance paid by January 5 of the next year. Children of ministers were given a tuition reduction of 15 percent. Tuition was raised once in the school's short three-year existence and only for boys under fourteen boarding on campus. Their tuition rose to $250.00 for the 1915-1916 school year.[9]

3.5 The school admitted young women as day pupils because "they have made a most excellent record." If this photo of the 1914 sophomore class can be taken as representative, the ratio of male to female students was roughly two to one.

During the school's first year, Taylor saw to it that a number of extracurricular activities were organized. For boys, the school fielded football, basketball, baseball, and track teams. These teams competed with those from other area schools and served to rally Arlington residents behind the school. Not to be left out, the female students at Arlington Training School organized a basketball team. The school also started a band during its first term and held a series of band concerts for parents and the general public. A school newspaper titled *The Reveille* made its first appearance in November 1913. At the close of the 1913-1914 school year, the school held its first graduation and awards ceremony, complete with a band concert, declamation contest, and all of the pomp and circumstance characteristic of such occasions. Thomas Spruance, Jr., Chester M. Willingham, and James H. Netherby were the school's graduates for the year.[10]

Also during the school's first year, Taylor worked hard to bolster the support in the community for the institution and to strengthen the school's financial condition. In fall 1913 and spring 1914, mass meetings were held in Arlington to address the financial health of the school. Chairing these meetings was Thomas Spruance, who, as the individual owning much of the school's property, had a personal interest in seeing the school succeed. In these meetings, Taylor argued that support from local residents was absolutely essential *before* the school could expect to draw pupils from a distance. Taylor proposed to sell sixty scholarships to Arlington residents to finance the school, and the idea was met enthusiastically. At a meeting held on February 28, 1914, Taylor succeeded in selling all sixty scholarships. Moreover, the attendees of the meeting formed a permanent organization called the "Busy Men's Forum" to help the school. Thomas Spruance was elected president of the forum, and W. A. Bowen, the editor of the *Arlington Journal,* was elected chairman. Soon afterwards, a board of advisors for the school was also organized. It included all of the individuals who owned the school property. Just a couple of months earlier, in January, Taylor had agreed to lease the school and grounds for $1,400 a year for the next two years. He also agreed with the property owners to spend $500 in repairs during each of these two years.[11]

Pleased with what looked like adequate community support, Taylor made plans for the next school year. These plans included recruiting a few new faculty members, upgrading the science labs, repairing facilities and improving the grounds, and building a band pavilion and grandstand. Arlington Training School began its second year on September 16, 1914. Of the faculty, only Major Grant did not return. Godbey became commandant in his place, and a number of new faculty members were hired. The faculty were touted as being "experienced, skillful, and exemplary Christians." In addition to its teachers, the school also promoted its large ten-acre campus and a physical plant which consisted of eleven buildings, a gym with pool and showers, and a campus with natural gas, electricity, city water, and modern sewage disposal.[12]

In terms of enrollment, the 1914-1915 academic year was a relatively good one for the school, as ninety-five students attended the fall and spring terms. The school also added a number of extracurricular activities in the academic and cultural areas, such as forensic clubs, literary societies, drama groups, and musical and martial organizations. Sports continued to play an important role in campus life with a number of the school's teams compiling impressive records. The football team won four games and tied one for the year; the basketball team went undefeated in nine games; and the baseball squad amassed a fourteen and two record. The school also added tennis for both boys and girls. The school graduated ten students in May 1915, including Edward E. Rankin, Jr., and Edna Rankin,

3.6 By 1908 downtown Arlington had become an important railway stop between Fort Worth and Dallas. As the community's economy grew stronger, its commitment to Arlington Training School did not waver. In fact, the school's 1915 *Blue Bonnet* stated that the school owed its existence to the good business sense of the Arlington community.

two grandchildren of Edward E. Rankin, the driving force in establishing Arlington College.[13]

Despite what seemed to be improved prospects for the school—and certainly they did improve relative to its first year of operation—none of the improvements or repairs Taylor had promised were done during 1914-1915, except for the construction of grandstands at a cost of $125. The *Arlington Journal* reported that the failure to improve the property, a stipulation of Taylor's January 1914 contract with the property owners, was the result of a "difference of opinion regarding the value of the property." This was the first instance of disagreement between Taylor and the school's advisory board. It would not be the last.[14]

The disagreement with the board—e.g., the property owners—seemed to be shortlived. Indeed, the newspaper reported on April 2, 1915, that Taylor had reached an agreement to greatly enlarge and improve the school. In a letter published in the *Arlington Journal*, Taylor announced that in the near future the school would be incorporated and the public would have a "splendid opportunity for a profitable investment" by purchasing stock in the school. Taylor revealed his plan to improve the buildings on campus, erect a new building for laboratories and other classes,

3.7 While the school's aim in teaching may have been to "give a common sense and useable knowledge of scientific principles that will prepare boys for becoming more intelligent farmers," there were also women who desired the same vocation.

and perhaps, most dramatically, to convert the school into a junior college which would offer classes in agriculture, manual training, and home economics. Taylor also envisioned the school having an experimental farm and demonstration service in agriculture and home economics for Tarrant and Dallas counties. This was a bold plan indeed![15]

Taylor sought to bolster community support for the plan by holding a public meeting in mid-April to discuss it. At the meeting, Clarence Owsley, the director of the extension department at Texas A&M College, and G. W. Eudaly, Tarrant County farm demonstrator, spoke in favor of changing the school into a junior college. Owsley even suggested that Texas A&M could help to supervise the campus. After the meeting, the newspaper reported that a "Committee of Eighty" had pledged to purchase stock in the school. Shares were to be $100.00 each and sold at $.90 on the dollar. Shareholders with one share of stock were entitled to purchase a five-year scholarship at a 10 percent discount; shareholders with two shares would receive a 20 percent reduction; and those with three shares would get a 33 percent reduction. The shares would earn 6 percent interest (after the first year) for four years.[16]

Thirty thousand dollars worth of stock was to be issued, with $15,000 of the net proceeds used to pay for the present site and buildings. The balance was to be set aside for new construction, improvements and upgrades, and new equipment. The school was to incorporate under Texas law and the stockholders were to elect a board of directors. The board was to lease the school to Taylor for five years and

3.8 Although young women were not permitted to room on the school's campus, Arlington Training School did have many activities for the female students, including a basketball team.

he was to assume responsibility for operating the school. During the first year of his contract, Taylor would pay no rent to run the school, only insurance fees. But after the initial year, Taylor agreed to pay $1,800 per year (6 percent of the total stock) for rental of the property. Taylor could decide on the improvements to be made, but the contract stipulated that the board had to approve them and their cost could not be "less than $10,000."[17]

In July 1915, the Arlington Training School was incorporated with a capital stock of $15,000, half the amount originally planned. One-hundred-fifty shares were purchased before the end of summer. The board of directors for the new corporation included Frank McKnight, president; W. C. Weeks, secretary-treasurer; and W. M. Dugan, M. H. Cravens, A. W. Collins, J. H. Watson, and J. W. Burney. Optimistic that the school was on firm financial ground—at least firmer than before—Taylor pushed for making the improvements stipulated in the contract. In the summer and fall of 1915, a rather extensive program was begun to renovate the buildings on campus and construct a new one. A new two-story frame building was erected just southeast of the classroom building. The new structure housed the library, science labs, business office, literary society halls, and other activities. The school's auditorium received a face-lift as well as "new opera seats" and "a drinking fountain." Virtually all of the school's other buildings were redecorated and repaired. The cost of these repairs and new construction was $10,000.[18]

Prospects looked bright for Arlington Training School at the start of the 1915-1916 school year. Only two teachers, Wiley and McMillan, failed to return for the year, and they were replaced by Captain John H. Bower, who taught modern languages and directed the musical activities for the school, and Elizabeth Crocker, a home economics teacher. Two of Taylor's sons, Walter and H. K., Jr., also joined the school as business manager/librarian and secretary to the president respectively. Enrollment did not change much from the previous year, as ninety-three students greeted the school staff on opening day. Newspaper coverage of the school's activities, however, was all but non-existent during the year, foreshadowing some sort of problem on campus.[19]

This problem did not become obvious until the spring of 1916. Once again financial trouble and recriminations leading to law-suits raised their ugly heads, and the school was thrown into a temporary tailspin as a result. The cause of the problem was a serious disagreement between Taylor and his board of directors over the $10,000 repairs completed in the summer and fall of 1915. Taylor accused Weeks, the secretary-treasurer, and other members of the board of conspiring to take most of the money earmarked for school expansion and improvement and using the money for themselves. Taylor eventually filed suit against Weeks demanding $9,276.90 for remuneration, claiming that he was

3.9 Regarding athletics, the school's 1915-1916 *Announcement* states that although "physical training must be correlated with intellectual and moral development . . . sports are not to be given an undue and hurtful prominence." Pictured is the school's 1914 basketball team.

3.10 Part of the Fort Worth Interscholastic League, Arlington Training School's 1915 baseball team boasted a 14-2 season.

unable to run the school properly because too few improvements had been completed. In the court papers, Taylor characterized the improvements made as leaving the buildings in an "unfinished, unsanitary and unsightly condition. . . ." He also argued that the school lost enrollment as a result of insufficient facilities. In March 1916, Taylor informed the corporation's stockholders that he would not lease the school after the close of the term in May. This essentially broke the contract he had signed in the summer of 1915, in which he had agreed to lease the property for five years.[20]

Obviously angry over Taylor's actions, the board filed a breach of contract suit against him in the 17th District Court of Tarrant County on June 5, 1916. Taylor countered by arguing that the Arlington Training School board was the first party to breach the contract when it failed to make all of the necessary repairs and improvements on the school property. The jury, however, agreed with the board and, on February 13, 1917, ruled against Taylor. The jury ordered Taylor to pay the board $1,497.50 plus court costs, and cleared Weeks of any wrongdoing in the process.[21]

By the time the verdict was handed down, Taylor had left Arlington to serve as extension agent for Texas Woman's College in Denton. He later joined the faculty of Southern Methodist University in Dallas in 1922, where he taught until his death in January 1934. Taking his place in Arlington was John B. Dodson, most recently from Dallas. Dodson was born in Tennessee in 1861 and received his B.A. and M.A. degrees from Carson-Newman College in 1884. Before moving to Arlington to attempt to revitalize the former Arlington Training School, Dodson had served as superintendent of schools in McKinney, Texas; superintendent of Oak Cliff schools and president of Oak Cliff College; and head of the University Military School for Boys in Dallas. Like Taylor, Carlisle, and the others before him, Dodson hoped to operate a viable and profitable school in Arlington—a school he would call Arlington Military Academy. And like the individuals before him, he would fail.[22]

3.11 John B. Dodson, who organized Arlington Military Academy in 1916, was the last person to attempt the creation of a military school in Arlington.

Arlington Military Academy lasted for only one school year, 1916-1917. Its goals, like its forerunners, were to train students in "all rudimentary education," preparing them for a university education to follow or a life in business. Writing in the July 7, 1916, issue of the *Arlington Journal*, Dodson discussed some of his ideas about education and his plans for students. He promised strong courses in literature, an emphasis on athletics, offerings in music and domestic science, and advanced courses in oratory. The school, he said, would also stress military exercises and the discipline which comes through rigorous military training. The school was open to boys and girls and actively recruited both. The school's advertisements promised that the faculty would stress all social amenities, including "dining room manners, street politeness, good behavior at Church and all public places, and especial deference to Seniors in age, and the deepest respect for parents."[23]

Dodson also organized a "Board of Reference" to advise him and his faculty and to generate community support. The board was comprised of several leading Arlington businessmen and clergymen, including Arlington mayor R. H. Greer; James Ditto, president of Arlington National Bank; Frank McKnight, president, First State Bank; J. B. Berry, pastor of the Methodist church; S. M. Bennett, pastor of the Presbyterian church; A. G. Gustavus, pastor of the Baptist church; Patrick Henry, pastor of the Christian church; and William Bowen, editor of the newspaper. There is no doubt that Dodson knew he would need all the help he could get.[24]

Little is known about the year in which Dodson operated Arlington Military Academy. Few records of the period are extant, and the local newspaper essentially ignored the school, except for a mention here or there of a play, or a minstrel show, or other performance by the students. Enrollment must have been disappointing because the school's promotional ads published in December 1916 promised a "much larger attendance" in the spring session to follow. Judging from the school's quick demise in May 1917, the hoped-for boost in students never came.[25]

3.12 Arlington Training School's Music Department included not only basic courses in piano, but also the opportunity to be part of the school's military band.

Arlington leaders had other plans for the school grounds and facilities and did little to salvage Dodson's academy. In fact, rather than rally to save Arlington Military Academy, local businessmen, convinced that a private academy would never be viable, met on January 27, 1917, to organize a communitywide effort to pressure the Texas legislature to establish a "Junior Agricultural, Mechanical and Industrial College" in town. Community leaders had adopted the idea first advanced by Taylor of using the school's grounds for a junior college. The junior college would eventually come, but it would come at the expense of Dodson's academy.[26]

The closing of Arlington Military Academy brought to an end the efforts of educators and the Arlington community to support a private intermediate and secondary school in town. Each of the schools—Arlington College, Carlisle Military Academy, Arlington Training School, and Arlington Military Academy—had opened with high hopes and closed amid mounting financial pressures and even lawsuits. In the end, the Arlington community proved unable—or unwilling—to provide the support necessary to keep these private schools operating. Despite the schools' ultimate failure, they had provided parents with an alternative to the public schools, educated hundreds of children over a twenty-two year period, and built a campus with adequate physical facilities. By 1917, however, Arlington leaders believed that the community would benefit more from a junior college than from a private academy. Consequently, these leaders set out to do everything in their power to convince the legislature that Arlington would be an ideal location for such a college.

3.13 During Arlington Training School's short history, its yearly *Announcement* functioned as both a catalog and yearbook, chronicling the events of the school.

The Kind of Boys We Want

The following excerpt comes from the Arlington Training School catalog for 1913-1914. In it, H. K. Taylor summarizes the kind of student the school hopes to attract.

Arlington Training School's seal.

We take only a limited number of pupils. We want and are desirous of welcoming boys who are at least in possibility imbued with manly hopes and ambitions. The Arlington Training School is essentially a training school for gentlemen's sons, and we want only such in our school. We want young men who are willing to work heartily during study time, and play heartily during play time. Young men who will at all times be high-toned, courteous gentlemen in the fullest sense. For the boy who believes that he desires to be all this we have a hearty welcome and the assurance that we will do all in our power to help him climb to the pinnacle of noble ambition.

This is not a school for reforming vicious boys. Any boy who shows himself incapable of responding to kind, but firm, treatment cannot continue in the school. The influence of one such boy will contaminate the spirit of the whole school if allowed to remain one of the student body.

CHAPTER FOUR

A Hard Road to Travel

The push which culminated in the establishment of a junior vocational college in Arlington in the fall of 1917 actually began shortly after the turn of the twentieth century. In 1902, William A. Bowen, editor of the *Arlington Journal,* started a campaign to convince state legislators and officials at Texas A&M College (at this time officially named the Agricultural and Mechanical College of Texas) to consider placing a junior branch of the college in North Texas, preferably in Arlington. For the next fifteen years, Bowen used his newspaper to advance this cause and to emphasize the advantages of Arlington. According to Bowen, Arlington's location made it an ideal site for a college because it lay in the center of the most heavily populated region of the state. Moreover, the Arlington community was willing to donate both the land and physical facilities to get the college started. He also emphasized several of the area's other geographical advantages, such as rich soil, moderate climate, accessibility to adequate water, and its proximity to the State Fair of Texas in Dallas and the Fort Worth Stock Show.[1]

Bowen's arguments did not fall on deaf ears. Indeed, a number of Texas newspapers, including the *Houston Post,* the *Dallas Times Herald,* and the *Fort Worth Star-Telegram*, lent their editorial support to starting an A&M branch campus in Arlington. At the time, Texas A&M had only one branch campus, Prairie View A&M, which was for the education of African Americans. The issue of Texas A&M's expansion, whether at College Station or in other parts of the state, was being debated in Austin, College Station, and throughout Texas. Most people agreed that the College Station campus and buildings were inadequate to meet the needs of the state's students who wanted an agricultural or mechanical education. In the century's second decade, A&M strained to accommodate 500 students, 150 of whom were agricultural students and the balance engineering students. The state press characterized the A&M campus as "overcrowded" and "inadequate," with too many students being denied entrance as a result. The press urged college and state officials to find a solution to this problem. Eventually, two positions developed on the issue of A&M's development. The first called for the expansion of the College Station campus so that it could serve a student body of 3,000. The second position—and the one which would eventually win out— called for the expansion of the A&M campus *and* the opening of branch campuses throughout the state. In either case, more students hoping to study agriculture or

4.1 Grubbs Vocational College carried on the tradition of military training that began during the Carlisle period. Here, the Student Army Training Corps practices a bayonet drill on the school's parade grounds.

the mechanical arts could be accommodated in Texas.[2]

By 1917, the A&M issue had been discussed in the press for a decade and a half, and the call for action was becoming louder. Vincent Woodbury Grubbs sensed that now was the time to act. Grubbs was a strong proponent of the state's developing a comprehensive system of industrial schools and junior agricultural, mechanical, and industrial colleges "for the poor boys and girls of Texas." In 1902, he led the efforts to establish the College of Industrial Arts (CIA) in Denton, Texas (now Texas Woman's University), and, some fifteen years later, was ready to lobby the legislature for other vocational schools.

4.2 In 1917 Vincent Woodbury Grubbs, who believed that the higher education system in Texas catered only to the wealthy, lobbied for the establishment of a state-supported vocational college in Arlington.

Born in Calloway County, Kentucky, on May 1, 1848, Grubbs, after the death of his father, came with his mother and two brothers and two sisters to Texas in 1855. They settled near Crandall, in Kaufman County near his maternal grandmother's land. Three years later, his mother, Anne Utley Wade Grubbs, married R. O. Anthony and moved the family to Ellis County. During the Civil War, the family moved back to Kaufman County, where young Vincent worked on a farm and as a cow driver. In 1869, Grubbs entered Trinity College, in Limestone County, graduating in 1872. In 1874, he received his license to practice law and opened an office in Kaufman, Texas. Here he handled cases and also wrote for the local newspaper. He ran for district judge of the county's Eighth Judicial District in 1884, but lost the election. Dejected, he left for Greenville, Texas (Hunt County), in 1885 to work as a newspaper columnist, and later became co-owner of the town's newspaper, the *Herald*, for two years. After his brief stint with the newspaper, Grubbs devoted his time to practicing law in Greenville and working for industrial education in Texas. At the turn of the century, he represented Hunt County in the Texas legislature for one term and continued to work to broaden the educational opportunities for Texans. By 1917, Grubbs was intimately familiar with the education system in the state and with the lawmakers in Austin.[3]

Grubbs strongly believed that the higher education system in Texas was unfair and limiting. According to him, the colleges in the state catered to the "boys and girls of city people, and of rich people, or at least the well-to-do" at the expense of the kids on the farms. Most colleges aimed at providing students a professional education, preparing them for

4.3 Soon after the bill establishing Grubbs Vocational College as a branch of the Agricultural and Mechanical College of Texas was signed by Governor James Ferguson in March 1917, the Arlington Business Men's League purchased one hundred acres of land west of the campus from J. P. Fielder to be used as the college farm.

careers as lawyers, doctors, bankers, teachers, and merchants, he argued. There were few opportunities for industrial or agricultural education in Texas, and he set out to change this. By broadening the educational system, he hoped to draw the "sons and daughters of farmers, mechanics, and other of us common people" into the college classroom. Grubbs devoted the last three decades of his life to working and lobbying for this change.[4]

It was in his capacity as a lobbyist that Grubbs offered his services to Arlington in 1917. Just before approaching the Arlington community, Grubbs had worked to establish a junior college in Campbell, Texas, and had had discussions with the city leadership in Commerce about converting East Texas Normal College (now East Texas State University) into a state-supported vocational school. Both of Grubbs' attempts were unsuccessful. Stung by these failures and aware of the sentiment in Arlington for a junior college, Grubbs wrote J. A. Kooken, the superintendent of Arlington public schools, and offered to visit the town to discuss "the feasibility of securing the passage of a bill by the Texas legislature then in session establishing a Junior Industrial College at [Arlington]. . . ." The Arlington city leadership, already thinking in these terms, accepted Grubbs' offer to speak and arranged a community meeting to hear him. A meeting was held on January 27, 1917, where Grubbs outlined his plan to bring a junior college to town provided he could muster the necessary support in the 35th legislature. Grubbs predicted success and offered his services to Arlington in exchange for the community's paying his expenses while he was in Austin. Grubbs was optimistic because the state's Democratic party had come out in favor of an A&M extension college in North Texas and the A&M president had also recommended several branches be built. Arlington's leaders agreed to Grubbs' terms and organized a finance committee to raise the money to defray his expenses. Other than his expenses, Grubbs received no other money or compensation from Arlington.[5]

4.4 After removing the central tower from the original Arlington College building, Grubbs Vocational College used this structure for classrooms and, later, as a freshman dormitory.

Grubbs promptly left Arlington for Austin. Upon arriving in the state capital, he met an old friend, A. D. Jackson, with whom he had worked earlier on the industrial education movement in the state. Grubbs asked Jackson to recommend a name for the proposed industrial college and Jackson responded without hesitation, "Grubbs Vocational College." After receiving permission to use the name from the Arlington committee sponsoring his trip, Grubbs inserted it into the bill he had drafted which would establish the school. Grubbs then gave the bill to the Tarrant County delegation in the House of Representatives, and they introduced it as House Bill 656 on February 12. The representatives sponsoring the bill were Charles A. Burton, C. E. Walker, and I. T. Valentine.[6]

A few days after its introduction, the bill was sent to the House Committee on Education, where it met stiff opposition led by Representative William Fly of Gonzales. Hoping to forestall a defeat, Grubbs issued an appeal to Arlington leaders to join him in Austin to help lobby legislators. A number of individuals responded to his call, including Frank McKnight and Leslie P. Coulter. He also made a few minor revisions to the bill and gave it to State Senator O. S. Lattimore of Tarrant County. On March 1, Lattimore introduced the legislation as Senate Bill 449. Unlike its reception in the House, the bill was referred to the Senate's Education Committee and was passed on March 10 without a dissenting vote. The bill then reached the House and was referred to the House's Education Committee, where it had been stalled before. Grubbs, the Arlington businessmen, and the county's representatives and senators lobbied zealously for its approval by the committee. The committee vote on the bill ended in a tie, but committee chairman W. E. Thomason of Nacogdoches broke the deadlock by casting the deciding vote in favor of the bill. This occurred on March 15. Having cleared both the House and Senate committees, the bill made its way to the floor of each body for final vote. On March 20 it garnered in the House the two-thirds vote necessary to become law, with seventy-one representatives voting in favor and thirty-two opposing. The Senate passed the measure without opposition. The next day the Texas legislature adjourned. Five days later Governor James Ferguson signed the bill into law.[7]

The bill that the governor signed provided for the establishment of Grubbs Vocational College as a "Junior Agricultural and Industrial College" to be located in Arlington. In return for the college, the citizens of Arlington were required to donate one hundred acres of "good tillable land" to the state and the "Carlisle Military School property, with all buildings, dormitories, barracks, etc., belonging thereto." The school would be under the direction of the "board of directors" of Texas A&M and would also have its own five-person advisory "local board of managers," to be appointed by the governor. The two boards were to work together, but the A&M directors were to have ultimate authority. The local board was to meet as soon as possible in Arlington to elect officers, get organized, and, with the approval of the A&M directors, appoint a dean and faculty for the college. The bill defined the mission of the college as being for "the education of white boys and girls in this State in the arts and sciences in which such boys and girls may acquire a good literary education . . . together with a knowledge of agriculture, horticulture, floriculture, stock raising and domestic arts and sciences. . . ." At the same session, the legislature also established John Tarleton Agricultural College in Stephenville as another extension of Texas A&M.[8]

4.5 Described as dilapidated, the gymnasium with its indoor pool was renovated and converted into a mess hall in 1918.

After the bill's passage, Arlington hosted a banquet in early April to recognize and thank Grubbs and the state delegation from Tarrant County for their fine work. Grubbs was the keynote speaker, and he entertained the audience with stories about the bill's passage. He also implied in his remarks that he might be moving to Arlington in the next few months—obviously a reference to his desire to administer his namesake school. After being feted for his success, Grubbs returned home to Greenville, but not before he told Arlington's civic leaders that he wanted to be informed when the local board of managers was to meet to select a dean and faculty. He wanted to be in Arlington for that meeting. Unfortunately for Grubbs, he was neither informed of the meeting nor asked to run the school, a slight which made him bitter toward the school, A&M, and Arlington in general.[9]

4.6 While young men typically learned the skills associated with agriculture, young women enrolled in classes in the household arts, such as sewing.

Summer of 1917 found feverish activity in Arlington and at its new college. By this time, the Arlington Business Men's League, the group organized to pay for Grubbs' lobbying activities, had retired the $11,000 debt of the now closed Arlington Military Academy in preparation for transferring the campus to the state. Additionally, the league had purchased one hundred acres of land west of the campus from J. P. Fielder to be used for the demonstration farm for the college. In June, the deed to this land was given to the state to fulfill the requirements of the bill establishing Grubbs. In July, William B. Bizzell, president of Texas A&M, arrived in Arlington to organize the school and hire its administration. Meeting with Bizzell was the recently appointed local board of governors, which included James Ditto, president; Frank McKnight, treasurer; Webb Rose; Leslie Coulter; and J. P. Fielder. Bizzell guided the deliberations and ran the meetings.[10]

From the beginning, Grubbs Vocational College was considered by Bizzell and the A&M directors to be a branch of Texas A&M and, as a consequence, Grubbs' chief executive officer was given the title of dean, not president. The dean of Grubbs reported directly to the president of Texas A&M. Bizzell appointed a friend and colleague to this position, Myron L. Williams. Joining Dean Williams in the college's administration was R. T. Bruce, registrar and accountant, and Mattie Louise Thomas, secretary to both men. Once Grubbs read about the college's organization in his local newspaper, he became critical of Bizzell's methods and argued that the vocational college was *not* intended to be a branch of A&M, only an "affiliate" of the college. He also characterized the college's organization as being "clandestine and palpably illegal" because the local board had not met with the A&M board of directors. Grubbs, obviously hurt that he had not been asked to manage the college, remained bitter and antagonistic toward the college for the rest of his life. Despite his sniping at Bizzell, Grubbs and his complaints had no effect on the school.[11]

4.7 Directing nine years of the school's growth, Dean Myron L. Williams guided GVC and, later, NTAC with his motto, "Let us press forward."

When Williams arrived in Arlington on August 7, 1917, he found much that needed doing before the college could open on September 20. With just over a month to prepare, Williams had to hire a faculty, decide on school policies and regulations, recruit students, upgrade the campus and its facilities, and work within the A&M chain of command to do it all! But he proved up to the job. Born in Oenaville, Texas, in 1875, Williams' early education was spotty at best. By age twenty, he had only completed the seventh grade. In 1895, however, he went to work at a hotel in Miami, Texas, where he met Lieutenant Governor J. N. Browning. Taken with young Williams, Browning offered him a scholarship to Sam Houston Normal Institute, provided he complete his intermediate education first. Williams accepted Browning's offer, completed his preparatory education in Mobeetie, Texas, and went off to attend Sam Houston, where he graduated in 1899 with the equivalent of a high school diploma. After graduation, Williams held a succession of teaching and administrative jobs in such Texas towns as Amarillo, Miami, and Clarendon. He also continued his education in the summers, attending the University of Texas, where he graduated in 1908 with an A.B. in education. Williams then joined the faculty at CIA in Denton, teaching education courses until 1917. Also during this time, he received his M.A. from Columbia University, taught summer classes at his alma mater in Austin, and befriended President Bizzell of A&M. Bizzell, in the summer of 1917, hired him from CIA and brought him to Arlington to open Grubbs.[12]

4.8 Working just west of the main campus at the college farm, young men learned to erect a poultry house.

Upon arriving in Arlington, Williams was not impressed with what he saw. In his first biennial report to President Bizzell, Williams wrote that he found the campus "badly neglected." "The school buildings," he complained, "were in a state of decay and with practically no furniture or equipment for school purposes, the sewer, water, gas and light systems out of order, the campus grown up in weeds and grass, the fences down and most everything dilapidated."[13]

Williams went on to discuss each of the structures on the twelve-acre campus and how the school used them. His report provides an accurate look at what the campus was like—physically at least—at the opening of Grubbs Vocational College. The buildings mentioned in his report were:

Academic Building—This was a two-story wooden frame building, 50' x 60', with a two-story annex, 30' x 60'. After the building was thoroughly cleaned, stated Williams, it was used to house classrooms for English, history, mathematics, languages, education, and science. The building also accommodated laboratories for physics, chemistry, and biology and the college's library with "about $500 worth of books."

East Barracks—Williams reported that the barracks was a one-story brick building, 25' x 300', with twenty-seven bedrooms, each 9' x 15', two toilets, and one bathroom.

Woman's Dormitory—The woman's dormitory was a two-story wooden structure which had to be overhauled and renovated to be usable. In it were installed laboratories for domestic science and domestic art classes and a kitchen and dining hall were furnished and outfitted. The college furnished the remainder of the building with shades, beds, dressers, tables, and chairs to accommodate women residents.

West Barracks—This barracks was a one-story brick structure, 25' x 125'. During Grubbs' first year, the building was used for applied arts and Red Cross work, as World War I raged in Europe. In the fall of 1918, the building was converted to an auto machine shop.

Gymnasium—The gym was so dilapidated that it was not used at all during the 1917-1918 school term. Williams described it as a "wooden building, boxed and stripped, 40' x 60', with a leaky concrete pool, 20' x 30', adjoining." The gym, however, was renovated the next year and converted into a Mess Hall.

4.9 The courses at Grubbs Vocational College did not focus only on agriculture and domestic science. In the department of Commercial Arts, for example, students could take courses in stenography, commercial law, bookkeeping, and banking.

Mess Hall—The Mess Hall was a small wooden frame cottage with a kitchen and dining hall large enough to handle forty students. In 1918, the building was changed to a domestic science cottage, with laboratory and dining hall for students enrolled in those classes.

Dean's Cottage—The dean's cottage was on a block of land immediately north of the campus and was purchased by a special appropriation of the state legislature.

Campus—Williams reported that the campus was cleared of grass and weeds, the fences repaired, and sewer, water, and gas lines put in working order.

Farm—The one hundred acres of land deeded by the citizens of Arlington to the state for a demonstration farm were located approximately one-half mile west of the campus, where Maverick Stadium and the J. D. Wetsel Service Center are currently located. During the school's first year, the property was fenced, a cottage and barn built, teams and farm implements purchased, and milk cows and hogs placed on the property.[14]

While Williams and his small administrative staff worked to get the campus ready for students, they also went about hiring a faculty. Making up the fourteen-person faculty on opening day were C. H. Alspaugh, assistant professor of horticulture; Berlie Bolton, professor of domestic science; Thomas E. Ferguson, professor of English; Sallie Byrd Henry, professor of domestic arts; Adeline Holloway, instructor of music; Jesse R. McElroy, director of physical training and athletics; J. S. Mendenhall, professor of mathematics; Cora A. Reynolds, instructor in applied arts; J. Mc. L. Ridgell, professor of agriculture; John W. Scott, professor of history and rural economics; Dora Ella Watson, instructor in modern languages; B. W. Wells, professor of biology; H. S. Woods, professor of chemistry and physics; and J. A. Evans, "pecan specialist."[15]

Grubbs Vocational College opened to students on September 20, 1917, with a curriculum consisting of two years of secondary school work and two years of college work. To be admitted, a student had to be fourteen before September 1, show evidence of good "moral standing," be free from contagious disease, and, if a male, able to perform the activities of a cadet. Students were placed in Grubbs' various classes based on the amount and success of formal schooling they had received. At the school, the freshman class was the equivalent of today's tenth grade; the sophomore class, the eleventh grade; and the junior and senior classes, the first two years of college. At Grubbs, the high school students (freshmen and sophomores) took the traditional academic courses of English, mathematics, science, history, and modern languages, and could select electives in agriculture, foods, clothing, manual training, military science (for men), physical training (for women), and home economics.[16]

At the college level there were initially two basic tracks in keeping with the school's agricultural and vocational roots. The tracks were agriculture, which was for young men, and household arts for female students. The agriculture students enrolled in such classes as agronomy, animal husbandry, horticulture, veterinary medicine, agricultural engineering (repair of farm machinery, farm concrete, irrigation techniques, etc.), and economics (rural life problems and rural sociology), as well as the basic academic regimen of English, science, military training, and electives. Household arts students took the traditional academic classes and also courses in clothing (textiles and sewing), foods (cooking and preserving), sociology of the family, and physical training. The curricula was modeled on that of the parent institution and was intended to dovetail into A&M's programs so male students could transfer into advanced college courses without loss of credits and time. The school year was divided into two eighteen-week semesters—fall and spring—and the school offered a summer school for students. Grubbs also offered "short courses" or one-year courses in agriculture and home economics aimed at men and women who could not pursue a degree but who wanted to improve their lives by broadening their education in these areas. During the summers, Grubbs was the site for the summer schools for the city's normal school students. Grubbs also offered college courses over an eight-week summer semester and one-week courses in home economics and agriculture.[17]

Students wanting to attend Grubbs had to pay an annual $3.00 registration fee, $2.50 library and lab fee, and a $5.00 fee for "incidentals." Those living on campus paid an additional $20.00 monthly for room and board. The college also estimated that each student would spend another $15.00-$20.00 a year on textbooks. These fees fluctuated and increased over time, as new fees were added. There was no tuition fee at this time. Despite the school's low fees and its advantageous location between the rapidly growing cities of Dallas and Fort Worth, its first year enrollment was a disappointing sixty-six students, twenty-six of whom were young men and forty were young women. The relatively small number of male students can be explained, in part, by the nation's involvement in World War I

4.10 Although the college had a lower enrollment due to U.S. involvement in World War I, trades courses, such as auto mechanics, electric shop, welding, woodworking, and carpentry, helped to increase male enrollment by the early 1920s.

and the fact that young men were being drafted to fight in the war. According to Dean Williams' official report, the classes broke down as follows:

Freshman Class	21
Sophomore Class	13
Junior Class	17
Senior Class	1
Special Class	14

Williams attributed the meager enrollment to several other factors as well, including the relatively late date in the summer that the college was organized and the debate being waged in the Texas legislature on abolishing the school.[18]

Indeed, while Williams and his staff struggled to build a viable school in Arlington that first year, the legislature's Central Legislative Investigating Committee was looking critically at higher education throughout Texas. In early 1918, the committee recommended the repeal of the act which established Grubbs Vocational College because it believed Grubbs should not be a junior agricultural and mechanical college. The committee report stated:

> There seems little reason to justify the efforts for the development of a junior agricultural and mechanical college at Arlington; land is high in that vicinity, and it will be quite expensive to secure enough advantageously located for the purpose. . . . As a location for a junior agricultural and mechanical college, the school at Arlington has been the source of criticism. . . .

While the committee took exception to the college's original mission, it did conclude that Grubbs could better serve the state in general and the North Texas area in particular by focusing only on vocational instruction and the manual arts. The committee went so far as to offer a bill which would have transformed Grubbs to fulfill its members' vision.[19]

Dean Williams and President Bizzell viewed the committee report as a threat and rallied public opinion in Arlington and College Station against it. They also took their fight to Austin, eventually convincing Governor William P. Hobby to oppose the committee's efforts. Hobby's opposition to the committee's recommendation sealed its fate, and Grubbs' mission was not changed.[20]

Though the committee failed in its ultimate goal to abolish Grubbs and redefine its purpose, the school did change in response to the committee's findings. In fact, during the 1918-1919 school year, the college began offering a one-year course in "automobile repair work" with the intention of "training and equipping mechanics for garages." Additionally, commercial courses in shorthand, typewriting, and bookkeeping were introduced and, like the automobile classes, proved to be popular. Despite these changes, the college still billed itself as a school for "young men and young women who desire not only a liberal literary education but also practical instruction that will prepare them for the vocations of farming, manufacturing, and homemaking." The world war in Europe also impacted the college and precipitated changes. In the fall of 1918, Grubbs College started its Student Army Training Corps (SATC), which was open to all men over

4.11 In 1918 the Texas legislature appropriated $112,500 for the construction of a new Administration Building. The structure, which was completed by the spring of 1919, boasted an auditorium "equipped with a moving picture machine and stereopticon for illustrating various kinds of manufacturing processes."

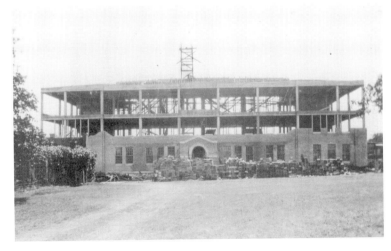

eighteen who planned to go to college. The purpose of the SATC program was to provide scholastic and military training to students before they were sent to officer training camps and then on to active military duty. They were allowed to register for the draft and were immediately inducted into the army as SATC privates. At school they received army pay and military training. Sixty-two men were part of the SATC during the 1918-1919 year, but none of them saw active duty in Europe because the war ended in November 1918. To make room for these men, the school converted the Woman's Dormitory into a barracks.[21]

The war generated on campus a great sense of patriotism, excitement, and support. Williams reported to President Bizzell that his faculty had all "contributed liberally" to the Red Cross and the United War Work Fund and had purchased Liberty Bonds and War Stamps. Students also donated money, time, and energy to the war effort, particularly making surgical dressings for the injured. The college's Clothing Department sewed for the Belgian relief effort and the Red Cross, while the Foods Department stressed the conservation of certain foodstuffs being urged by the U.S. Food Administration. Williams wrote in June 1919 that the "war spirit" had touched the entire campus, even to the extent that "the young ladies were desirous of being organized into a drilling company."[22]

Grubbs' second year brought dramatic enrollment increases of nearly 200 percent, with the student body numbering 192. Young men made up the majority of this total with 143 enrolled, while there were 49 young women at the school. An additional 32 disabled soldiers back from the war attended that year and 88 summer school students, but Williams' totals did not include them. Dean Williams reported the following figures to Texas A&M for the 1918-1919 year:

Freshman Class	26
Sophomore Class	18
Junior Class	26
Senior Class	9
Specials	2
SATC	62
Mechanical	33
Commercial	16

In addition to the growing student body, the campus was also undergoing changes. The legislature had appropriated $112,500 for the construction and furnishing of a fire-proof Administration Building, which was completed in the spring term of 1919. The building, now known as Ransom Hall, still stands on campus. The building measured 149' x 65' and included three floors. The first floor housed the administrative offices,

library, and laboratories for the various agriculture classes. The second floor included classrooms for history, languages, domestic science, domestic arts, and education, and laboratories for botany and clothing. The third floor had classrooms and offices for English, mathematics, and applied arts, and an auditorium furnished with "312 opera chairs and motion picture and lantern slides machine." The school bragged that the new building was "lighted by electricity and heated by steam" and was "fire-proof and modern in every detail." The building's formal opening took place on May 1, 1919, with a standing-room-only ceremony open to the public.[23]

Williams and his staff were obviously pleased with the school's progress, but were not complacent. Williams characterized the approximately twelve-acre campus as "entirely inadequate," and recommended to President Bizzell that "immediate steps" be taken to enlarge the campus to at least thirty-six acres. He also urged Bizzell and the A&M directors to add three new buildings to the campus: a woman's dormitory, a dormitory for men, and an auto mechanics shop. Williams estimated that the expansion he proposed would require $310,000 of state funds, exclusive of furnishings. Williams expressed confidence that the school would grow rapidly, and he was determined to have a physical plant capable of accommodating the student body.[24]

Williams' optimism about the college's future was not unfounded. Indeed, the college experienced steady growth as a result of its location, its improving reputation, and the fact that the end of World War I had prompted returning servicemen either to start or to continue their educations. By the 1919-1920 school year, the college's total enrollment had climbed to 444, and these students came from fifty-four Texas counties. During the 1920-1921 year, 511 students attended Grubbs, while the next year, 1921-1922, saw 680 students enrolled. During the 1922-1923 year, 808 students enrolled in the various courses and programs offered at Grubbs.[25]

Struggling to keep pace with this rapid growth, the college refurbished existing structures, built new buildings, upgraded furnishings, and added equipment. In 1919-1920 alone, for example, Grubbs converted a two-story wooden frame building to a ninety-eight bed dormitory, built a Mess Hall for the disabled soldiers who had started attending the school, opened a new auto shop and machine shop, began construction on a new Mechanical Arts Building, and added five new tennis courts. Also during the year, the college added courses in woodworking, mechanical drawing, machine shop, and the commercial arts, in addition to a complete program for disabled soldiers. Rapid growth also prompted the administration to enlarge the size of the faculty. By the end of the spring semester

4.14 In addition to a tennis team, Grubbs also boasted basketball and volleyball teams for women. Pictured is the 1921 basketball team.

of 1920, there were twenty-eight faculty members at the school (double the number that opened the school in 1917), including seventeen with the rank of professor, one associate professor, two assistant professors, and eight listed as instructors. For the most part, the faculty was young and relatively inexperienced, with twenty-five having had fewer than six years of teaching experience. In considering the highest academic degrees held, five faculty members had earned masters degrees, twelve had bachelors, and eleven, primarily those who taught vocational subjects, had no college degrees. If his reports to A&M are an accurate barometer, Williams had a difficult time retaining faculty because the college's salary scale was not competitive.[26]

4.15 The school's new Administration Building replaced the original Arlington College building, which became a dormitory. Pictured here is the 1918-1919 student body in front of, what is now, Ransom Hall.

Contributing to the college's relatively poor pay scale was the school's inability to attract more than modest funding from the legislature. State appropriations for Grubbs started at $164,300 for the college's first academic year and dropped to $115,100 for the fiscal year ending August 31, 1923, a reduction of 30 percent, and this at a time when the student enrollment had increased dramatically. It certainly should be no surprise that Grubbs started levying additional fees on students to make up for the falling appropriations from the state. By the early 1920s, Grubbs had increased its fees substantially, most notably by charging students an $86.40 maintenance fee for the fall semester and a $64.00 fee for the spring. Like today, schools such as Grubbs in the early twentieth century can best be characterized as state assisted rather than state supported.[27]

While Dean Williams and the faculty concerned themselves with expansion, planning, and running the school, the students at Grubbs enjoyed a number of varied campus activities and a rich social life. Sports, as always, played a big part of campus life, and the school fielded teams in football, baseball, basketball, tennis, and track. The school also sponsored a basketball team for female students. The school's teams were known as the Grubbworms for the first four years of the college's operation, but in 1921, the mascot name was changed to the Hornets. The school's colors were blue and white. These teams competed against those from other schools in the Texas Junior College Athletic Association. For students with other interests, the school sponsored a number of clubs and organizations. For the young men, the Wilsonian and the Star Literary societies offered training in debate and practice in public speaking. Young women had the Round-Up and the Gro-Voco clubs for social entertainment. There was also a Chorus Club for women and a Glee Club for men as well as an orchestra and band. These clubs and groups gave frequent programs for the student body and the general public. The Dramatic Club, open to both men and women, performed plays and other productions throughout the year, and the college touted its "good motion picture machine," which it used to show educational and entertainment films to students. The college also sponsored a chapter of the Young Men's Christian Association.[28]

Beginning in April 1919, the students began publishing a monthly magazine called *The Shorthorn*, the forerunner to today's campus newspaper of the same name. *The Shorthorn* replaced an earlier student publication entitled *The Grubbonian*, which came out only once in February 1919. The title "Shorthorn" was selected by the student body after a campus-wide contest solicited possible names from students. Dean Williams offered $2.50 of his own money as a prize to the student who submitted the winning name. Subscriptions for *The Shorthorn* sold for $1.50 per year, with single copies selling for $.25 an issue. The monthly publication included everything from sports news to student poetry, and from essays to information about campus activities. *The Shorthorn* also published an occasional column by Dean Williams. The magazine proved to be so popular with students and faculty that in 1922 it changed from a monthly to a weekly publication.[29]

For the young men at the school, military training consumed much of their time and energy. The school required that all male students enrolled in the college's high school and junior college programs be cadets. This was in keeping with the college's ties to Texas A&M, a school where the corps of cadets was an influential and prestigious group; its link to Carlisle Military Academy, which had its own military tradition; and the martial spirit of the early twentieth century. This training was designed to "coordinate the mind and muscles," "develop quickness of decision and executive ability," "develop respect for authority," and "increase . . . physical fitness." The military organization at the college at this time included one battalion, which was comprised of four companies and eight platoons. As cadets, the young men received rigorous physical training, practiced military drills, and adhered to a rigid code of conduct. *The Shorthorn* of April 1919 outlined the cadets' daily routine. All young men were awakened at 6:00 a.m. and had fifteen minutes to dress and meet in formation. After an exercise period, the students marched off to breakfast at 7:00. Rooms were inspected at 7:45 each weekday morning except Sundays, when the inspection occurred at 9:30. Classes began at 8:00 and ran until 12:30 p.m. Lunch was at 12:45 and classes resumed at 1:30 and lasted until 4:30 each afternoon. On Tuesdays and Thursdays, the cadets drilled from 4:30-5:30. Supper was at 6:00 and each cadet had to be in his quarters at 7:15 studying, unless he had a pass. Cadet guards walked posts to ensure this was done. If a cadet were caught out without a pass, he was usually given demerits, extra duty in the Mess Hall, or some other punishment. Tattoo

4.16 **Beginning as a monthly magazine in 1919,** *The Shorthorn* **became a weekly newspaper in 1922. Pictured is the 1920** *Shorthorn* **staff.**

came at 9:45 and taps at 10:00, when rooms were again inspected and students were expected to be in bed. Day in and day out, the students followed this routine.[30]

The college established the Reserve Officers Training Corps (ROTC) in the fall of 1921. The War Department assigned Captain Carl A. Bishop to the school as professor of military science and tactics, and Lieutenant L. W. Caine worked as his assistant. Because of the ROTC program, cadets, after graduating from Grubbs, could seek commissions from the military by going on to finish their last two years of college and ROTC at a four-year institution such as Texas A&M. Captain Bishop organized the college's rifle team shortly after he arrived, and the team placed third in the National Inter-Collegiate ROTC match of 1922 and fifth in 1923. Because of the college's military traditions and the administration's desire for order and decorum, a student's dress was prescribed. The school's catalog for 1921-1922 specified in great detail the military uniform for men:

> Present cadet cap; woolen serge blouse, English cut, pleated back, bellows pockets, color patch on the arm of service, four inches long and one and three-quarters inches wide at bottom and one-half inch wide at top worn on each side of the collar just above the lapel of the coat; R.O.T.C. button in metal at the top of said patch; insignia of arm of service embroidered on patch extending from lower part of patch upward to a distance of two inches and being one inch in width, embroidered in black silk; insignia of rank of officers to be worn on shoulder loops; present insignia of rank to be continued; insignia of rank of non-commissioned officers to be the regulation chevron worn on both right and left sleeve three inches above the cuff of coat; gold star on right sleeve, corresponding position; commissioned officers to have one-half inch wide brown braid on sleeves three inches from cuff; in addition, commissioned officers to wear the Sam Brown Belt; all enlisted men to wear leather belts same as officers excepting the shoulder strap; shirt O.D. (with collar attached) to be woolen, linen, cotton, silk, depending on weather; black tie. For evening or chapel formations white linen or silk shirts with detachable white roll collar and black tie and white cuffs will be worn. Breeches same as at present. Spiral wrapped leggings as used at present, and in addition the mounted reinforced leather and canvass leggings for the mounted branches and for drill formations only. Leather leggings for all dismounted officers; boots and spurs or leather leggings for all mounted officers, spurs to be worn at all times when the boots are worn.[31]

4.17 By 1920, Grubbs Vocational College was a mixture of different building types. The west barracks served as a machine shop while the old superintendent's house served as a women's dormitory and dining hall. The newly-erected Administration Building housed most of the school's academic classes as well as the library and auditorium.

Women too were required to wear uniforms while on campus or when they left the school in a group. Their uniforms were described as:

> Blue chambray dresses, trimmed only in white, made by any pattern; blue uniform suits and hats. Black or brown shoes, black or brown hose. White wash middy blouses without colored trimming, or white wash blouses; blue serge or flannel middy-blouses trimmed with white. Red or blue ties, black or blue hair ribbons. Tan or dark blue rain coats and caps; long coats may be worn in extreme weather. Dark blue sweaters and caps. White dresses may be worn by those taking part in recitals.

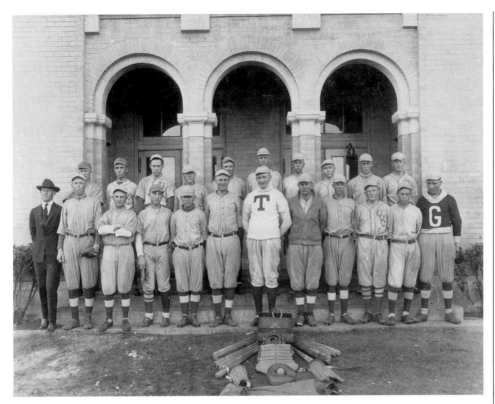

4.18 In addition to baseball, men's athletics included football, basketball, tennis, and track.

Men and women were given demerits by faculty for being out of uniform, not maintaining a spotless room, being tardy to class, or for breaking any one of the college's many rules of conduct. Rosemary Ribbon, a Grubbs student in 1919, complained that "you get demerits for everything you do and for everything you don't do."[32]

Students attending Grubbs could live on campus in dormitories—or barracks for the young men—or at home or in approved boarding houses. The school advertised its dorm rooms as being "furnished with gas or coal stoves, electric lights and bathrooms, tables, chairs, single beds and mattresses." The college inspected the students' rooms daily and required that they be kept neat and "thoroughly sanitary." Room and board for each student cost approximately $15-20 a month, not including laundry. By the early 1920s, however, Williams characterized the school's dorms as "fire traps, uncomfortable and unsightly." In Dean Williams' report written at the close of the 1921-1922 academic year, he listed the building of dormitories as the college's greatest need. The college also offered to a limited number of "industrious young men" the opportunity to work at the school to defray a part of their school expenses.[33]

4.19 This baseball medal was awarded to 1921 Grubbs College graduate, Chester W. Ditto, whose father, James Ditto, was president of the local Board of Managers for the school.

Field trips were an activity enjoyed by many students. *The Shorthorn* frequently reported on trips by students and campus clubs and organizations to such places as Camp Bowie, a military base in Fort Worth; the State Fair in Dallas; and the Fort Worth Fat Stock Show. Oftentimes the students and their faculty sponsor would catch the interurban to their destination in the morning or early afternoon and return to Arlington that evening. Picnics too were a popular activity, and it was common for the faculty and students to plan one picnic each semester. Students also attended chapel services held three to four times a week. Occasionally Dean Williams would fill in by preaching when ministers were unavailable.

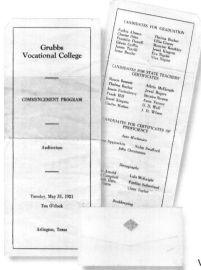

4.20 According to this commencement program, there were twelve graduates completing their second year of college-level work at the May 1921 ceremony. In addition, there were fifteen others who received certificates of proficiency in the mechanical and vocational programs.

Williams also forbade dances and smoking on campus during his tenure.[34]

Students, of course, attend college to receive an education and to graduate. The number of graduates of Grubbs Vocational College climbed slowly and steadily during the school's six-year history. The numbers of students graduating with a two-year college certificate were as follows:

Year	No. of graduates
1918	None
1919	8
1920	5
1921	12
1922	13
1923	23

The class of 1923 was the last class to graduate from the school when it was known as Grubbs because by the next school year, 1923-1924, the college's name had been changed.[35]

The impetus for renaming the school came from Dean Williams, with the approval of President Bizzell and the A&M directors. Basically, Williams wanted to remove the "limiting word" "vocational" from the name and, if possible, shed the image of the school as a private institution. With a name like Grubbs Vocational College, most people believed the college to be privately funded. Williams may have also wanted to remove Grubbs' name from the college because of Grubbs' critical remarks about it, President Bizzell, and A&M. Williams got what he wanted in July 1923, when the Texas legislature changed the school's name to North Texas Junior Agricultural College. Shortly after this, the word "junior" was dropped from the name to shorten it. From this point on, the college was called North Texas Agricultural College, or NTAC (pronounced "N-tack") for short.[36]

During the six-years that Grubbs Vocational College existed as a branch of Texas A&M, the school underwent rather dramatic change and growth. Student population grew from 66 in the fall of 1917 to 808 by the close of the spring semester in 1923. Much needed repairs, renovations, and new construction were completed on the campus' infrastructure and physical plant. The curricula and

4.21 Despite its small size, the Grubbs College library, located in the new Administration Building, was a popular study area for students.

course offerings evolved from the rather narrow focus on agriculture and household arts in 1917 to a more diverse inventory of courses covering everything from arithmetic to zoology. Dean Williams provided the school solid executive leadership, and his personal relationship with President Bizzell ensured that Grubbs would be given serious consideration by A&M at all times. State funding, while inadequate for everything Williams wanted to do, was relatively stable and could be counted on to provide a basic level of support. Students seemed to enjoy the school and its Arlington location and developed a rich campus life as a result. Arlington residents and the city's leadership also were strong supporters of Grubbs, seeing the college as an asset to the town and the region.

Not all problems had been solved. Dean Williams had to constantly contend with high faculty turnover because of low pay, and physical facilities, while improved, were still inadequate for the school's rapid growth. But for the first time in the history of a campus which had undergone multiple name and affiliation changes, the future looked bright. The individual, however, most responsible for establishing the college was Grubbs himself. Ironically, after leading the efforts in Austin to secure legislative approval for the school, Grubbs, to his great disappointment, never held a position at the college. Without Grubbs' lobbying efforts—however self-serving—there would have been no state school in Arlington. Grubbs died in Riverside, California, in 1928 a bitter man, hurt by what he believed was mistreatment and a total disregard for his hard work in Austin on Arlington's behalf. The school for which he worked so hard, however, lived—lives—on.[37]

Diary of a GVC Girl

In the November 1919 issue of *The Shorthorn,* the following excerpt was printed from a diary purported to be by a young woman who attended Grubbs Vocational College. Though the diary is attributed to a "Rosemary Ribbon," there is no record of a student by that name ever attending the college. The passage that follows reflects both the pleasures and frustrations students feel when they are away at college for the first time.

I have decided to keep a diary of my college days here at Grubbs. I just know it's going to be lots of trouble to keep up, and I imagine it makes a person feel perfectly peculiar to put down all her secrets and beautiful thoughts on paper, but I think I will need a diary or something to prove that I have been to college, because if things don't go different from the way they have been, I won't have any sense to prove it. I don't know where I'm going to keep this little book so no one can see it. I might let it stay under my pillow, but then I'd be sure to leave it there when I'm rushing off to a 7:30 class. I wouldn't make the Dean or anyone feel bad, or wouldn't say anything that could make G. V. C. a disgrace to A. and M., but personally, I think this is a night school. Anyway, I'm sleepy all day long.

I like G. V. C. perfectly dear. At first I thought it would be a nuisance, because for three days straight out, I didn't do anything but chase through forty rooms trying to get registered. I just thought if I had to keep that racing stunt up all through the whole year I wouldn't do anything but bump into people at every turn of the stairs. But now I have so much work to do I never even think about it when I bump into people. I guess those things have to happen when you're having a college career.

The only thing I don't like is the demerits. You get demerits for everything you do and for everything you don't do. The other day I was standing in the hall just talking plain to some of the G. V. C. boys, and a lady came along and said I mustn't talk to boys in the hall. I kept perfectly calm and told her all right, and just asked her where could I talk to them then? I don't see anything wrong asking for information you don't know, but she acted real peeved. I guess I got some demerits for that. And yesterday, I just didn't have time to comb my hair nice for 7:30 class, so after it was over, I just stopped for a few minutes to fix my hair and powder my face. I was just a little late for my next class and that perfectly horrid teacher sent in a tardy report. I didn't think I ought to have to tell him why I was late, so I just acted perfectly calm and told him I couldn't help it. He ought to have known that I wouldn't have been tardy if I hadn't had some important business to attend to. Some people are so dense. But I suppose all that has to happen when you're having a college career.

I like the members of the student body perfectly dear. There are some right nice boys here. Sometimes they act like heathens in the hall. Some of them are real funny, and don't seem to know much. There's a boy in English 301 who doesn't even know how to keep his hat off in the room. I guess he can be excused for that though, for he said he had to be taught everything. And the other night at the "get acquainted" party the boys acted like they would know all the girls all their lives, but the other day when we went to the fair they didn't act as if they knew us a bit. But they acted like they knew a whole lot of girls they didn't know, especially when they were riding the mammoth racer and the old mill. They thought they were acting cute, but I don't guess anyone cared. I know I didn't. I expect the girls had as much money as they did.

I think going to college is real romantic. It makes you feel like the stories of

college girls in the Ladies' Home Journal. I don't think the boys are very roman-tic. The other morning I was going down stairs with a girl and she fell clear down from the top to the bottom. A boy was right behind us, but he didn't even offer to help me pick her up.

But there may be a few of the boys who are nice and polite. That afternoon I was telling some of the boys about it, and one of them wanted to push me down stairs just to show me that he was polite. It may be that boys are afraid of the rock pile. I wonder what that is. I've looked all around and never have seen it, only I know it's the place the boys have to go to and break up rocks with picks and shovels when they get a whole lot of demerits.

Well guess I'd better not write any more now. Somebody might find it out and give me some demerits. You just have to take what you get when you're having a college career. I'll write some more soon. I don't know whether I'd better wait for an inspiration like some poets do, or just be like the poet who lets his poems gush from his heart.

4.22 According to the 1923 *Bulletin*, all young women at Grubbs were required to take one hour of physical training each school day.

CHAPTER FIVE

Northaggieland

Grubbs Vocational College became North Texas Agricultural College in 1923, a name the school held until 1949, a period of twenty-six years. For twenty-one of these years, Edward Everett Davis served as dean of the school, leaving his personal stamp on all phases of the college's operations. Davis replaced Williams as dean on August 26, 1925, and led the college through a tumultuous two decades. Williams had left the Arlington school to accept a teaching position at Southwestern University in Georgetown, Texas. During Davis' tenure as the college's chief administrative officer, the school was buffeted by national and international events beyond its control. It was a roller coaster ride for Davis, the faculty, staff, and students who struggled to bring stability and growth to a campus that was hit first by the depression and later by World War II. Despite the problems caused by recession and war, NTAC made significant strides under Davis' administration, which proved itself to be innovative and adaptable. In fact, C. D. Richards, a former professor at the college, characterized Davis as "one of the finest administrators in Texas."[1]

Off campus Davis was a fun-loving man and a practical joker. He especially enjoyed outdoor activities, such as gardening, boating, and fishing, and looked forward to weekends boating on Lake Worth or summer vacations on the Texas coast. On campus Davis had the reputation of being "fair and square, but hard," as former director of business and finance B. C. Barnes recalled. Davis was born on March 21, 1881, in Williamsburg, Missouri, the son of Martha Caroline Davis and Robert Augustus Davis. The Davises moved to Texas in 1885, eventually settling in Erath County. From 1888-1895, Edward attended a community school in the county financed by his father and a few others. In 1899, he entered John Tarleton College in Stephenville, Texas, earning a bachelor of literature degree in 1906. For the next four years, Davis held a number of jobs in West Texas, including principal of the public school at Lingleville, employee at a lumber company in Big Spring, and employee for entrepreneur C. W. Post. Davis admitted in 1939 that it was while working for Post that he decided not to waste "a perfectly good life on the ignoble pursuits of vulgar dollar chasing."[2]

From 1911-1913, Davis, with a renewed commitment to education, attended the University of Texas at Austin and earned an M.A. The next year he joined the UT staff as a "rural research specialist," his responsibilities being to publish bulletins and pamphlets examining rural issues and deliver lectures on rural topics. He held

5.1 In 1934 NTAC constructed a new gymnasium to replace the one built during the Carlisle era. The building served not only for basketball and other sporting events, but also for dances and school plays.

this position until 1923, when he joined Dr. A. W. Birdwell to help organize the education department at Stephen F. Austin State Teachers College (SFA) in Nacogdoches. Two years later, Davis was lured away from SFA by the prospect of serving as dean at NTAC.[3]

When Davis arrived on campus in late summer of 1925, he found the physical plant "run down and poorly kept," the student body "small and lacking in the attitude and *esprit de corps* essential to the spirit and success of such an institution," and, worst of all, a faculty containing a number of individuals, who "were both incompetent and incapable of working harmoniously with their co-laborers."

5.2 By the late 1940s, the North Texas Agricultural College campus had assumed a familiar look. Centered on west Second Street, the main campus occupied eight city blocks.

Davis and Associate Dean George L. Dickey studied the school's problems and, in a fairly short period, decided on a course of action which Davis later described as "positive and decisive" and one that would "either make or break the institution." Their decision was to "purge" the student body of undesirables and "rehabilitate" the faculty with "virile, competent, young people of high attainments and proper educational perspective." To drive the point home to the students and faculty, they adopted the slogan, "High class educational workmanship and no dead-beats in faculty or student body."[4]

Davis and Dickey did not waiver from this course. In the first year alone, 1925-1926, 102 of the 456 students then enrolled were dismissed from the college or left because of bad grades, illness, rules infractions, or behavior problems. By the opening of the 1927-1928 school year, twenty-three faculty members, out of a total of approximately forty, had been replaced with individuals who fit Davis' conception of an effective teacher. In Davis' mind, the best teacher for junior college students was someone who was energetic, capable, enthusiastic, and under thirty-five years old. In a 1941 letter, Davis readily admitted his preference for young faculty members and his strong bias against older faculty:

> I have the highest respect for gray hairs and venerable old age, but I think the instruction of this modern youth should be entrusted to educators in the prime of life. In other words, I think that there is no other curse comparable to the curse of senility in a lot of our college faculties. There are too many good old boys and girls occupying instructional positions with one foot in the classroom and the other foot on the edge of the grave.

Given Davis' attitude and inclination to have a young faculty with, as he put it, no "antiquated, senile human fossils in it," it should come as no surprise that his teachers were relatively inexperienced. In the 1920s, for example, there was not

5.3 A familiar sight in Arlington was the NTAC gateway located at the intersection of Abram and College streets. In the distance can be seen the school's Administration Building, or what is known today as Ransom Hall.

an individual on the NTAC faculty with more than six years of college teaching experience.[5]

While Davis was able to mold the faculty to meet his expectations, he was, in the 1920s, only moderately successful in addressing the physical needs of the college. He did lobby and cajole the A&M administration for increased resources for physical improvements to the campus, but, all too often, his requests fell on deaf ears. The A&M board dutifully forwarded his funding requests and budgets to the Texas legislature, but the lawmakers in Austin were tightfisted for the most part. Before the depression hit Texas hard in 1930, Davis pushed for budget supplements to build a new science building, library, mechanical arts building, and a girls' dormitory (there was not one on campus); expand and improve the college farm and dairy; purchase land adjacent to the campus; upgrade and replace lab and instructional equipment; and demolish some of the older buildings on campus.[6]

Davis did not come away empty-handed. Funds were appropriated to build a new library (now College Hall) in 1926 and a science hall (now Preston Hall), which opened in 1928. The last of the old barracks was demolished. Moreover, more than 4,000 square yards of streets inside the campus were paved, including "College Avenue from the car line to the flag pole in front of the Main Building." Davis also boasted in 1928 that First Street was extended west to Cooper Street and the college had hired a "full-time yard man with a power-driven lawn mover." Once the depression hit, however, funds for such improvements virtually dried up until the mid-1930s.[7]

Dean Davis not only attended to the college's faculty, student body, and physical plant, he also looked at NTAC's curriculum to determine whether it was meeting the needs of students and area businesses. At the time of his arrival, the college had a two-track curriculum, with a college track and a trades/vocational track. The college track was designed to give a student the first two years of a college education in a variety of fields, including agriculture, household arts, pre-medical, and an area the college labelled "general," which was a general course of study to prepare students to transfer to a senior college. The trades/ vocational track was intended to train students to work in auto-mobile repair, engineering, agriculture, business administration, carpentry, machine shops, stenography, accounting, and the electrical trades. To enter the college track, a student had to have a high school diploma or be admitted by special permission of the dean. There was no such restriction for vocational students. The college also offered the last two years of a high school

5.4 During his tenure as the college dean, E. E. Davis resided at the Dean's Cottage, located at the corner of First and College streets. The house, built in 1926 for $10,000, was last occupied by President Woolf before being demolished in the 1960s.

5.5 Post cards were a popular and inexpensive way for students to communicate with friends and relatives. These NTAC post cards show a view of the Administration Building from College Street (right) and the newly erected Science Building, today's Preston Hall (below).

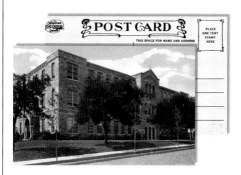

education in what it called its "sub-college division," but restricted the students in this program to the "under-privileged boys and girls from rural communities—those who have not been in reach of a standard high school and have attained an age where they cannot pursue their high school courses in the average high school. . . ." Most of the high school students were from Central and West Texas and, on average, were older than the students enrolled in the college courses.[8]

Upon arriving in Arlington, Davis and his administration surveyed the businesses and industries in the North Texas area to determine if any changes in the curriculum were needed. The survey took two years and revealed that industry needed more employees "between the highly trained technician and the common laborer," particularly in the fields of mechanical engineering, aviation, the electrical trades, dairying, and animal husbandry. Armed with this information, Davis and his administration steadily began to enrich the school's course offerings in these areas. The college also was innovative in the way it delivered these courses, introducing more of them in summer school, allowing students to work in their chosen fields and attend school part-time, offering more classes at night, targeting the needs of particular groups and formulating courses to meet these needs, and making direct recruiting appeals to older and married students. In the 1920s, the overwhelming majority of new courses introduced at NTAC was in the vocational and technical areas, prompting Cothburn O'Neal, a faculty member for the college track, to characterize Davis as being "anti-intellectual."[9]

True to the college's mission of providing educational opportunities to the less fortunate students of the state, fees were kept relatively low. For the 1926-1927 academic year, for example, the fees were:

Registration fee	$ 3.00
Late registration fee	1.00
Course change fee	1.00
Diploma fee	4.00
Certificate Fee (for one-year courses)	1.00
Semester Fees (charged in fall and spring)	
Incidental fee (for office expenses)	7.50
Hospital and medicine fee	3.00
Student activities fee	7.50
Room and board	125.00

The college also charged what it called special courses fees. These were fees levied on students enrolled in vocational courses, such as auto mechanics, machine shop, accounting, typewriting, music, electrical work, and welding. These fees ranged anywhere from a low of $10 per semester for typing to a high of $30 for an intensive automobile mechanics course. In addition, the young men and women in the college program had to spend approximately $50-60 for appropriate uniforms. The only students exempted from wearing uniforms were married students, individuals over the age of thirty, and vocational students. Davis, the hard-nosed administrator that he was, tried to keep these fees as affordable for his students as possible.[10]

Davis' policies produced results. College enrollment at the school climbed from 451 in the 1925-1926 school year to 821 in 1929-1930. One would think that Davis would have taken great pride in these dramatic increases, but instead he expressed deep concern about the number and quality of the students entering college. He especially deplored the trend that thousands of students each year were being admitted to Texas colleges who could not do college work. He lobbied hard for strengthening college entrance requirements. The solution he advanced was to require all students wanting to enter college to take an entrance exam, which would demonstrate their basic mastery of certain high school subjects. He was convinced that requiring only a high school diploma to gain entrance into college was not enough. Writing in 1928, he argued that the "high school diploma is no longer an adequate guarantee of one's fitness and ability to do college work."[11]

He also criticized his colleagues in higher education for being "obsessed with the mania for numbers." He believed that entrance requirements were intentionally kept low in order to boost college enrollments. With growing enrollments, an administrator could then make a convincing case for increased funding for his college. Davis viewed this

5.6 Located just west of Davis Street, the land that made up the NTAC farm is now occupied by the police and J. D. Wetsel Service Center buildings, and the Maverick and Allan Saxe stadiums. The intersection of Second and Davis streets is in the lower left corner of the photograph.

position as shortsighted, arguing that it was unfair to the students allowed entrance to college without the necessary skills to succeed and it was expensive for the legislature to increase its support to schools whose enrollments were "artificially" high. Davis estimated that 25 percent of the state's appropriations for higher education "was practically wasted on inferior students." Despite his efforts, the school did not change its entrance requirements until 1965, the year it entered the University of Texas system.[12]

The Great Depression, which hit the United States in 1929, ended NTAC's steady progress of the twenties and ushered in a six-year period of retrenchment.

The effects of the depression were felt immediately after the opening of the new decade. In the 1930-1931 school year, enrollment plummeted to 657, down a whopping 164 students from the year before. It was not until the 1933-1934 year that enrollment climbed above that of 1929-1930, reaching 954 for the year and 1,023 for the year after. The economic crisis and the accompanying industrial recession had an especially deleterious affect on the school's vocational classes. With jobs drying up and the local economy shrinking, vocational training to learn a specific skill became less attractive. As a result, fewer students enrolled in vocational classes. This trend was exacerbated by the inability of many families to send their children to college. By the early thirties, three departments were especially hard hit: agriculture, home economics, and trades and industries. A cooperative program where students worked in local industry part of the time and attended school part-time disappeared entirely. Based on the University of Cincinnati-Antioch College plan, this program, at its peak in 1930, had 192 students in it, but by 1933 it had been discontinued because of a lack of jobs for the students.[13]

5.7 Trimming the fat had little to do with finances at the college farm. Here, students in an animal husbandry class get hands-on experience in pork preparation.

Accompanying the decline in vocational classes was a steady increase in students enrolled in general college courses. Davis speculated that two factors drove this growth in the school's collegiate division. The first was that the school was receiving more transfer students from private schools because state-supported schools like NTAC were more economical and affordable. The second factor was the general feeling on the part of students and their parents, brought on by the depression, that a general, liberal arts education was more adaptable and marketable than a highly specialized education. Fall enrollment figures for 1930-1933 show this dramatic shift in students:[14]

ENROLLMENT

	Oct. 1930	Oct. 1931	Oct. 1932	Oct. 1933
College	308	405	543	603
Vocational	141	79	54	72
Sub-college	68	61	36	46

The Davis administration responded to these enrollment trends by reorganizing some departments; reducing the number of small classes; reducing the number of teachers at the college, especially in the vocational area; and increasing the teaching load for faculty by enlarging the size of classes in the collegiate department. Davis also recommended, and the A&M board agreed, that the college abolish its sub-college division after the 1933-1934 year, due to a drop in enrollment. While teaching loads became heavier and a few teachers lost their jobs, the state slashed salaries by 25 percent and the college's maintenance and operations budget was reduced.[15]

Despite Davis' efforts to respond to the vagaries of the economic recession, the college came under biting criticism in late 1932 from the Joint Legislative Committee on Organization and Economy, a committee of the legislature whose purpose it was to reduce state spending in all areas possible. The firm of Griffenhagen and Associates, self-described "specialists in public administration and finance," conducted the study on state supported higher education, including looking critically at NTAC's operations. The committee's report was published on December 31, 1932, and must have hit Davis and his faculty like a bombshell.

The committee pulled no punches in its recommendations after studying the school from top to bottom.[16]

While the committee recognized that the school had responded to some of the changes brought on by the depression, it concluded that Davis and his administration had not gone nearly far enough. Instead, the committee called for a drastic reorganization and redefinition of the college.

5.8 Constructed in 1926, College Hall not only housed the college library, but also the student lounge.

Perhaps its most shocking—and threatening—recommendation was that the state "abandon" the college and withdraw state support. The committee concluded, after looking closely at NTAC's enrollment figures, that the school served primarily a local clientele. Indeed, the committee report showed that 88 percent of the student body commuted to school from homes in Fort Worth, Dallas, Arlington, and the surrounding area. In the early 1930s, only 45 students lived in the men's dorm and only 30 women students boarded in homes in Arlington, this out of a student population of approximately 650. In short, the school was a commuter school, where students drove, carpooled, or rode the interurban to campus. Zelda Ramsey, a teacher at the time, recalled that the school was known as a "college on wheels" because of the commuting students. Recognizing this fact, the committee urged Dallas and Tarrant counties to create a "joint county" junior college district to assume control of the college. The committee report prophesied that if the two

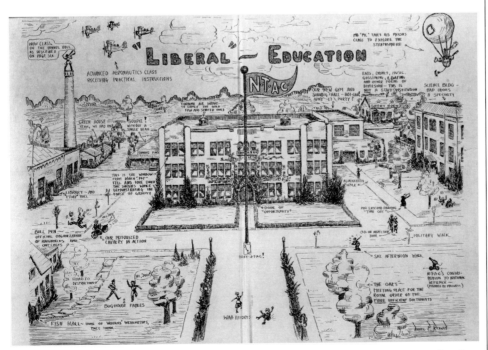

5.9 As this cartoon shows, the school's focus began shifting in the 1930s from a purely vocational and agricultural curriculum to a more traditional liberal arts education.

counties did not do this, then "sooner or later" both would establish junior colleges. The committee was careful to point out that "this is not a recommendation to close the institution, but a recommendation to place the burden of its support upon the people whom the College benefits."[17]

The committee report did not stop there. The committee also recommended a number of major and minor changes for the college, including:

abandoning the agriculture department, closing the college's farm, and removing the word "agricultural" from the school name;

discontinuing all courses in education;

reducing the number of courses offered in engineering to only "pre-engineering training" classes and continuing home economics courses on a "minor scale;"

prohibiting any class be taught with fewer than ten students and greatly reducing the number of subjects offered;

eliminating fourteen faculty positions in the vocational and fine arts fields primarily;

restructuring faculty rankings to shift more faculty to lower ranks;

reorganizing the administration to eliminate the associate dean position and the bookkeeper;

abolishing most student assistant positions on campus;

eliminating summer school sessions because they are not economical;

developing a curriculum which meets the needs of the North Texas community rather than one which mirrors that of A&M;

and forbidding the construction of any additional dorms.

5.10 Prior to World War II, aero mechanics was a popular and well known focus of study at North Texas Agricultural College. The classes were conducted about five miles east of the campus near the present site of the Grand Prairie Municipal Airport.

The report also took Davis and his administration to task for promoting and advertising the college too much. It argued that "state colleges should not need to use advertising methods to attract students" and "state college administrators should be mainly concerned about building up better, rather than larger, institutions," a charge that Davis himself also levelled at his colleagues.[18]

Luckily for Davis and NTAC, the committee report proved as unpopular in other parts of the state as it had in Arlington. Consequently, few of its recommendations were adopted and NTAC remained a part of the A&M system. Occasionally, however, the school would experience repercussions stemming from the report, with the most serious one coming in 1935 when there was an abortive attempt in the state legislature to abolish the school. After 1935, however, the

5.11 Davis Hall, now known as Brazos House, was completed in 1936 with federal funding through the Public Works Administration. According to the 1937 _Junior Aggie_, a student described it this way: "Remember splintered feet, cold showers, shaving rushes, freezing mornings, blown fuses—them days are gone forever, we're living in a real Ho-tel!"

college did not experience another serious threat to its state-supported status.[19]

By the mid-1930s, the college slowly began recovering from the worst effects of the depression. Enrollment climbed once again as students returned to campus and new students enrolled. There was a concerted effort on the part of the administration to push enrollment above the 1,000 mark, a feat accomplished for the first time in the 1935-1936 school year, when 1,007 students enrolled for fall and spring classes. There was steady enrollment growth throughout the remainder of the thirties; the decade closed with the student population reaching 1,632 in 1939-1940. A number of factors fueled this growth, but perhaps the two most important were the college's location and its state-supported status. Because of its Arlington location, NTAC was in the heart of the most populated metropolitan area in Texas. Davis made it a habit of reporting that 10 percent of the young people of college age in the state resided within fifty miles of the school. This, coupled with the fact that NTAC was the only state-supported college close to Dallas and Fort Worth, seemed to ensure growth.[20]

The enrollment growth also made it easier for Davis and his staff to alleviate one of the school's inefficiencies pointed out in the Organization and Economy Committee's report—that is, allowing classes with ten or fewer students in them. Small classes were simply not an efficient way to utilize the college's faculty resources, and this concerned the Davis administration. In 1932, 36.1 percent of the school's classes had 1-10 students, raising the ire of the committee. By 1940, only 7 percent of its classes fell into this category, the lowest percentage in Texas for state schools. Moreover, Davis bragged that the improved efficiency—and greater workload—of his staff gave NTAC the lowest cost per credit hour for instruction of any Texas college. Growth and a judicious reduction in low-enrollment classes made this possible.[21]

The school that emerged after the depression still offered a curriculum based on vocational and general studies. In the vocational area, students were offered a number of classes in agriculture (general agriculture, agricultural administration, agricultural education, agricultural engineering, and pre-veterinary medicine), business administration (general business, secretarial, and bookkeeping), education (elementary and high school), and engineering (chemical, civil, electrical, mechanical, petroleum, and aeronautical). Under general studies, students enrolled in a full array of classes in the arts and sciences in preparation for continuing on to a senior college.

5.12 As this advertisement in the 1929 _Junior Aggie_ indicates, the interurban was the easiest form of transportation between Dallas and Fort Worth for NTAC students. An Arlington interurban depot, located at the corner of Center and Abram streets, was just a short walk from campus.

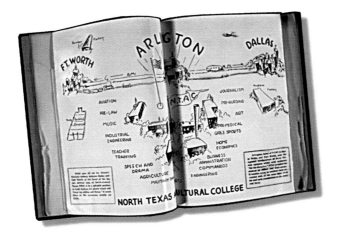

5.13 Dean Davis believed that education was a vital part of the war effort. In this drawing for the 1942 *Bulletin*, NTAC is depicted as a central part in the metroplex's contribution to an Allied victory in World War II.

Students also had the option of concentrating their studies in home economics, music, pre-journalism, pre-law, pre-medicine, and speech and dramatics. While there was occasional friction between the vocational and academic faculties, Davis managed to ameliorate differences when they occurred.[22]

The college did add two new buildings during the 1930s, both constructed without heavy use of state funds. The first was a 96' x 116' brick building located just behind the Administration Building to be used as a gymnasium and an auditorium. The building was completed in 1934 and financed with local funds the college had saved over a five-year period. The other, completed two years later, was a men's dormitory built with federal money through the Public Works Administration (PWA), one of President Franklin Delano Roosevelt's alphabetical agencies. At the time it opened, the dorm was called Davis Hall, but today it is known as Brazos House. The addition of these buildings only reinforced the feeling of the Davis administration that the twelve-acre campus was too small to meet the needs of the school. Davis lobbied hard for A&M to purchase land adjacent to the campus to accommodate the school's growth, but the decade of the thirties ended without the campus grounds being enlarged. At the school farm west of campus, new barns were constructed in addition to housing for the agriculture students. These improvements were financed by the Works Progress Administration (WPA) and cost $59,000. Just after the new decade of the forties began, the Mechanical Arts Building opened on campus, complete with classrooms, workshops, and offices.[23]

Just as NTAC's recovery appeared to be assured and sustainable at the close of the 1930s, the college, in the first half of the 1940s, was once again thrown into a tailspin by international events. The cause this time was the outbreak of World War II in Europe and the United States' entry into the war after the Pearl Harbor attack in December 1941. As the depression had done in the early thirties, the war

5.14 Although military exercises in the 1940s, such as the rifle drill, were normally practiced only by the college's young men, NTAC also sported a young women's rifle team.

caused dramatic enrollment declines for the college, forced a revamping of the courses the college offered, and led to a large number of faculty members leaving campus to join the war effort. From 1941-1945, the war and the college's response to it forced a number of changes on campus.

Many of the changes, of course, stemmed from decreasing enrollments as more and more young men either volunteered or were drafted into the armed services. While the number of women students was relatively stable throughout the war years, remaining at around 300 a year, the number of men attending the college dropped more than 47 percent from 1941-1945. In fact, only 1,041 students enrolled in classes during the 1944-1945 school year, a decrease of 782 from four years before. The Davis administration tried to slow the enrollment drop by recruiting high school graduates under eighteen and more young women. The enrollment crisis would undoubtedly have been worse had the administration done nothing. Accompanying this loss of students was also a loss of faculty, many of whom went on leave to join the military or to work in war industries. During the course of the war, the full-time faculty dropped from seventy-seven teachers to fifty-three. Dean Davis tried his best to keep the faculty in the classroom, arguing that "total war calls for total mobilization" and "the teacher in the classroom may be as useful as the soldier in the trench." He and his administration routinely asked for deferments for teachers in the departments of engineering, chemistry, physics, biology, and mathematics, all subjects considered vital to the war effort. Those teachers who did remain on campus were required by the state to take a loyalty oath, affirming that they were "not members of the Communist, Fascist or Nazi Parties, nor members of any Bund, or any affiliated organization, and further stating that they will not engage in any un-American activities, nor teach any doctrines contrary to the Constitution and Laws of the United States. . . ."[24]

5.15 Due to the restructuring of the Texas A&M system in the late 1940s, Dr. E. H. Hereford (far left) became the first "president" of NTAC, succeeding outgoing dean, E. E. Davis (fifth from the left). The importance of this new title is seen in the 1949 *Junior Aggie*, which called the first inauguration a "coronation."

The focus of many courses changed as the result of WWII and the all-out national effort to defeat the Axis Powers. Physics students learned photography and the techniques used to interpret aerial photographs, while students taking geology learned map skills. Biology teachers concentrated on clinical laboratory techniques, while business professors taught industrial accounting. The war's causes, the Allies' aims, and the hoped-for shape of the postwar world were all topics considered in history, government, and economics classes. A member of the art department taught classes in camouflage. The war effort even removed the gender barrier in engineering classes, as young women were allowed to enroll in these classes beginning in 1943. ROTC cadets learned commando techniques and spent forty-five minutes a day in rigorous physical training, followed by lessons in jujitsu and Japanese. The war spawned new programs at NTAC, many of them financed by the federal government. One of these was a pilot training program, where students divided their time between the classroom and local airports. Another federal initiative was the National Defense Program, which trained students in the technical trades of aircraft sheet metal, machine shop, and jig building. In 1943, the Bureau of Naval Personnel designated the college as an instructional center for 350 trainees in the Navy's V-12 program. Four Navy and three Marine platoons were assigned to NTAC during the last two years of the war. Because of all of these changes, the college's promotional materials appealed to prospective students to "find your opportunity in NTAC's war program."[25]

In April 1945, as the war was coming to a close, Dean Davis prepared a report for the president and board of Texas A&M on the state of NTAC and its prospects for the future. The report was an optimistic document, revealing, through Davis' eyes, what had been accomplished at the school and what had yet to be done. In the report, Davis alluded to his approaching retirement and predicted that the school would have an enrollment of 2,500 in the "immediate postwar period." Because of this expected spike in the student population and because campus facilities could only accommodate 1,900 students, Davis argued that an auditorium, a new classroom building, and a library needed to be built. Davis also called for further development of vocational courses for women and the construction of a women's dorm. Davis pointed with pride at the school's accomplishments in its engineering, agriculture, arts and sciences, and fine arts courses, and he forecast further development of the school's guidance and counseling program, which, he wrote, was in its "pioneering stage." Davis concluded that "a brighter day [was] dawning" provided the legislature—or A&M for that matter—did not financially strangle the institution.[26]

Davis retired as dean on June 1, 1946; he was sixty-five years old. He had taken the school through the depression and the Second World War and positioned it for steady growth and development in a postwar world. The optimism Davis revealed in his 1945 report was not unfounded. Indeed, his prediction that the school would have a student body of 2,500 shortly after the war proved accurate, when, in 1946-1947, enrollment climbed to that level. A brighter day was indeed

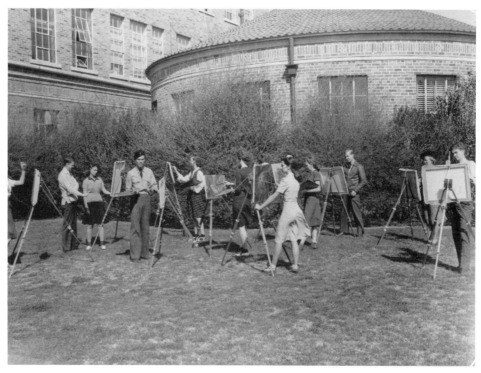

5.16 Professor Howard Joyner and his outdoor painting class just behind the Roundhouse, c. 1946.

dawning on the NTAC campus when Davis retired to his home near the southwest corner of Park Row and Davis, his namesake street.[27]

Taking Davis' place as the school's chief administrative officer was Dr. E. H. Hereford. Hereford was appointed acting dean in 1946 and the college's first president on October 28, 1948, in a public inauguration ceremony. Hereford was a native of Llano County. He received his undergraduate education at North Texas State Teachers College in Denton and Baylor University in Waco, his M.A. from Southwestern University in Georgetown, and his Ph.D. from the University of Texas in Austin. Prior to coming to NTAC as registrar in 1942, he had served as ward school principal in Llano from 1916-1921; teacher at Southwestern and UT while pursuing his graduate education, 1921-1932; superintendent of schools in Corpus Christi from 1932-1935 and president of Corpus Christi Junior College from its establishment in 1935 to 1938; state college examiner and curriculum director for the Texas Department of Education from 1938-1941; and dean of staff and director of public relations at the Hockaday School in Dallas for one year. At NTAC, Hereford was groomed as Davis' likely replacement, being promoted from registrar to acting associate dean in 1943 and acting dean after Davis' retirement three years later.[28]

5.17 In the 1940s the Fine Arts Department, which included music, art, and speech, was housed in this structure located on the present site of the Fine Arts' Mainstage Theater.

Like Davis before him, Hereford was criticized by some faculty as being "autocratic" and "egotistical in attitude," with his solutions, in his mind at least, always being the right ones. C. D. Richards, while recognizing Hereford's immodesty, characterized him as a "sophisticate" and a president who preferred the "scholastic" side of the school over the "vocational." Cothburn O'Neal remembered Hereford's push to upgrade the faculty by requiring doctoral degrees whenever possible as a prerequisite for new hires.[29]

Hereford was the first *president* of NTAC and the first individual to have to work within a restructured Texas A&M system. In fact, the new A&M system was formally created on September 1, 1948, and included A&M, NTAC, Tarleton, and Prairie View A&M. The chief administrator of the system was called chancellor, and the former deans of the branch campuses became presidents. The newly titled presidents reported to the chancellor and ultimately to the board of directors for the system. This reorganization was designed to give each school more autonomy and to free up the president of Texas A&M from having to serve as both college president and essentially chancellor. With the change, the College Station campus would have its president and the system a chancellor. Despite the reorganization, Hereford still had to work within the system's rigid administrative structure and its philosophy to keep the branch schools subordinate to the College Station campus.[30]

As of fall 1948, NTAC's administration included Hereford as president; J. S. Hopper, dean; Maxine Mitchell as dean of women; B. C. Barnes, registrar; Joe Bailey, business manager; and Orsen Paxton, commandant of the ROTC. The Hereford administration concentrated its attention in the 1940s on managing the many changes to the college brought on by the end of WWII. Spurred on by the G.I. Bill of Rights, returning soldiers enrolled in NTAC in droves, sometimes accounting for as much as 46 percent of the student body. As the college enrollment grew to well over 2,000 students, new teachers had to be hired and returning ones assimilated back into the classroom.

The college also was under contract with the Veterans Administration to provide former servicemen training in the fields of agriculture, trade, aviation, and electrical trades, and, for women veterans, homemaking. The college initiated new courses, such as a four-semester program for cooks and bakers developed with the Texas Baking Association and a few classes on the new medium of television. Expenses for students were kept as low as possible. The college estimated that total expenses for a male student, not including room and board, was approximately $132.85 for nine months, while female students paid $88.00. The difference between the two was the cost of the uniform the young men were required to purchase. Moreover, for the first time, the Texas legislature, in the late 1940s, approved state colleges' levying higher fees on nonresidents as compared to state residents.

5.18 The most popular form of hazing at NTAC was the freshmen's traditional duck waddle from the campus to Arlington's mineral well, located at the intersection of Center and Main streets. Once there, each freshman was forced to drink the mineral water before staggering back to campus.

As was often the case, the school's budget, set by the legislature at $582,499 at the end of the decade, was $200,000 short of what the Hereford administration requested.[31]

In addition to the management of the campus, Hereford found himself having to strategize on ways to transform NTAC from a junior to a senior college. There had been a local movement afoot since 1937 to elevate NTAC to a four-year school and to change its name. This movement was being pushed by alumni, local citizens interested in seeing a state-supported senior college in the Dallas-Fort Worth area, local legislators, and cautiously by first Davis and then Hereford. The arguments used to try to convince both the A&M board and the Texas legislature that NTAC was deserving of four-year status were many and compelling. Davis articulated them as early as 1938 in a letter to the A&M president and board. In the letter, Davis pointed out a number of reasons for advancing the school, including its location "near the center of the state's greatest population area;" availability of ample part-time employment opportunities for students; satisfactory facilities, such as labs and the library; the large size of the school's freshman class (the basis upon which the success of senior rank would be determined); and the relatively low cost of instruction at the college (at this time NTAC had the second lowest cost per credit hour ratio in the state).

Davis, always the shrewd administrator and politician, did not want to alienate A&M or any other senior-level school and, as a result, recommended that upper level instruction be allowed only in courses which would not conflict or compete with those offered in other institutions. Specifically, he argued that "the four-year collegiate service at NTAC might well be extended to include the subjects of government, history, economics, sociology, geology, biology, chemistry, journalism, business administration, home economics, English, and modern languages." The semi-technical industrial courses, such as aeronautics, electrical trades, radio, and machine shop, would remain on the two-year level. As a concession to A&M, he also recommended that the school not offer junior and senior level classes in agriculture and engineering. Davis concluded his letter saying these changes should be made "very slowly and conservatively; that new courses with small classes not be permitted under any circumstances; and that no new course be added until the demand for it gives absolute assurance that there will be a class of sufficient size to keep the unit cost of instruction in line with the average cost for similar services in other institutions."[32]

Other arguments that were used by the pro-senior college forces emphasized a negligible impact on the state's budget to elevate NTAC. In fact, the proponents argued that the college, being a commuter school, would need no expensive new dorms, only a parking lot to accommodate more cars. They also averred that no new faculty would be needed because the college was already offering more semester hours of classes than many of the state's senior colleges. Finally, appealing to social conscience, NTAC's administrators pointed out the need for educational opportunities at the senior college level for "the great middle-class of society" in the North Texas area. The college was not a "rendezvous for flappers and highsteppers," but rather an institution providing education for a more purposeful student body, they argued. By the late 1930s, the proponents of advancing NTAC to senior rank were working in concert with those people at Tarleton trying to do the same thing.[33]

Despite the best efforts of Davis and Hereford, the A&M board refused to budge on the senior college question. Most faculty members at NTAC believed, as did the alums, that the A&M board opposed four-year status for the college because it feared the Arlington school would quickly overtake the College Station campus in size and prestige. Whatever the reason for the board's opposition, there was also great resistance to the idea in the legislature and the governor's mansion. All legislative bills introduced in the 1930s and 1940s to elevate NTAC's status failed in the Texas legislature. Many legislators believed that adding more schools to the senior college ranks would dilute state support for the schools already at that level. Texas Christian University in Fort Worth and Southern Methodist University in Dallas, both private schools, viewed a four year school in Arlington as unwelcome competition, and opposed the plan too. In short, the lobbying efforts to make NTAC a senior college stalled in College Station and Austin. It was not until 1959 that the college became a four-year school.[34]

Though NTAC's supporters were unsuccessful in the 1940s on the senior college question, they did win a significant victory in

5.19 According to the 1938 *Junior Aggie*, the purpose of girl's athletics was to teach the "mechanisms" of the human body, its diseases, and its care. Pictured is the 1938 women's tumbling class.

NOW DO YOU KNOW WHY I WANT TO SIT THIS ONE OUT?

JITTERBUGGING....REMEMBER?

5.20 Popular culture took its toll at NTAC in the form of the jitterbug. By 1941, the dance was so unpopular that a petition was circulated to stop all jitterbugging at formal dances. The debate ended in a compromise, however, as jitterbugging was allowed in only certain areas of the dance floor.

1949 when the school's name was changed. Throughout much of the forties, the school's supporters believed that the school's name was inadequate and actually misleading to the general public. They especially wanted to see the word "agricultural" removed from the name because agriculture courses were only a small—and at this time minor—part of the curriculum. They argued that by keeping "agricultural" in the name, many potential students would be misled about the nature of the courses offered at the college. On this question, NTAC's supporters received the blessing and support of A&M board. With the support of A&M behind them, NTAC proponents began to lobby the Texas legislature for a name change. The name they preferred, and one which the A&M board rallied behind, was Arlington State College.

In summer of 1949, Senate Bill 93 passed the Texas legislature, formally adopting the new name for the school. The bill stated that the old name was "insufficient to properly designate the purposes for which said College was founded, and who may attend said College. . . ." The bill also abolished the local board of managers for the college and transferred the board's powers to the A&M board of directors. This change had virtually no impact on the college's operation because the local board had never exercised any real authority over the college since its creation in 1917.[35]

Students and ex-students were pleased with the change and played a major part in lobbying legislators and even, early on, the college administration for it. They believed that such a change would boost the college's prestige and the value of their diplomas as a result.

There is no doubt that alums of NTAC looked back with fond memories of their college years. In fact, student life at NTAC was rich, diverse, and, according to many alumni, just plain fun! Generally speaking, students saw themselves as either day students, that is students who commuted to campus, or boarding students, those who stayed in dorms or in boarding houses close to campus. Most student activities were open to both groups. *The Shorthorn*, throughout the NTAC years, continued to be published weekly, keeping students abreast of news of events and activities both on and off campus. The newspaper's staff was made up of from twenty to twenty-five students, and these students were responsible for all aspects of the paper's operation. A student editor was selected each year to direct the week-to-week activities of the paper, and faculty members, such as W. A. Ransom and Duncan Robinson, served as sponsors. In 1923, the first annual, the *Junior Aggie*, was published by a student staff. The school annuals, covering as they do all aspects of campus life, were popular mementos of college life and today, of course, serve as historical sources for examining the college's history.[36]

For young men, ROTC continued to play a major role in their college lives. True to the college's roots as a military academy and to its ties with Texas A&M, the NTAC cadet corps included virtually all of the male students, except those who were married and those over thirty. The corps was intended to instill in students the traits of loyalty, cooperation, honesty, initiative, punctuality, leadership ability, and commitment. Because the number of ROTC students fluctuated in direct proportion to the college's enrollment from year to year, the number of military companies also fluctuated. In 1933, "The Crack Platoon" was founded as NTAC's military drill team. The platoon changed its name in 1937 to the Sam Houston Rifles. The Rifles, nicknamed the "Jodies," are the oldest ongoing organization in the corps of cadets at the college. During the NTAC years, a strict military hierarchy existed, complete with a rigid code of honor. Freshmen, or "fish," had to defer to the sophomores in the corps, and hazing was so common many "fish" adopted the motto: "When in Rome, do as the Romans do; when at N.T.A.C., do as the old men say."

In fact, hazing was so common that Dean Davis tried in vain to end the practice by expelling students guilty of it and formulating policies against it. Despite the dean's efforts, hazing in the form of paddling underclassmen was widespread throughout his administration. He could not overturn or reverse years of tradition. The poem that follows, entitled "Good Will," was written by a student whom Davis expelled for hazing and reflects one student's desire to maintain this tradition:

> Hazing, they say is against the law,
> The deal they give us is always raw.
> To oust such boys as Geran, Westbrook, Trainer
>   and Greene,
> Is mighty fine sport for our dear old dean.
>
> Our love of love is oh so true,
> With old N-Tac I'll bet he's through.
> To give the dean waddin', he did desire,
> Now, boys, it's time for return of fire.
>
> Although, the dear dean loves us well(?)
> He damns us plenty and gives us hell.
> So play the game fair and let him rave,
> To a damn good school, we'll somehow pave.
>
> When hazing(?) is stopped in this grand old place,
> The dog that claims it will have little race.
> So, beat a little ??? at your own good will,
> We unfortunate Sophs will foot the bill . . .

"Fish" or freshmen in the corps were also the target of a campus-wide practice which involved the town's famous mineral well located just south of the railroad tracks on Center Street. About the third week in the fall semester the corps held "Mineral Water Day," where NTAC freshmen cadets were marched down to the well and forced to drink from it. Because of the water's purgative properties, it was considered great fun to watch the freshmen literally run back to campus in search of a bathroom![37]

In addition to ROTC, there were a host of clubs and organizations open to students. In 1933, for example, there were more than twenty-five such organizations, including clubs for students from Dallas and Tarrant counties and West Texas. For students with an interest in a subject or activity, there was the Agriculture Club, Home Economics Club, Engineering Society, Pi Mu Club (pre-med), Commercial Club, Art Club, Women's Athletic Association, Tennis Club, Athenian Club (literary), Dramatic Club, and Coop Club. Students with an eighty-nine average overall could join Phi Kappa Theta, an honorary society. For students with an interest in music, the Aggie Melody Men, Treble Club, and Glee Club offered opportunities. The Bull Pen Society promoted "good fellow-

5.21 **Minnie Pearl of the Grand Ole Opry hosted NTAC's first dance of the 1948 fall semester.**

ship" among the "off-campus" male students, while the "T" Association was restricted to male students who lettered in one of the school's major sports (football, basketball, tennis, track). The social clubs open to the young women on campus included La Docena, Avolonte, and Sans Souci. All of these clubs sponsored meetings and activities open to their members and oftentimes other students.[38]

A "Students' Council," organized in 1919, dealt with "breaches of military discipline and of the honor system" and worked with the administration to improve student life. Additionally, the council planned picnics and other activities throughout the year. Among the activities the students enjoyed were trips to Dallas, Fort Worth, and other surrounding towns to participate in parades, competitions, and contests. The school band performed in the North Texas area, while ROTC drill teams competed for awards at local, regional, and, at times, national competitions. Perhaps the students' favorite activity was dances held throughout the year at the school. Marcella Bonte Wilemon, an NTAC student in the late 1930s and early 1940s, remembered the dances as being a very special part of college life. The young men, she recalled, looked dashing in their dress uniforms and boots. Sometimes even the dances caused a stir on the campus, such as when, just before WWII, a group of students petitioned the college administration to prohibit "jitterbuggers" at college-sponsored dances. The petitioners argued that the wild gyrations of the "buggers" were obstacles for the other dancers. Davis wisely stayed out of this debate. Martha Hughes, a former teacher at NTAC, remembered spontaneous dances the students held at noontime across the street from the gym, much to the chagrin of Davis.[39]

NTAC also sponsored lectures and performances which had broad appeal to both students and the general public. Guest speakers addressed weekly assemblies at the school, and included everyone from politicians, to authors, to academics. For example, in 1936 the school hosted Ruth Bryan Owen, the U.S. minister to Denmark; Frances Perkins, U.S. Secretary of Labor; Agnes MacPhail, member of the Canadian Parliament; Upton Close, historian and lecturer; William McAndrew, superintendent of the Chicago public schools; and Edward Howard Griggs of the Brooklyn Art Institute, just to mention a few. Other noted individuals who spoke at the campus were J. Frank Dobie, Texas writer and folklorist; historian Walter Prescott Webb; Texas governor Buford Jester; and historian Arnold Toynbee.[40]

Lectures were balanced by the many athletic contests in which the school participated. Of the various sports, football attracted the largest crowds and the most local support, and the team played a schedule of seven to nine games a year. The NTAC Hornets, as they were called, played junior college teams and junior varsity teams from senior colleges, including such schools as Decatur Baptist College, Terrell School of Dallas, Peacock Military Academy of Dallas, Texas Military College of Terrell, Paris Junior College, Hillsboro Junior College,

5.22 In sports, NTAC's great rival was John Tarleton Agricultural College, or JTAC. Pictured is the crowd, the coaches, and the 1939 NTAC football players as they prepare for the annual Thanksgiving Day match-up.

Marshall Junior College, and Texarkana Junior College. Without a doubt, NTAC's fiercest rivalry was with John Tarleton Agricultural College (JTAC) in Stephenville, its sister school in the A&M system. Almost every year, NTAC and JTAC faced each other in a game which was the "homecoming" game for the home team. In true Aggie tradition, the school hosting the game prepared a bonfire and held a pep rally before the game. The rivalry became so intense that it was considered great sport for students of the opposing school to sneak to their rival's campus and ignite the bonfire prematurely. Former students still remember the incident in fall of 1939 when two NTAC students piloted a Taylorcraft airplane to

Stephenville and dropped a phosphorus bomb on the JTAC bonfire. Before the Arlington students could turn the plane and head for home, however, a Tarleton student grounded the low-flying aircraft by throwing a piece of wood into its propeller. After the plane crashlanded, the pilot and his friend were dragged from it and a large "J" was shaved on their heads. Dean Davis ended the bonfire ritual after this episode.[41]

The NTAC Hornets played their home games in a stadium which was located about where the Activities Building is now. It was not uncommon for the stadium to be sold out for these games. The student body and the local community supported the team and were enthusiastic boosters, and the strains of "Northaggieland," the school's fight song, were heard after each Hornet score. The song, written by the legendary NTAC band director Colonel Earl D. Irons with words by Enid Eastland, went like this:

5.23 As stated in a wartime bulletin, "Your country needs you strong. Good health is a necessity forced upon us by the stern demands of war. Consequently the college is striving to keep alive its program of inter-collegiate athletics." Here, NTAC takes on Tarleton in front of a home-team crowd in 1946.

> There is a land fair—
> Northaggieland!
> And it's a land where
> Each man's a man;
> There is a charm
> Where Hornets swarm
> That's not in any other place on earth you'll find.
> Hornets! That is our name!
> Fair play! That is our fame!
> For true to thee,
> N.T.A.C.,
> We'll ever be—until the end of time—
>   (That's the old fight, boys!)
> For we are Aggies,
> North Texas Aggies,
> And we've got that old fight to the end!
> Quit never!
> Stand by them ever!
> That blue and white that we defend.
> Oh, we sting'em hard, we sting'em fast, we sting'em till they swell,
> We give'em war, we give'em woe, we give'em worse—and— well—
> We are the Aggies,
> North Texas Aggies,
> And we've got that old fight to the end!
>   (That's the old fight, boys!)[42]

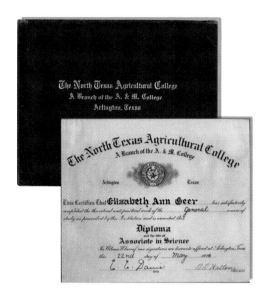

5.24 NTAC's general studies program was popular with those students desiring to obtain the first two years of coursework leading toward a bachelor's degree at a four-year school.

In addition to football, NTAC fielded a men's track and field team, tennis team, and basketball team. Because women were not allowed to compete interscholastically, the college in 1927 organized the Women's Athletic Association and established a system where they could earn a "letter" by participating in several sports, including basketball, indoor baseball, volleyball, tennis, hiking, and gymnastics. The college's coaching staff was minuscule, and generally included an athletic director who coached football and basketball, a track and tennis coach, and a "coach of girls' athletics."[43]

The student body elected six cheerleaders a year—three men and three women—after interested students "tried out" at the first home football game of the season. Elections were also held for class officers each year and for the king, queen, escorts, and princesses for a spring coronation dance. Five students, also elected, served on the important Student-Faculty Committee, which helped to establish rules and regulations for the campus.[44]

Students' behavior was strictly controlled on campus. Boarding students were required to live in dormitories or in approved boarding houses near campus. Car radios could not be played on campus during the daytime, and dancing, "on or near the campus except as regularly scheduled and under college control," was forbidden. All boarding students were required to remain in their rooms from 7:20 p.m. to taps—this being the evening study period. Anyone wanting to leave campus for an evening was required to request a pass from the commandant, in the case of men, or from the dean of women, in the case of female students. Firearms and explosives, except for ROTC purposes, were not allowed on campus, and the use of tobacco was prohibited everywhere except in the dorms and dining hall. The college maintained a record of demerits for each student, and students could be dismissed if they amassed more than twenty demerits per term. Demerits were given for rules infractions and shortcomings observed in inspections. Cadets residing on campus had to wear their uniforms until after supper every day and women students had to as well. The school mandated that the deportment of students "be dignified and courteous under all conditions and

5.25 One of the more popular events at NTAC was the annual coronation ceremony of the queen of the student body. Pictured is the 1935 ceremony, which took place in the newly-constructed gymnasium.

circumstances" and that they be held accountable for their actions both on and off campus.[45]

During the NTAC years, students going to school fulltime generally had classes five days a week, with lecture classes scheduled for the mornings and labs in the afternoons. Students spent the majority of their time on campus, eating lunch in a cafe called the Shorthorn or at the Student Exchange. The library was open six days a week and was a popular spot to study or do assignments. Meetings of the various campus clubs and organizations were generally held on Thursday afternoons, and most social functions were held on either Friday or Saturday evenings. Former students often look back on campus life during these years and characterize it as being rich, fulfilling, and innocent.[46]

As the decade of the forties came to a close, the college had a new name, a new president, a vibrant campus life, and was operating in a newly reorganized Texas A&M system. The depression and world war of Davis' time had given way to a period of greater stability, both economically and in international affairs. With this stability came more and more students and the pressure their numbers exerted on the college's inadequate campus and physical plant. Additionally, the depression and the enrollment patterns it produced had changed the college in a fundamental way, causing the administration to place more resources and emphasis on the general collegiate programs as opposed to vocational areas. The college that emerged on the eve of the 1950s, Arlington State College, was no longer content with its two-year status or the limited educational role it had played in the Dallas-Fort Worth area. Indeed, it would fall to President Hereford, the faculty, staff, and the college's many supporters to try to move the school to the next level of development—senior college ranking.

A Student Remembers NTAC

Marcella Bonte Wilemon attended North Texas Agricultural College from 1938-1940. Born and reared in Fort Worth, Wilemon graduated from Paschal High School in May 1938 and enrolled at NTAC the following September. She was sixteen at the time. Wilemon was a pre-journalism major, completing the two-year program in May 1940. In April 1994, Diana Mays, a graduate student in history at UTA, interviewed Wilemon about her years at NTAC. In the interview excerpts that follow, Wilemon fondly remembers the college, its rules, and student activities.

Well, I'll have to tell you how the school worked. If you were married, you had no privileges at all. You could not be an officer in any of the organizations. You could not play football. You were not part of the military. You just could not do anything if you were married. That was one thing. One of the years, and I have forgotten which one it was, there was a story on campus that the dean of women had made the rounds of the girls boarding houses which were one or two. And in one of the rooms she found two girls, one in pajamas and the other in a nightgown. And she told them that they needed to change their night clothes because what they were wearing was very suggestive. A little later on, the same woman . . . sent one girl home because she didn't have socks on with her loafers. And yet, we were just like every other teenager, every other college freshman. Our rules were strict, but we were so innocent and so naive. . . .

The first year out here the girls wore blue chambray dresses with white pique collars and white pique cuffs and little short sleeves. In the fall and winter when it got cold, we had a navy blue wool dress. The only time you were allowed out of uniform was during dead week. . . .

Everybody looked just alike, the fellas in their uniforms and we were in our uniforms. And that is one reason why I do not possess anything in my wardrobe that is denim or chambray. (laughter) When you wear it day in and day out, you don't like it at all.

[In response to a question about dances, Wilemon answers:] Oh! That was what we did! That was our pleasure—dancing. If you went to NTAC, you were a dancer. You danced every

5.26 The college's 1942 *Bulletin* not only boasted an "all out for victory" academic program, but also stressed the fact that NTAC did not overlook the importance of social activities. With nine social clubs on campus during the 1940s, a week seldom passed without a dance in the college gym or library.

opportunity you had. There was a place, they called it "the coffee shop," in downtown Arlington, where you could even dance in the daytime to the nickelodeon. In the fall, the different girls' clubs always had costume dances, Lil' Abner dances . . . and all different kinds of theme dances. And then in the spring time, the [young women] wore beautiful formals. Just absolutely gorgeous formals. Twice a year they had a corps dance with the fellas with a grand march and always silver taps. . . .[Silver taps were when] someone from the band would get out on the quadrangle out in the front of the Administration Building and would play taps at midnight. Everybody would stand at attention. . . . You got a lump in your throat and tears in your eyes every time it happened.

Official Program

$.4808 Selling Price
$.0192 Sales Tax
TOTAL PRICE

50¢

Eleventh Annual Junior Rose Bowl Game

Sponsored By

PASADENA JUNIOR CHAMBER

OF COMMERCE

Arlington State College
Arlington, Texas
vs.
Compton College
Compton, California

SATURDAY, DECEMBER 8, 1956 • **1:30 P. M.**

CHAPTER SIX

We Are
at the Crossroads

*W*hen Arlington State College (ASC) opened with its new name in September 1949, few people could—or would—have predicted the monumental changes in store for it. Indeed, during its eighteen years as ASC, the school underwent fundamental changes in all aspects of its operations, going from a junior to a senior college, moving from the A&M to the University of Texas system, adding graduate-level education, and beginning the peaceful integration of African Americans into the student body. And these were only a few of the changes that took place. During the ASC years, the college became a *cause celebre* for students, faculty, alums, North Texas residents, and local politicians, and it was these groups who pushed and pressured for change, often over the objections—or at the very least, disinterest—of the A&M board of directors in College Station. Without a doubt, the ASC years were the most important ones in shaping the university we know today.

As ASC entered the decade of the 1950s, it was the largest state-supported junior college in the Southwest. This did not, however, prevent it from experiencing an enrollment decline in the late 1940s and early 1950s brought on by the end of large numbers of WWII veterans returning to school and the beginning of the Korean War. Fall enrollment dropped from 1,790 in 1949 to 1,322 in 1952. By the mid-1950s, the trend reversed and enrollment rebounded strongly, reaching an all-time high of 6,528 students by the end of the decade. ASC's growth was so rapid that the college moved from fourteenth in size among state-supported educational institutions in 1951 to fifth in 1959. Arlington itself experienced growth equally as dramatic, going from a town of 6,000 residents in 1950 to a city of 45,000 in 1960. Tarrant and Dallas counties, the two counties from which the college attracts the overwhelming majority of its students, also enjoyed significant population gains in the fifties.[1]

The rapid urbanization of the North Texas area not only impacted enrollment, it also had a major affect on student attitudes and educational interests. In the fifties, ASC students began turning away from courses which they believed were not relevant to their lives and careers—courses such as agriculture and home economics. In their place, students registered in record numbers for classes in engineering, business, and the arts and sciences. From 1953 to 1956, for example, the number of ASC students preparing for careers in engineering almost quadrupled, increasing from 445 to 1,635. By contrast, the enrollment in agriculture for the

6.1 In 1956 and 1957 ASC won back-to-back Junior Rose Bowl championships. On the facing page is a program and ticket for the December 8, 1956, game with Compton College.

same three years increased only from 108 to 173. Home economics fared even worse, as only 36 students enrolled in its courses in 1956. The college's administration realized that this shift in student interests reflected a national trend and was not likely to reverse itself. Aware that ASC students would have to compete for jobs in an increasingly sophisticated, technically advanced world, the college's administration dropped the agriculture and home economics programs in 1957 and 1959 respectively.[2]

Even after these changes were made, students in the fifties at ASC still had plenty of options to pursue. The college offered the first two years of preparation to students working toward a B.A. in English, mathematics, modern languages, and the social sciences, or for those

6.2 Parades were a significant part of homecoming festivities during the Arlington State College years. This entry not only sports the Rebel theme, but also signifies the importance of football in the early 1960s.

working toward a B.S. in geology, math, or science. The college also offered a two-year associate degree in general studies. In engineering, students could take the first two years of study which would lead to a professional engineering degree in either aeronautical, chemical, civil, electrical, mechanical, or petroleum engineering. In the popular "semi-professional" engineering program, students could study aviation maintenance, applied civil engineering, industrial baking, industrial electrical, or industrial mechanical engineering. In the area of business, students could enroll in two-year programs in accounting, merchandising, and secretarial training or, for those working toward a B.B.A., they could take the first two years of the four-year degree at ASC. The college also offered course options in art, music, speech, and physical and health education, as well as "pre-professional" courses in journalism, law, medicine, nursing, and dentistry. In 1954, young men were no longer required to participate in the cadet corps, and ROTC became an option in the curriculum just like any other. ASC college catalogs recommended that a student register for an average of sixteen to twenty hours a semester.[3]

Also during the late 1940s and 1950s, the college initiated a much needed building program and began preparing a master plan for land acquisition and planned growth. The college had many needs in terms of space because there had been no permanent classrooms constructed in thirty years, and the size of the student body and the faculty and staff had increased dramatically. In fact, the last buildings constructed on campus had been the engineering drawing building, completed in 1940, and the aeronautical engineering building, completed the following year. In December 1949, after eight years of construction inactivity, ASC dedicated a new men's dorm, Pachl Hall, to the more than two hundred former students killed during WWII. The dorm was named in honor of Delmar Pachl, an NTAC art teacher who lost his life during the war. Eight years later, a women's domitory, Lipscomb Hall, was formally dedicated and named for Ina Lipscomb, dean of women from 1927-1945. During the fifties, the Texas A&M system, spurred on by the passage of a constitutional amendment which allowed ASC to share in the Permanent University Fund for building money, opened its pocketbook for ASC construction, budgeting more than $6.5 million for this purpose. In rapid succession, a new science building opened in the fall of 1950, construction of an engineering technology building was begun, and a student center was completed in 1953. Other improvements were also funded in the early fifties, including the construction of steam tunnels between some of the buildings, the building of a maintenance shop, the construction of a steel-decked football stadium called Memorial Stadium, the paving of some streets on campus, and the building of tennis courts.[4]

In the late 1950s, the college administration revealed its plans to acquire numerous lots surrounding the campus on both sides of Cooper Street. In March 1958, Dr. M. T. Harrington, chancellor of the A&M system, met with Arlington city officials to discuss the college's expansion plans. During the meeting, Harrington argued that this land was needed to meet the demands of a rapidly growing school. ASC's President Hereford argued for the expansion, explaining that if it were carried out and if the college's athletic facilities were moved to the west farm acreage (the site of current Maverick Stadium), then the college's acreage would be adequate for years to come. A&M planned to finance the purchase of the land through the sale of the college's 237-acre "east farm" located on east Park Row, approximately five miles from campus on the Tarrant and Dallas county line. Hereford announced a ten-year, $10 million building program planned for the proposed new sites. Among the buildings the college president said were being considered for the land were a new science hall and engineering building, "contemporary library," physical education building complete with a swimming pool, auditorium, fine arts building, and administration building. City officials greeted the college's plans enthusiastically and the acquisition process began in earnest. When the college confronted landowners who refused to sell their property, condemnation suits were filed by the Texas attorney general for the land. These legal proceedings were used only as a last resort.[5]

Land acquisition and the construction of new buildings did not stop in the 1950s. In fact, the A&M board of directors budgeted millions of dollars to ASC for new construction, especially after the school achieved senior college rank in 1959. Construction crews were a normal part of the campus landscape as the school struggled to provide adequate space for an expanding student body and a burgeoning faculty. A master plan for the college was unveiled in November 1960, calling for more land acquisition east and south of campus and the creation of a landscaped quadrangle "immediately south of west 3rd Street." The plan located a new

6.3 Courses in livestock were conducted just west of the main campus until they were abolished by President Hereford in the early 1950s.

science building north of the quadrangle, a new library east of it, a fountain in the center, and an administration building west of Cooper Street. The placement of new buildings after 1960 have generally followed the master plan.[6]

In 1960, a new engineering building opened at a cost of $2.25 million and, three years later, a $2.1 million science building housed its first classes. A year later, the school constructed a new library, at this time consisting of two floors and a basement, at a cost of $1.5 million. After the library opened, the legislature appropriated $120,000 to renovate the interior of the old library building to provide space to house music, military science, and student personnel. ASC also turned to innovative ways in which to finance improvements and new construction. In fact, the college was one of the first institutions in the state to use "revenue financing" to build facilities. These revenues generally came from two sources: regular income, such as dormitory room rents and parking fees, and building use fees levied on students as part of their tuition. With funds from these two sources often used to match low interest federal loans, ASC funded a new gymnasium (1962), an addition to the student center (1961), an expansion of the football stadium (1962), and the construction of new dormitories for men (Trinity House) and women (expansion of Lipscomb Hall). In the mid-1960s, ASC added a new student health center with thirty-six beds, built another addition to the student center, constructed an auditorium and theater, expanded parking facilities, and upgraded the physical education building.[7]

6.4 Pachl Hall was named for Delmar Pachl, an art instructor killed in action during World War II. Despite the quiet appearance of students studying in its lounge, this men's dormitory was famous in the 1950s and 1960s for its Tuesday evening dances.

Shortly after ASC left the A&M system to join the UT system, the UT Board of Regents approved the construction of a four-story addition to the library at a cost of $2.1 million, a $1.4 million mathematics-language building, and a $350,000 addition to the men's physical education building. The library addition and the mathematics-language building were partly financed by federal grants. By the mid-1960s, the college campus consisted of approximately 130 acres on the main campus with another 100 acres of former farm property located three blocks west of the main campus. Despite the construction of the fifties and sixties, the college still operated on considerably less classroom and office space than other state-supported colleges and universities of comparable size. To maximize the use of its building space and to cater to a student body which was largely commuter-based, ASC offered classes from 8:00 a.m. to 10:00 p.m. Monday through Thursday and from 8:00 a.m. to 4:00 p.m. on Friday.[8]

The move to the UT system also prompted ASC to re-examine and revise its master plan drafted in 1960. The revised plan followed fairly closely the earlier one, but strove to make the campus more student-pedestrian oriented. The plan called for the closing of a number of streets which bisected the campus, but not Cooper Street. The assumption was that Cooper brought people to campus and could not be closed without jeopardizing enrollment. The revised plan established as the ideal that students not have to walk more than 2,000 feet from class to class. The plan also recommended a compact campus with low-slung buildings, a concession to the fact that tall multi-story buildings with several elevators were more expensive to build and to maintain. The library and auditorium, which faced each other on either side of Cooper Street, were considered campus axis buildings and the plan recommended that new construction occur on the south side of the quadrangle for the sake of "balance." The plan also called for developing the southern edge of campus along Mitchell Street into a "beauty spot." The college's administration adhered to this plan whenever possible when new construction was initiated.[9]

6.5 The original Student Union Building was constructed in 1952 for $238,000. Although this structure makes up less than one-fourth of the present E. H. Hereford Student Center, it originally housed the college exchange store, post office, confectionery, and recreational facilities.

In the midst of ASC's building boom, a tragedy befell the campus on November 24, 1958, when Dr. Hereford suffered a fatal heart attack in his office. Though Hereford had had an earlier attack in July, his death took everyone on campus by surprise. Shortly after Hereford's untimely death, the A&M directors appointed ASC dean, Dr. Jack Royce Woolf, as acting president. In June 1959, the directors named Woolf president of the college. He was thirty-five years old at the time. His Texas upbringing and Aggie background and education made him the directors' first choice. Born in Trinidad, Texas, to Mr. and Mrs. Jeff Woolf and raised in the small East Texas town, Jack served in the Army Air Corps during WWII, rising to the rank of first lieutenant commanding an engineering company. After the war, he attended Texas A&M and graduated with both a bachelor's and master's degree in mechanical engineering in 1948. Three years later, he received his Ph.D. in engineering from Purdue University and then spent five years at Convair as supervisor of propulsion. While at Convair, he taught engineering at SMU in Dallas in the evenings. Woolf left Convair in the summer of 1956 to return to Texas A&M to teach. Woolf came to ASC the following year when A&M decided it wanted to start a graduate school in engineering on the Arlington campus. Though the graduate school did not come about, Woolf was made dean of the college in 1957. The following year, President Hereford died.[10]

At his inaugural ceremony held on February 27, 1960, Woolf and the audience heard Walter Prescott Webb, historian at the University of Texas in Austin, compare the president's position to being in the middle of a see-saw. In this position, Webb maintained, the president would teeter-totter between the college's directors on one end and the faculty on the other. Webb advised that Woolf keep these two different groups apart and, if necessary, protect the faculty from the directors. The historian also said that the president must be able to understand both groups, be tolerant of both, and be capable of explaining one to the other. Webb warned the young president that "since you have not yet refused . . . requests or declined advice, it is possible, in fact it is quite probable, that you now stand at the peak of your popularity as a college president." Webb's words proved prophetic.[11]

When Woolf was designated as ASC's acting president after Dr. Hereford's death in 1958, the movement to make the college a four-year school was coming to a head. As discussed in the preceding chapter, the push to elevate the school to senior status began in the 1930s, but ran into enough opposition by the end of the forties to make the change impossible. Dejected but not defeated, proponents of four-year status once again marshalled their forces, honed their arguments, and initiated a new push in the fifties. This new push was led by President Hereford;

ASC's faculty, students, and alums; the state senators and representatives from Tarrant and Dallas counties; local business leaders; and Arlington's newly elected "boy mayor," Tommy Vandergriff. The proponents of change realized that rational reasons alone would not be enough to carry the day. Indeed, the final decision would be made in the Texas legislature, where logic and rationality sometimes give way to pettiness and parochial vision.

Initially, ASC supporters had little success in Austin. Bills proposing elevating the school to four-year status were introduced in the state legislature in 1951, 1955, and 1957, but each died in committee or on the legislative calendar. Not one came to the floor of the respective chambers for a vote. Also during the first half of the fifties, the proponents of senior college status encountered less than enthusiastic support from the A&M board of directors. In 1955, Chancellor Harrington mailed a telegram to state representatives saying, "We [the board] do not consider it proper for us to support or oppose the change of status of Arlington State College from junior to senior college level." The board was concerned about the increased appropriation ASC would need if its status changed. Chancellor Harrington met the following year with Arlington officials, telling them that the board would not support a change of status unless it was assured that Arlington and its citizens would make adequate land available to meet the needs of an expanded curriculum. Harrington explained that the A&M system had no funds to aid an expanded ASC. Arlington officials did pledge their support in acquiring more land for the campus, and, in 1958, A&M decided to help fund campus expansion by selling off the east farm. By this time, the A&M board had thrown its support behind the effort to make ASC a senior college.[12]

6.6 As the ASC campus expanded south and west along Cooper Street, some Arlington residents found themselves in the way of the school's progress. When the library's foundation was poured in 1962, a wood-framed house stood directly in front of the construction and beside the Science Building.

In 1957, the question of senior rank for ASC was referred to the Texas Commission on Higher Education (TCHE) for consideration and recommendation. The commission, established in 1955, was the forerunner to today's Coordinating Board. Its purpose was to study questions relating to higher education in the state and make recommendations to the legislature. Senior college proponents knew that the commission's findings would carry much weight with legislators. ASC supporters got the chance to present their arguments to the TCHE in an hour-and-a-half session on February 28, 1957. Leading the Arlington delegation was Mayor Vandergriff, who was accompanied by Harold Bodley, director of engineering personnel for Convair; Nevin Palley, vice president in charge of engineering for Temco; J. W. Larson, assistant chief engineer for Chance-Vought; Estil Vance, president of Fort Worth National Bank and chairman of the Dallas-Fort Worth Municipal Industrial Commission; and a number of other supporters. Most of their remarks emphasized the great need of local industries for more engineers, the college's ideal location in the rapidly growing Dallas-Fort Worth metroplex, and the college's capacity to accommodate senior status without much additional construction. Chancellor Harrington also spoke in favor of four-year status.[13]

6.7 **With the two-story library in the background, members of the ASC security force keep watch as area commuters attend classes.**

The delegation was crestfallen, however, when the TCHE announced shortly after the presentations that it would study the question further. The commission did promise to hand down a decision on April 8, a mere forty days before the end of the 1957 legislative session. Knowing that such a delay essentially killed any four-year status bill's chances for passage, supporters on and off campus greeted the news with disappointment and even hostility. *The Shorthorn*, on March 5 in a banner headline, complained "Hearing Result May Be Death Blow." Vandergriff conceded that the delay meant defeat until the next legislative session. *The Dallas Morning News*, in a March 1 editorial, urged the commission to make a "quick decision." Matters were made even worse when, in April, the TCHE postponed any decision until an indepth study could be made. The commission estimated that such a study would take between fifteen and eighteen months. After hearing this news, a torchbearing crowd of angry ASC students streamed out of their dormitories to express their resentment over the delay. Local police quickly moved in to ensure order. Two days later, an effigy, with a sign reading "Texas Commission on Lowering Education" with a hanging noose around its neck, was found in one of the college's parking lots. Frustration had replaced optimism over the college's chances for senior status.[14]

In fairness to the TCHE, it did need more time to conduct a careful study because the ASC issue had been combined with the fate and futures of four other colleges. In fact, joining ASC in pressing for senior status were Tarleton State College in Stephenville and Del Mar Junior College in Corpus Christi. Also, Midwestern University in Wichita Falls was lobbying for full state support, and the University of Texas system had asked to establish a state-supported medical school in San Antonio. Dr. Ralph T. Green, the commission's executive director, said that the TCHE had to decide "whether the state should bring education to the student or vice-versa."[15]

After more than eighteen months of study, the commission released its findings on December 15, 1958, just a few weeks after President Hereford's death. The commission concurred with the arguments presented by ASC supporters and recommended to the Texas legislature that the school be given senior status beginning September 1959. The report further specified that bachelor-level degree programs be created in the liberal arts in economics, English, foreign language, mathematics, history, sociology, and psychology; in the sciences in biology, chemistry, geology, and physics; in engineering in the specialties of aeronautical, civil, electrical, indus-trial, and mechanical engineering; and in business administration. Courses, but no degree programs, could also be offered in the fine arts (art, speech, drama, and music), vocational arts, and physical training. The TCHE report concluded by saying that "because of its favorable location, the relative ease with which it can be developed, the number of students which it will be able to serve, the fact that as a junior college it is now the sixth in size among the fully State-supported institutions, and the need for the State to provide in advance for increases in enrollment, Arlington State College merits serious and immediate consider-ation for elevation to senior-college status." The commission also recom-mended that the UT system be allowed to open a medical college in San Antonio and Tarleton be elevated to senior status. It ruled against the proposals from Del Mar and Midwestern.[16]

6.8 Consistent with ASC's Rebel theme, the college celebrated Old South Days each spring. While faculty members assumed roles, such as Robert E. Lee and Jefferson Davis, students were recruited into a "confederate" army. Instead of seceding from the Union, however, ASC ceremoniously seceded from the "harsh rule" of the Texas A&M system.

Reactions to the commission's findings in Arlington and the surrounding cities were immediate and positive. Acting President Woolf commented that the college community was "heartened by the action of the committee," while Mayor Vandergriff said he was "immensely gratified." Corporate officials at Texas Instruments, Convair, Chance-Vought, and Temco characterized the news as beneficial for their companies and North Texas residents. Vandergriff warned, however, that there was still much work to be done before a bill elevating the college to senior rank could pass both houses of the legislature. With the 56th Texas legislature scheduled to convene on January 13, 1958, ASC supporters mobilized once again on behalf of the college. With Vandergriff taking the lead as chair of the Arlington Chamber of Commerce's Education Committee, thousands of letters of support for four-year status were mailed to parents of students, ex-students, and influential political and business friends of the college. Vandergriff cautioned against overconfidence and stressed that businessmen and politicians outside the Dallas-Fort Worth area would have to be convinced to support an ASC proposal as well.[17]

Shortly after the legislature convened in early 1959, ASC bills were introduced in both the House and Senate. Representative W. A. "Red" Cowen of Tarrant County introduced a bill in the House of Representatives along with thirty-nine other cosponsors, and, in the Senate, Doyle Willis of Tarrant County and George Parkhouse of Dallas County cosponsored the ASC bill. Both bills were quickly referred to the appropriate committees for hearings. The State Affairs Committee of the House held its hearing on February 18 and the Senate State Affairs Committee considered the Willis-Parkhouse measure on February 23. Bodley of Convair, Chancellor Harrington, Dr. Green of the TCHE, and Gus F. White, executive secretary of the Texas Society of Professional Engineers, testified before the committees in favor of four-year status. The only significant opposition to the ASC bills came from Representative Alonzo Jamison of Denton, who argued that a statewide policy on higher education should precede the elevation of any college. Jamison's district, of course, included North Texas State College and Texas Woman's College, and it was clear that he did not want a four-year college in Arlington to compete with the two Denton schools. Despite Jamison's opposition, both committees reported favorably on the ASC bills and referred them to the floors of the House and Senate for debate.[18]

6.9 Marching on Center Street in downtown Arlington, homecoming was celebrated by ASC students, alumni, and Arlington citizens alike.

The House made quick work of its ASC bill, passing it by voice vote on March 4, 1959. It was in the Senate, however, where legislative maneuvering, the press of other business, and an unsuccessful filibuster by William Moore of Bryan prevented the bill from reaching the floor for six weeks. Moore opposed the bill because he did not want A&M to become a branch of ASC! This changed, however, on April 20, 1959, when the Senate voted 17 to 12 in favor of the House bill, which had been slightly revised by Senator Willis. Because of the revision to the bill's preamble, it was referred to the House for final approval. This approval came exactly one week later, when the House approved the bill by a voice vote. The bill was then sent to Governor Price Daniel for his signature.[19]

The news of the bill's approval reached campus at 2:15 p.m. on April 27, the day the House conducted its vote. A spontaneous celebration erupted on campus and classes were suspended at

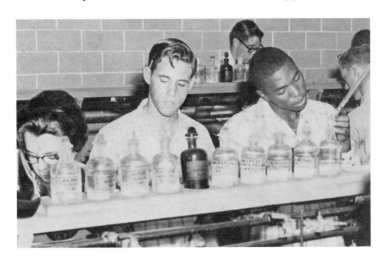

6.10 Accepting African-American students for the first time in 1962, ASC became the first integrated college in the Texas A&M system. According to the 1963 *Reveille*, "ASC witnessed a peaceful integration which produced no display of prejudice among students or faculty."

2:30 as wild bell ringing signalled the long-sought victory. Students, faculty, and staff gathered in front of the student center for a hastily planned celebration and to hear President Woolf, Mayor Vandergriff, and Arlington Chamber of Commerce President Rayborn Dews deliver speeches about the bill's passage. Their remarks were punctuated with "Rebel yells" from the audience of 800 because the school's mascot at the time was a Rebel. After the speeches, the students paraded through Arlington with a police escort and eventually returned to the student center for a dance and more celebrating. The next day *The Shorthorn* emblazoned across its front page in two-inch letters the headline "MADE IT AT LAST." [20]

At 11:00 a.m. on May 5, a delegation from Arlington and the North Texas area witnessed Governor Daniel's signing of the ASC bill in his executive office suite in Austin. Attending the signing were President Woolf, Mayor Vandergriff, the House and Senate delegations from Dallas and Tarrant counties, representatives from both Arlington newspapers, and A&M officials. The bill the governor signed into law followed closely the recommendations of the TCHE, creating four-year degree programs in the liberal arts, engineering, science, and business. The bill further mandated that ASC add third year college courses in the fall of 1959 and fourth year courses in 1960. The signing ceremony in the governor's office capped a drive for four-year status which had begun more than two decades before and changed the character and scope of the college in a fundamental way. During the same session, the Texas legislature passed legislation which would make Tarleton a senior college and would extend full state support to Midwestern. The legislature also approved the UT system's request to build a medical school in San Antonio.[21]

When ASC achieved senior rank in 1959, it was a college open only to white students. Admission policies of the A&M board prohibited the enrollment of African Americans in all of the system's colleges except Prairie View A&M, which was the only state-supported college for people of color in Texas. The Texas constitution legitimatized segregation by calling for separate schools where "impartial provision" could be provided for both whites and blacks. This separate and presumably equal system of education had existed in the state since the adoption of the constitution in 1876. By the late 1940s and throughout the 1950s, legal challenges to what was obviously an inequitable and discriminatory education-tion system began to produce results for African Americans. In cases like *Sweatt v. Painter* (1950) and *Brown v. Board of Education of Topeka* (1954), the United States Supreme Court's rulings began making it possible to dismantle segregated educational systems. In September 1956, for example, the University of Texas at Austin, after fighting integration through the courts, became the first major institution in the South to admit African Americans as

6.11 Flanked by legislators and ASC supporters from the North Texas area, including President Woolf (pictured directly behind the governor's nameplate), Governor Price Daniel signed the bill making ASC a four-year institution in 1959.

undergraduates. By the late 1950s, it became obvious that segregated schools and school districts could not withstand legal challenges. The civil rights movement was forcing change.[22]

ASC students seemed willing to accept integration long before the A&M board was. In 1956, *The Shorthorn* published the results of a poll which had asked ninety-six students, "Would you be willing to attend classes with Negroes?" The poll revealed that seventy-two students said they would be willing, while twenty-four students answered no. Despite the feelings of the students, the Woolf administration in the late fifties and early sixties continued to enforce the restrictions against admitting black students. Whenever a student of color applied, the college registrar would write a letter to the applicant explaining that "present regulations" prohibited his admission to the college. The registrar would also forward the

6.12 In the 1950s student life was under the supervision of a dean of men and a dean of women. Consistent with this separation of the sexes, there were no co-ed dormitories at ASC.

request to Prairie View A&M for consideration. This response worked until 1962, when Ernest Hooper, Jerry Hanes, and Leaston Chase III were denied admission to ASC. Rather than accept the ASC policy, these three men called on the Dallas branch of the National Association for the Advancement of Colored People (NAACP) to help them gain admittance to ASC. In the spring of 1962, the NAACP agreed to represent the three. The matter was turned over to the organization's Legal Redress Committee, which was chaired by Dallas attorney Fred J. Finch, Jr.[23]

On May 25, 1962, Finch wrote a letter to President Woolf advising that he had been retained by Hooper, Hanes, and Chase to help them secure admission to the college. Finch informed Woolf that the three men had submitted completed applications and had satisfied all other requirements for entering freshmen. Finch closed the letter with a thinly veiled threat: "I am sure it will not be necessary to resort to the courts in this matter due to the present status of the law in this regard." Though Woolf never answered the letter, he moved quickly to inform Chancellor Harrington of it. Woolf, a practical man by nature, advised the chancellor that "a court fight of this case could lead only to hard feelings and the outcome would be the same." He recommended that the A&M board allow ASC to change its policy and no longer "discriminate against any person on [a] racial basis." Harrington took the question to the next regularly scheduled board of directors meeting on June 29, and polled the board on whether ASC should be allowed to change its admission policy immediately. The directors, realizing that they could not win in court, approved the integration of ASC. Harrington, shortly thereafter, telephoned Woolf and told him of the board's decision. ASC was to be the first school in the A&M system to integrate its student body.[24]

Pleased with the decision and not wanting to hide it from the local community and the media, President Woolf called a press conference for July 10. News of the policy change, however, was leaked by the *Fort Worth Press* a day before the news conference and this served to heighten media interest. The press conference was held as scheduled at the Inn of the Six Flags, and Woolf announced ASC's integration to the eighteen to twenty reporters there. That same day, Woolf sent a memorandum to the faculty and staff of the college briefly explaining the new policy. Two months later, the first African-American students enrolled in ASC classes. Arlington State became the ninth state-supported college (out of nineteen) in Texas to remove its racial barriers for admissions.[25]

Reaction to the change of policy was mixed. Both Arlington newspapers, the *Daily News Texan* and the *Arlington Citizen-Journal*, supported the school's decision and reasoned that the change was inevitable in light of recent court decisions. Interviews conducted on campus just after the policy change revealed that the majority of students and faculty favored integration and believed that African Americans deserved a higher education "just like us." It should not be a surprise then that the integration of the campus was

6.13 A necessary and traditional beverage for many students, coffee has been dispensed from automatic coffee machines on campus since the late 1950s.

accomplished peacefully. President Woolf, however, did receive a number of letters from local residents hostile to the change and vehemently opposed to racial integration. Most of these letters came from individuals in Dallas County, and their tone was similar to that expressed by Arthur F. Stovall in his letter of July 25, 1962: "The decent white people of this State will never forget your actions in this instance. They will never forget that you did not have the backbone to tell these N_ _ _ _ _ _ that you would not have them in the school under *any* circumstances." Some of the segregationists who wrote argued that integration was a communist plot to mongrelize and then enslave white America. Mrs. F. G. Ogden of Richardson, Texas, wrote Woolf, saying, "The N.A.A.C.P. is a Communist front organization and their goal is to mix the white and black blood and some years from now have a mongrelized nation." Carey Daniel, a Dallas Baptist minister, agreed, stating, "We will soon have a *mulatto* nation and a *Communist* nation." [26]

Despite the concerns expressed by several fanatical segregationists, ASC started a slow and gradual process of integration. The number of African-American students who registered for classes in September 1962 was small, estimated by President Woolf to be "twenty-five or thirty" students. During the following spring semester, that number inched upward to approximately thirty-two out of a total enrollment of more than 9,000. Throughout the latter part of the sixties, African-American enrollment hovered somewhere between 1 and 2 percent of the school's overall enrollment. While some areas on campus were integrated immediately, such as classrooms, bathrooms, dining areas, and social functions, other areas, namely housing and sports, were integrated gradually. Nevertheless, by 1965, ASC was "fully integrated" and had removed all policy barriers aimed at preventing African Americans from fully participating in all areas of college life. ASC integrated its athletic teams in 1963 just after joining the Southland Conference and opened its dorms to African Americans in 1965.[27]

The removal of policy barriers, however, did not ensure that all of the school's fraternities, social clubs, and academic clubs would integrate. In 1965, for example, only fourteen of ASC's sixty-one organizations, which were integrated in policy, were integrated in fact. Also, African Americans on campus formed their own clubs, with Kappa Alpha Fi, begun in the 1963-1964 school year, being the first established. ASC's initial move to integrate did not apply to the faculty. At the press conference announcing the change in admission policy, President Woolf announced that the school had no plans to hire African-American teachers. In fact, the pressures from the courts to integrate schools emphasized student facilities and activities, not faculties and administrations. It was not until 1969, four years after joining the University of Texas system, that the college hired its first African-American administrator, Reby Cary. Cary's position was associate dean of student life.[28]

The elevation of ASC to a senior college and the integration of the campus three years later had a dramatic impact on the school. Enrollment quickly grew to 6,388 for the fall 1959 semester, the first semester that the school offered junior-level classes. This growth reflected a gain of 1,209 students from the fall of 1958. A year later, enrollment grew to 7,444, as the school added senior-level classes. By fall 1963, enrollment had increased to 9,116, outpacing that of Texas A&M. During fall of 1965, the first semester ASC was a part of the UT system, enrollment had ballooned to 11,849, despite a 15 percent decrease in freshmen enrollment caused by the adoption of selective admission standards. Indeed, beginning in September 1965, all freshmen entering ASC for the first time were required to show aptitude for doing college work in addition to having graduated from an accredited high school. A combination of SAT scores and high school class ranking determined whether a student was admitted into ASC.[29]

In the mid-1960s, male students consistently outnumbered female students by a ratio of three or four to one. Moreover, 60 percent of the student body was twenty-one or older and 34 percent were married. Tarrant County continued to supply the largest number of students, followed closely by Dallas County. The largest group of students outside of Texas came from California, while Iran was the home country of most of the foreign students at the time. Sixty-one percent of the student body worked at least part-time and 44 percent worked twenty hours a week or more. ASC, like its predecessors, was a commuter college where the overwhelming majority of students lived off campus. In 1962, for example, the college dormitories housed 338 male students and 144 female students. About 30 percent of the students attended the college in the evening, and, because of the large number of students working and attending school part-time, the number of full-time equivalent students was about 80 percent of the total student population.[30]

Beginning in September 1959, after the passage of the bill making it a four-year school,

6.14 The characterization of ASC as "an island of enlightenment among a sea of parking lots" accurately describes this aerial view of the college in the late 1960s.

6.15 Accompanied by his wife, Vice President Lyndon B. Johnson visited ASC in December of 1962. His visit included an inspection of the Sam Houston Rifles, a speech to approximately 2,500 students, and a luncheon in the student center.

ASC promoted itself as a regional college offering degrees in the liberal arts (economics, English, history, modern foreign languages, and psychology) and sciences (biology, chemistry, geology, mathematics, and physics), and professional degrees in engineering (aeronautical, civil, electrical, industrial, and mechanical) and business (undifferentiated). By 1966, ASC had added baccalaureate programs in accounting, government, and sociology, as well as offering a secondary teaching certificate to students majoring in biology, chemistry, English, languages, history, math, and physics. *The Dallas Morning News* in 1963 said the college was "geared to the space age and also to the North Texas business and cultural community of which it is a part." The college also offered the first two years of classes for students working toward degrees in education, art, music, speech, journalism, architecture, and physical education. Additionally, ASC offered two-year terminal programs in commercial art, secretarial science, and aeronautical, civil, electrical, and mechanical technology. Among the electives offered at the time were philosophy, sociology, military science, and religious education.[31]

The distribution of students in the four-year programs for 1959-1968 can be found in the table below. During this period, the number of business majors doubled, while those in science and liberal arts more than tripled. The number of engineering majors at the college remained strong at approximately 3,000 for the nine-year period, making ASC's engineering school one of the largest in the Southwest.

MAJORS BY PROGRAM

Semester	Business Adm.	Engineering	Science	Liberal Arts	Social Work	Total
Fall '59	1,512	3,015	797	1,064		6,388
Fall '64	3,434	3,393	1,975	2,711		11,513
Fall '68	3,123	3,306	2,331	3,769	27	12,556

Administratively, ASC, from 1959-1965, was divided into two schools: the School of Arts and Sciences, which oversaw the programs in liberal arts, science, and business; and the School of Engineering, which administered the five engineering degree programs. Dr. Wendell Nedderman was hired in 1959 to be the first engineering dean, while Dr. S. T. Keim, Jr., was appointed the first dean of arts and sciences. Because of the rapid growth in enrollment in the non-engineering programs, ASC requested and received approval from the A&M board to divide Arts and Sciences into three separate schools in 1965: the School of

6.16 When the Engineering Building was built on the old college parade grounds in 1960, it not only enjoyed the distinction of being the largest classroom building in the Texas A&M system, but also completed the present configuration of buildings along Second Street.

Liberal Arts, School of Business, and School of Science. The first deans appointed to lead these schools were Dr. Charles Green, liberal arts; Dr. Wallace B. Nelson, business; and Dr. Peter Giradot, dean of sciences. As a result of this division, Dr. Keim, former arts and science dean, became dean of academic affairs, a new position. In the 1963-1964 school year, President Woolf created the office of dean of students and appointed Dr. Robert Dollar, formerly of Oklahoma State University, to head it. Dr. Dollar's office administered the activities of the deans of men and women, student housing, student activity, and student life.[32]

To accommodate the exploding student population, the Woolf administration added faculty as fast as the budget would allow. In 1963-1964, for example, thirty-two new faculty positions were added, twenty-five of which were in the Arts and Sciences. This brought the total number of faculty members at the college in the mid-sixties to approximately 400. At the time, more than 40 percent of the science and liberal arts faculty held Ph.D.s, while 50 percent of the engineering faculty did. The Woolf administration made a concerted effort to raise ASC faculty salaries, and had some success. When Woolf became president, salaries at the school were the lowest of all of the state-supported schools in Texas; when he left the presidency in 1968, salaries had climbed to fourth highest in the state. In 1966-1967, the average nine-month faculty salary range was: $12,441 to $13,511 for full professor, $10,444 to $11,206 for associate professor, $8,713 to $9,270 for assistant professor, and $6,938 to $6,990 for instructor. The student-to-teacher ratio at the college was about 25 to 1, and each faculty member taught, on the average, four classes.[33]

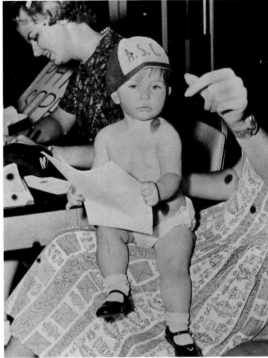

6.17 Distributed by a spirit group known as the Rebel Rousers, ASC beanies were worn by both current and future students of the college.

Faculty expressed a number of concerns during ASC's period of rapid growth in the 1960s. One common complaint was the lack of an "intellectual atmosphere" on campus. Faculty members believed that the college's commuter students and their jobs mitigated against developing an atmosphere where the campus would become the center of cultural, social, and intellectual life for students. Faculty also criticized the low academic level and anti-intellectualism of many students. To address some of these problems, the faculty suggested improving faculty-student communication through personal conferences, expanding counseling services, and creating student-faculty discussion groups. In addition, faculty members believed that they should increase their own intellectual activity through research and writing. Finally, surveys indicated a strong desire on the part of the faculty to establish graduate studies at the college. To the administration, the faculty urged the creation of a "faculty forum" where members could air their grievances; the addition of more faculty privileges, such as discounts at the bookstore, keys to the library, and private offices; and an articulated policy on academic freedom. Faculty also lamented that tenure at state-supported schools in Texas did not exist at the time.[34]

The concerns of the faculty did not prevent—or even delay—accreditation for the college. After becoming a four-year college in 1959, ASC received general accreditation in 1962 from the Association of Texas Colleges and Universities. The Southern Association of Colleges and Schools also granted general accreditation in December 1964 after an extensive self-study conducted in 1962-1963.

6.18 Jack R. Woolf, who became president of ASC after the untimely death of President Hereford in 1958, had a large impact on the college's physical plant expansion. Here B. C. Barnes (left), the college's director of business and finance, and President Woolf (right) look over plans for the school's new auditorium.

Each of these actions came at the earliest possible time given the general rules and regulations of the accrediting associations. In the fall of 1965, the Engineer's Council for Professional Development (ECPD) granted accreditation to the college's electrical engineering department for the maximum period of six years. The ECPD also granted the school's two-year engineering curricula accreditation in 1959, and renewed it in 1963 for another six years.[35]

A sizable budget increase helped to finance the rapid changes and growth at ASC after it achieved four-year status. When ASC began its first year as a senior institution, the college had a total budget of $3.1 million. This figure grew to $9.4 million for the 1965-1966 school year. During this same year, the college set aside a paltry $41,538 for organized research, and research programs financed by off-campus grants totaled $53,086. Some of the departments on campus devoted a part of their operating budgets to help support faculty research as well. The college estimated that the total dollar volume of research at ASC for 1965-1966 was less than $200,000.[36]

Despite ASC's improving budget situation and the volume of building which took place on campus in the fifties through the mid-sixties, there was an undercurrent of tension between the campus and A&M over the future development of the Arlington school and who would shape its course. Many students, alumni, faculty, and metroplex residents believed—and rightly—that ASC's interests were consistently subordinated to those of College Station by the A&M board, and this rankled ASC supporters. The college and its proponents no longer wanted to be the poor "stepchild" of A&M. In addition to this general uneasiness developing between ASC supporters and the board, the faculty in Arlington was growing increasingly dissatisfied with the A&M administrative style, which was characterized by a rigid chain of command and few opportunities on the part of faculty members to discuss and influence policy decisions. Additionally, faculty and others generally believed that A&M was not investing the resources necessary for the college to adequately handle its enrollment growth. Too many faculty members were teaching in inadequate buildings and many had no private offices. This dissatisfaction and tension bubbled to the surface in December 1964, when rumors began to circulate in Arlington that the A&M board was planning a reorganization of the A&M system along the lines of the University of California system.[37]

The rumors proved to be true when, on December 17, 1964, four members of the A&M board of directors (Sterling Evans, John Newton, L. F. Peterson, and C. H. Wells) met in Arlington and presented a plan of reorganization to a select group of ASC administrators, faculty members, and students. Basically, the plan consisted of four proposals. The first would change the name of ASC to Texas A&M University at Arlington. The second proposal called for an administrative reorganization which would more closely integrate ASC into a revamped system, though details of the new structure were sketchy. The third recommended the inauguration at ASC of graduate programs on the master's level in eleven fields, including seven in engineering, three in science, and one in mathematics. These graduate programs would be directed by the dean of the graduate school on the College Station campus, and the degrees granted in the name of Texas A&M University. The last proposal called for a sharing of faculty and facilities of A&M to enrich the graduate program at ASC. The A&M board of directors and the system administrators were unprepared—and totally surprised—at the firestorm of protests and hostility these proposals generated.[38]

At the meeting, the A&M board members did not ask for input or reaction from the ASC representatives. Rather, as Dr. Woolf recalled in a 1994 interview, "They came up with the attitude, well, this is what we're going to do and if you don't like it, you can lump it." In a letter written shortly after the meeting, Marvin C. Nichols, a local businessman and vice chairman of the Fort Worth Chamber of Commerce's Education Committee, characterized the meeting as being as "poor a piece of public relations as I have seen in quite some time. . . ." Nichols went on to observe that the reorganization plan had produced a "state of hot flux" on "the educational front" in the Dallas-Fort Worth area. Nichols had not exaggerated the situation either![39]

Once news of the reorganization plan hit the newspapers, reaction to it was swift and, for the most part, negative. Every part of the plan came under intense and biting criticism. Students, alums, faculty, and Arlington residents bristled at the proposed name change, fearing that the college would lose its identity and its relative autonomy if it were to become just another branch of the A&M campus. Arlington Chamber of Commerce manager Joe Wolfshol vowed, "This is something Arlington leaders won't take sitting down." Charles E. C. Brown, a former chamber president and an ex-student of ASC, said the plan was "harmful to the school." Mayor Vandergriff was less concerned about the name—though he expressed hope that "Arlington" could remain in it—than he was about the college being "a full working partner" in the A&M system. Jack McLaughlin, a member of the Tarrant County delegation in the Texas House of Representatives, told a meeting of 800 ASC students on December 18 that "I'll be damned if the name is going to be changed." Also on the 18th, the ASC student government passed a resolution "categorically opposing" the name change and reorganization. Students organized a "Save Our School Committee" to coordinate student opposition to the plan, and the committee went to work immediately. The Ex-Students Association also entered the fray, contacting its members to ask them to write A&M board members, legislators, and "political leaders" expressing opposition to the reorganization. In a letter dated December 28, James A. Cribbs, president of the association, informed members that the association's directors "have voted unanimously to begin a drive for separation from the A&M System."[40]

In an attempt at damage control, the Dallas and Fort Worth chambers of

6.19 When the first addition to the student center was completed in 1960, the building was named in honor of President E. H. Hereford, who helped establish the precedent for an aesthetically pleasing campus by planting flowers around the student center.

6.20 When Texas A&M proposed renaming ASC Texas A&M University at Arlington in 1964, students, faculty, and alumni opposed the change and advocated a complete separation from the A&M system.

commerce called an emergency meeting for December 22 to discuss ASC and its future with A&M. At the meeting were Robert Cullum, past president of the Dallas chamber; A. D. Turman, incoming Dallas president; Gifford Johnson, chairman of the Dallas chamber's Education Committee; Earle Cullum, chairman of the chamber's Higher Education Subcommittee; and Andy DeShong, the chamber's general manager. Attending from Fort Worth were J. Lee Johnson, III, president of the Fort Worth chamber; Nichols; Jack Key, secretary of the Fort Worth chamber's Education Committee; and general manager, M. A. Atkinson. Also present at the meeting were Dick Adams of General Dynamics, President Woolf, and Mayor Vandergriff. For several years, the chambers had been pressing for the introduction of graduate degree programs at ASC, and the individuals at the meeting believed that an escalating split between ASC and the A&M system would delay the implementation of graduate programs. After a frank discussion, most of the people at the meeting agreed that ASC should remain a part of the A&M system provided assurances could be obtained from A&M president Earl Rudder and the board that it was their intent to develop the Arlington school into one of the "first class with doctoral and post-doctoral curricula." If these assurances could not be given, then the chambers agreed to explore separating ASC from A&M and perhaps creating a regional university system which would include North Texas State and Texas Woman's, both in Denton. A delegation from both chambers, headed by Bob Cullum and Johnson, were to meet with Texas governor John Connally to ascertain his plan for higher education in the state and the role he envisioned for ASC. Only Vandergriff seemed inclined for separation, saying, "It seems that I have spent most of my adult life working on problems for Arlington State College. I worked on the four-year bachelor program for eight years, the first four of which I spent trying to persuade the Board of Directors of

A&M College that there was a real future for Arlington State College. . . ."[41]

ASC supporters received no assurances from Rudder, who was an irascible WWII hero with deep political connections and an ardent desire to build the College Station campus at whatever the costs. While president of A&M, Rudder had won the favor of the board and eventually was successful in supplanting Chancellor Harrington as the chief operating officer of the system. Once this happened, Vandergriff could see the writing on the wall for ASC. In fact, Rudder had told Vandergriff shortly after ASC received legislative approval to offer four-year courses that he and the college's supporters had made a "terrible mistake." As Vandergriff recalled in 1994, Rudder was blunt in saying, "You were one of the best junior colleges anywhere. You can never be anything but a run of the mill senior college. We don't intend to spend any of our resources there. . . . You should have stayed where you were." President Woolf remembered a similar conversation with Rudder when the then A&M president told him, "You're getting *our* building money." Rudder also alienated the Dallas-Fort Worth state delegation in December 1964 when, "in pretty blunt words" according to Nichols, he told them the name of the school *would* be changed. Moreover, he refused to discuss what ASC's future was within the A&M system.[42]

On January 6, 1965, Rudder and A&M board chairman Evans, in an attempt to allay the growing fear at ASC, met with college officials and student officers, representatives from the Dallas and Fort Worth chambers of commerce, Vandergriff, and Tarrant County state senator Don Kennard. Though the meeting lasted for two-and-a-half hours, little was resolved. The discussions centered on three topics, including the speed with which ASC could offer graduate programs, the college's need for additional building money brought on by rapid growth, and the role the college would play and the autonomy it would have in the restructured system. Rudder and Evans were noncommittal on all of these issues, but did promise that if ASC were a part of the new system it would receive its share of the revenues. Evans advised the ASC supporters that their request for more building funds was not possible in the foreseeable future. He suggested that they go directly to the Texas legislature for funding for an expanded physical plant. Rudder and Evans also speculated that under the new system, ASC would be able to offer graduate courses sooner—albeit in the name of the College Station campus—than if it left the system. In fact, the TCHE was already studying the question of implementing such courses in Arlington in September. Rudder and Evans were either unable or unwilling to give specific details on how the new system would operate in the areas of finances, administration, local control, and curriculum. In response to a pointed question by J. Lee Johnson regarding the type and amount of support ASC could expect from the A&M system, Rudder and Evans vowed that A&M and the board would *not* block a move by ASC to leave the system. President Woolf ended the meeting by appealing to the participants to put the controversy behind them and "get together on some kind of plan."[43]

The meeting and its aftermath served to reinforce the two positions which were developing on the issue. On one side, President Woolf, the ASC deans, and a number of the Dallas chamber officials favored staying with A&M in a revamped system. Shortly after the meeting, Woolf issued a statement which mentioned the college's building problems, but concluded "that these problems can most easily be solved

6.21 With the backing of legislators and area businessmen, ASC formally separated from the Texas A&M system and joined the University of Texas system in 1965. Present at the bill's signing were (left to right) UT Chancellor Harry Ransom, ASC President Jack Woolf, Governor John Connally, and Arlington Mayor Tom Vandergriff.

and the future potential of this institution as a university can best be realized by staying in the Texas A&M University System." Woolf, in an awkward position as ASC president requesting funds from a system that others were advocating leaving, had no other choice but to support the system proposal. Opposing the proposal were students, faculty, alumni, Arlington officials like Vandergriff, the Fort Worth Chamber of Commerce, and the Dallas-Fort Worth delegations in the Texas legislature. Unlike Woolf, they believed that ASC's interests would be better served outside of the A&M orbit, where the school would be allowed to develop to its full potential.[44]

On the weekend following the meeting with Rudder and Evans, a group of ASC supporters flew to Austin to meet with Governor Connally to get his support on separating ASC from the A&M system. Making the trip were Kennard, Johnson, Vandergriff, and Jenkins Garrett, a Fort Worth attorney and at that time a member of the governor's committee on higher education and chairman of the Fort Worth Chamber of Commerce's Education Committee. At the meeting, Connally, after telephoning Rudder and hearing that A&M would not oppose ASC's efforts to separate, agreed to help the effort. The governor did help matters a couple of weeks later when he introduced a bold and sweeping plan which called for restructuring higher education in the state. Connally's plan stemmed from the recommendations of a blue ribbon committee on higher education which advocated the creation of a "coordinating board for higher education" and the creation of three "super-systems" under its direction. Each of the state's twenty-two public colleges and universities would be placed in one of the newly created systems. The governor's plan called for ASC to become a part of the University of Texas system along with North Texas State, University of Houston, and Texas Western in El Paso. With the entire state buzzing over Connally's plan, local legislators in

6.22 Female students may have been a bit bewildered by this sign hung on the student center in 1958 which welcomed "dolls" to campus.

Fort Worth and Dallas, led by Senator Kennard, saw their opportunity to separate ASC from A&M.[45]

Even before the meeting with Governor Connally, Kennard had recruited a few faculty and staff members at the college to gather comparative information on Texas A&M and ASC. Kennard and what he called his "wrecking crew" had met secretly on and off campus to strategize ways to separate the Arlington school from the system. Among those who participated were E. C. Barksdale, chairman of the social science department and a personal friend of Kennard; Samuel Hamlett and Luther Hagard, both political scientists; John Hudson, director of libraries; and George Wolfskill, a historian. The "crew" researched and wrote a position paper for Kennard which compared the faculties, budgets, classroom space, student populations, degree programs, growth projections, and other relevant topics of the College Station and Arlington campuses. Kennard used the report to lobby his colleagues in the Texas House and Senate and to launch legislation to separate ASC from A&M.[46]

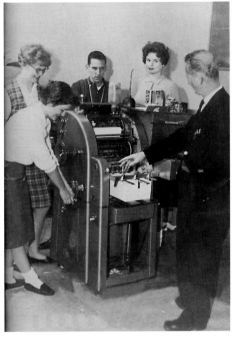

6.23 In 1962, this press supplied ASC with its weekly edition of *The Shorthorn*. By the early 1970s, however, the school's paper was printed four times each week.

Since President Rudder and the A&M board had agreed not to fight ASC's move from the system, and with the change of ASC to the UT system proposed in Governor Connally's higher education proposal, Kennard and other ASC supporters met little organized opposition in the legislature. In February, Kennard introduced Senate Bill 401, which proposed to move ASC from A&M to the UT system effective September 1, 1965. Kennard's bill cleared the Senate State Affairs Committee on March 16 without opposition, and came to the Senate floor for a vote on April 4. The measure won approval by a vote of 24 to 4, with only Bill Moore of Bryan, Murray Watson of Waco, J. P. Word of Meridian, and Dorsey Hardeman of San Angelo opposing. Shortly afterwards, the House also passed the bill. On April 23 at 11:30 a.m., Governor Connally signed the bill into law as Fort Worth and Arlington business, college, and civic leaders looked on along with members of the Tarrant and Dallas county legislative delegations. After the signing ceremony, the UT system, under the leadership of Chancellor Harry Ransom and W. W. Heath, chairman of the Board of Regents, hosted a luncheon at the Commodore Perry Hotel in Austin to celebrate the occasion. Regent Heath commented at the luncheon that ASC would be "an integral and important part of the University of Texas System," while Chancellor Ransom said, "I can't imagine a newcomer to the Texas System I would welcome with more confidence than Jack Woolf." President Woolf responded by saying, "This is one time I think I can speak for the faculty of my institution when I say that we are honored to become a part of the University System. . . ." Throughout the drive to get Arlington moved from the A&M system, the UT chancellor and regents had maintained a relatively low public profile, leaving it to the legislators to make the final decision. Nevertheless, Kennard, Connally, and other ASC supporters had been privately reassured that the UT system would welcome the school and work to offer graduate education and construct new buildings as soon as possible.[47]

Once word reached the ASC campus of the governor's signing the separation bill, the Vaqueros cannon team fired off the school cannon in front of the Hereford Student Center. With hundreds of students looking on, speeches were made commemorating the change, and a celebration began. Students had played a major role in garnering public support for the separation by leading a petition drive, writing and talking with legislators, and conducting orderly protests against A&M control on campus. President Rudder and the A&M board must have been relieved to be rid of the ASC problem because the Arlington school had, in terms of enrollment, outgrown the main campus and was constantly demanding more system money. At its heart, of course, the break between A&M and ASC was over money and status. ASC supporters were convinced that their school would always be treated as a "poor stepchild" in the A&M system, and the proposal to restructure the system and create "branch" campuses only reinforced this belief. Moreover, the president and board had made it clear that building funds in the system were running out and there were few prospects for ASC to receive more. Finally, the ASC faculty balked at the idea of introducing graduate programs in Arlington, but granting graduate degrees in the name of the College Station campus. ASC faculty felt confident that in many disciplines they had the credentials, expertise, and research background to handle graduate education. Separation became desirable, then, in both Arlington and College Station. *The Shorthorn*, pointing out that both A&M and ASC were pleased with the change, declared in an editorial that "this is probably the first divorce in history where everybody concerned lived happily ever after."[48]

The UT system administration moved quickly to make ASC feel welcome and to lay the groundwork for meeting some of the school's immediate wants and needs. Just a month after ASC joined the system, for example, the Board of Regents met on campus as a symbolic gesture of welcome. Just as importantly to many people on campus, the UT system made it clear from the start that the Arlington school was to be an equal among the six components in the UT system. It was not to be a branch campus. The system also emphasized that it supported the growth and development of ASC, unlike the attitude A&M fostered under Rudder's direction. Not surprisingly, the mood on campus improved tremendously as most faculty and students looked forward to UT affiliation. Chancellor

6.24 The high point of Arlington State College football came when, during its final years as a junior college, the school won back-to-back Junior Rose Bowl championships in 1956 and 1957.

Ransom and the regents did not disappoint, moving quickly to take steps to establish a graduate program in Arlington.[49]

For several years, the ASC administration, faculty, and supporters had pressured A&M for a graduate school in Arlington. They argued that the college's location in the middle of the Dallas-Fort Worth "industrial complex" and the growing need in area businesses for highly trained professional staff made the introduction of graduate programs absolutely essential to the growth and well-being of the region. Additionally, they used demographic and statistical data to prove that there was a built-up demand for graduate education which was not being met by the other local colleges and universities. The TCHE agreed, saying in 1963 that "the facts have been clearly established that modern industry has tended to follow brain-power, and as a result, is locating in those centers which provide graduate education and research." These sentiments were echoed by politicians, business and civic leaders, and alums, and slowly the A&M board came around to the idea of offering graduate programs in Arlington. Unfortunately, the board wrapped its proposal for master's level coursework at ASC into its broader plan to restructure the system, and dangled it before the college and its supporters as a type of carrot—the message was accept the plan and get graduate education in the process! As mentioned above, the entire proposal was scuttled in Arlington and with it went any hopes of introducing graduate classes in the fall of 1965. When ASC joined the UT system, any plan to introduce graduate education in Arlington had to start at "square one."[50]

In April, almost before the ink dried on Governor Connally's signature on the bill separating ASC from A&M, Chancellor Ransom asked Dr. Frank Harrison, the associate dean for graduate studies at Southwestern Medical School in Dallas (a UT component), to split his time between the Dallas school and ASC to get graduate programs started in Arlington. Harrison recalled that the chancellor "told me that the chief complaint of the faculty at the time, and the reason the faculty asked the legislature to change the school, was that A&M would not let them have graduate programs. He asked me, being the nearest graduate administrator in the UT system and knowing that I could commute out here, if I would come out and get graduate programs started." Harrison agreed to do this and for the next three years spent one-fourth of his time at ASC and the balance at the medical school. At ASC he reported to President Woolf and worked closely with Gordon Whaley, who was the dean of the graduate school at the University of Texas at Austin.[51]

Harrison methodically reviewed the vitae of all of the faculty members in the departments wanting to offer graduate programs. He looked for evidence demonstrating that a department's faculty was engaged in research because, as he mentioned some years later, "you have to have research faculty to handle the research programs of graduate students." He found six departments which met this criteria and later wrote proposals to the Coordinating Board, Texas College and University System (formerly the TCHE), seeking permission to begin graduate programs in these areas. The Coordinating Board approved the requests, and, in the fall of 1966, the school offered its first masters' programs in electrical engineering, engineering mechanics, economics, mathematics, psychology, and physics. Harrison, Woolf, and others at ASC also worked to change the school's image from a junior to a senior college. The introduction of graduate programs helped, as did the abolition of the last of the two-year programs in the college's Technical Institute. By the late 1960s, the college offered both undergraduate and graduate programs. Also, by the end of the decade, the school expanded its four-year programs by offering baccalaureate degrees in art, music, architecture, speech, and drama.[52]

The college's eighth name change occurred in March 1967, reinforcing the school's changing reputation to that of a senior and graduate-level institution. On March 13, ASC officially became The University of Texas at Arlington (UTA). The change was part of a bill which encountered little opposition in the Texas legislature. The bill, which was pushed by the UT system and signed into law by Governor Connally on March 6, changed the name of each of the components in the UT system to "The University of Texas at (location)." Unlike the furor which erupted when A&M wanted to rename the school in 1964-1965, little opposition arose over this change. In fact, most of the students on campus believed it would increase the prestige of their diplomas. Moreover, the faculty and administration argued it would make it easier to attract faculty and research dollars to the school. President Woolf commented at the time that "outside the state it will cause those in agencies of higher education and other universities to take a second look at this institution which they might not give an institution bearing the name 'State College.'" The first graduation ceremony where "The University of Texas at Arlington" appeared on diplomas was held on May 31, 1967. The Arlington school had become a university in name as well as in fact.[53]

Student life during the Arlington State College years was marked by rapid change. As the college moved from junior to senior level and from the A&M system to that of UT, students found an increasing number of clubs and organizations in which to participate. In addition, students throughout the fifties and

6.25 Part of ASC's graduation was the traditional march across campus. Students graduating in 1958 were also reminded of the school's recent football championships by the two goal posts which were taken from the Rose Bowl and erected in front of the student center.

sixties were given an increasingly greater voice in campus affairs. Sports continued to be a major focus of some students' life, and two ASC teams achieved national prominence for the first time. Except for the civil rights movement, which ultimately led to an end to the school's racially restricted admissions policies in 1962 (discussed above), the other societal pressures and movements of the sixties did not impact the campus in a significant way until after 1967. For the most part, ASC students concerned themselves with classes, grades, assignments, and fun rather than the broader social-political issues of the day.[54]

During 1949-1967, ASC actively encouraged the formation of organizations whose aims and activities furthered students' interest in literary, musical, professional, and social fields. The college encouraged all students to participate in the activities of one or more of the clubs or societies on campus. And the choices increased as the college grew and developed four-year and graduate programs. By the close of the ASC years, there were ninety-one organizations and clubs on campus, almost a four-fold increase from ten years before. Among these were twenty-one professional clubs, nine honorary societies, ten service fraternities and sororities (which were allowed national affiliations in 1966), fourteen social clubs, twenty-four special interest organizations (for example, Press Club, Architecture Society, Pre-Law Club), eight religious clubs, and five dormitory councils. Each student organization had a constitution and was regulated by the policies of the Committee on Student Organizations, and administered by the dean of student life and his staff. Students continued to fill all positions on *The Shorthorn* and yearbook staffs, and, in 1962, began producing the *Arlington Review*, a literary magazine devoted to publishing "articles on research, creative papers, art and poetry" by talented ASC students.[55]

6.26 Signed by members of the 1956 football team, the championship game ball as well as the championship cup testify to the importance of football during the ASC period.

In 1961, the college initiated a Student Activities Program with the hiring of its first student activities advisor. Gradually, the activities staff, with the assistance of student committees, began organizing dances, movies, guest speakers, and activities in the remodeled Hereford Student Center. In fall 1965, for example, campus activities included a "Howdy Dance"; Thursday night dances; parades; pep rallies; homecoming; a concert series featuring such performers as classical guitarist Andres Segovia, jazz great Lionel Hampton, and the Vienna Boys Choir; movies such as "To Kill a Mockingbird" and "Two Women"; a lecture series; and charm school. Although only 970 students lived in dorms on campus at the time, more than 5,000 people attended these programs.[56]

Also during the ASC years, students began to participate more actively in campus governance and policymaking. In the fifties, the president of the college appointed twenty individuals to the Student Council. This was changed in 1962, however, when the size of the council was increased to thirty, with fourteen students appointed by the president and sixteen elected at large and from selected organizations and classes on campus. Through the appointment of a number of student government committees, council members strove to increase services to students, improve communication on campus and between campus organizations, beautify the college grounds and make them safer, and consider questions of interest to the student body. In the 1966-1967 school year, student representatives, for the first time in the college's history, were placed on three university-wide committees and, by the end of the decade, students had a voice on eighteen such committees. On the eve of the UTA period, students had become truly incorporated into the university community and had a say-so in the formulation of a number of policies which affected them.[57]

ASC students rallied around their sports teams in the fifties and sixties. In fact, sports pulled the campus together and brought national recognition to the school in the 1950s for the first time. Indeed, the school and local community caught "football fever" two years in a row as the ASC Rebels football team played in Junior Rose Bowls in 1956 and 1957. The first year the Rebels were invited to play in Pasadena, California, they were coming off of an 8-1-1 season, losing only their final conference game to archrival Tarleton State College, and were co-champs of the Pioneer Conference. Nevertheless, the Junior Rose Bowl Committee selected ASC to play perennial power Compton College of California on December 6, 1956. As head coach of the Rebels team, Claude "Chena" Gilstrap, recalled, "We were most decidedly the underdog. Compton College . . . had played in it four successive years. They had a thirty-six game winning streak or something. And we were just supposed to be the opposition. And as a result of this, native Californians were pretty well up to here with Compton College. And so we were the fair-haired children. And by golly, we beat 'em!" ASC won the game by a score of 20-13, with diminutive running back Calvin Lee, the 5'8" and

6.27 A 500-pound cake made to celebrate ASC's 20 to 13 victory over Compton College in the 1956 Junior Rose Bowl.

147-pound "Comet from Comanche," scoring all of the Rebels' points. For Lee's inspired efforts, sports writers elected him the game's outstanding player and recipient of the Paul Helms Trophy. The game, played before 35,000 football fans, gave the Rebs a claim on the mythical title of National Champion.[58]

After the game, excited ASC supporters dismantled the Rose Bowl's goal posts, brought them back to Arlington, and erected them in front of the student center. On December 14, most of Arlington celebrated the Rebels' victory with a street parade; an appreciation ceremony on campus, complete with a 500-pound victory cake; and congratulatory speeches and presentations. Mayor Vandergriff, one of the the team's biggest fans and the announcer for the Rebs' home games, told the press, "We were so thrilled that I doubt I can put it into words, but our excitement and enthusiasm were so contagious that we transformed Pasadena into a suburb of Arlington!" In January 1957, Coach Gilstrap was named the Texas junior college coach of the year, the third time he received that honor. Assistant Coach Thomas Tinker observed that as a result of the Rose Bowl "football just consumed the town, the college, and everything else. We still tolerated the other sports, but football was it." In the spring, 520 fans attended the annual Gridiron Dinner to watch films of the memorable game.[59]

The roles were reversed a year later when the Rebels returned to the Junior Rose Bowl on December 17, 1957. This time they were carrying an undefeated record into California to play relatively unknown Cerritos Junior College, a California school in its first year of existence. Though the partisan California crowd threw its support behind Cerritos, ASC won the game 21-12 and brought back its claim to a second national championship. The 1957 Rebels team was a powerhouse, perhaps the best football squad in the school's history, with eight of its players named as All-Americans. Once again, Arlington and the college celebrated victory with a parade, pep rally, speeches, and dance. As a result of the two back-to-back Rose Bowl victories, ASC received national attention and notoriety. The school's reputation, no doubt, also improved because as Coach Gilstrap observed, ". . . it doesn't make any sense, but the man on the street measures the quality of the college by how it did last Saturday."[60]

The two Rose Bowl wins marked the pinnacle of success for ASC's football program. After this, the college became a four-year school in 1959 and was forced to compete with colleges at a different level. In 1963, ASC joined the newly created Southland Conference and fielded a team with African-American players for the first time. Though the Rebels remained competitive at the senior college level, they never again achieved national recognition for their football program. None of the college's administrations placed a great deal of emphasis on the sports program, but they did subsidize it heavily, especially football. A booster club also helped raise money for scholarships. Despite what the coaches perceived as a lack of adequate support by the school's presidents, ASC students and fans routinely filled the college's 10,000-seat stadium for home games. It was not until the stadium was demolished to make room for the construction of the Activities Building in the late 1960s and football games were played at Turnpike Stadium (a baseball field) that attendance began to dwindle.[61]

Football was not the only sport that attracted attention and support in the fifties and sixties. ASC's basketball team, led by Coach Tinker until 1965, played a full schedule in the Pioneer and later Southland Conference, and often competed in post-season tournaments and zone playoffs. Recalling his years as head basketball coach, Tinker admitted that "those zone playoffs were tough. The best we could ever do was finish second in one of those. . . ." ASC also fielded tennis, track, and golf teams for both decades. In the mid-sixties, ASC added swimming to its sports program under the direction of coach Don Easterling. In 1965, the swim team scored a first in Texas swimming by entering in competition the first woman to swim against men in the state. Dashell Maines was the woman and she, along with eleven men, earned swimming letters that year. Later in the 1960s, ASC and UTA swim teams, led by national record holder and 1968 Olympic gold medal winner Doug Russell, were consistent winners in competition. Also in the mid-1960s, the college started its intramural sports program, giving those students not on one of the school's athletic teams an opportunity to compete in such sports as touch football, basketball, bowling, and tug-of-war. By the time ASC became UTA, the only major gap in the school's athletic program was in women's sports—the school did not field a team in any sport for women.[62]

The Arlington State College years brought about the most sweeping changes in the school's history. During these years, the college gained senior status and added its first graduate programs. It also moved from the A&M to the UT system, integrated peacefully, began an aggressive land acquisition and building program, greatly enlarged the size and quality of its faculty, and saw enrollment grow from 1,790 to 11,873. And for the first—and last—time in its history, it gained national recognition on the gridiron. As students began the fall semester of 1967 at the University of Texas at Arlington, the university was poised for taking the next steps in becoming a research-oriented university.

6.28 Football games drew large crowds to ASC's Memorial Stadium. At this 1955 game, enthusiastic cheerleaders were not the only official supporters. Mayor Tom Vandergriff, known as the "voice" of ASC, announced football games from the 1950s until the end of football in 1985.

A Kinder, Gentler Time

6.29 ASC's own "marshal," who helped patrol campus in the 1950s and 1960s, was never without his famous six-shooters and gun belt.

Dr. Samuel B. Hamlett of the political science department has been with the university since 1956. In an oral history interview conducted in March 1994, Dr. Hamlett recalled his first impressions of the Arlington State College campus and some of the college's staff. Dr. Hamlett's recollections harken back to a time when the college was more intimate and casual than it is today.

I came here in the late summer of '56. The campus was not impressive at that time. There were a group of buildings built largely in the twenties. They had built a student center. There were old frame buildings as was true on most campuses built to accommodate the G.I. Bill and [the] swelling enrollments of the late forties and fifties. They used a lot of military buildings that were moved in. A lot of classes were in what had been barracks of various kinds. . . .

When I came here really for the first time, I drove up [Highway] 157, which is Cooper today. I drove, actually, through the western edge of the campus, unaware that I was on campus. [I] went downtown. [I] said, "Where is Arlington State College?" [People downtown] started describing where it was. I said, "Well, I guess I came through it." They said, "Yes, you did!"

I arrived here and found a place to park adjacent to what is now called The Roundhouse [the Planetarium], where they're constructing a new building. . . .

The first thing that I spotted as I drove in there was an elderly man in uniform—I can't remember his name—who was the sole campus policeman for the entire campus. He had a vision problem and was not very mobile. He had with him someone who appeared to be his assistant [who] was dressed in western garb. [The assistant was] very slender, maybe in his thirties or forties, and wore a large brim stetson. [He] had a badge, not quite like the badge of this policeman. [The assistant] had silver-plated . . . I think maybe there was one [pistol] on both sides of the belt. He was referred to as the "marshal." He stuttered a bit when he spoke, but he was clearly a part of the command procedure.

I was told I could park there. It was one of the interesting things which speaks to the nature of the campus and the college at that time. This person, whose name was actually Marshall Morton, lived off campus. His family had a home just off campus. He was, perhaps due to birth injury, mentally handicapped, but as an adult he had filled this role of assisting the campus police and city police. They accepted that. . . . He exercised authority without any official basis except the whole town knew about it and understood it. He was loved, really, as a town figure. At the football games for Arlington State College, he was given a place on the sidelines. You would see him out there, sometimes even directing traffic.

He was an interesting and beloved figure, the "marshal." Of course, later on, the campus police force grew and became an important aspect of university life. In 1955-1956, it was constituted by one elderly man assisted by one unofficial person.

CHAPTER SEVEN

A Positive Slope Institution

When the school began its first fall semester as the University of Texas at Arlington (UTA) in September 1967, it was the only state-supported graduate-level university in the Dallas-Fort Worth metroplex. Because of its location in a rapidly growing urban area, many people on and off campus predicted it would eventually evolve into the "UCLA of the University of Texas system." All signs and trends looked favorable for the continued diversification and development of the school. Even an anticipated enrollment decline resulting from the fall opening of the first campus of the Tarrant County Junior College (TCJC) system did not occur, as UTA's enrollment reached an all-time high of 11,873 students, 372 more than the preceding year. Despite the prevailing optimism about the school, President Woolf realistically observed that a name change alone did not make a university. He warned the college community—and cautioned the UT regents—that while "we have reached a name which does not shackle the future development of the institution, university status cannot be conferred by writ. . . ." Recognizing how far the college had come in the past decade, but still attempting to focus attention on improvements that needed to be made, Woolf proposed "Pride Without Satisfaction" as UTA's motto.[1]

President Woolf, however, was unable to put his motto into practice as he was pressured out of office the following year. In the minds of many faculty members, he had come to embody the rigid hierarchical management style of the A&M system and its unwillingness to share information and reach decisions in a collegial way. His public stand against leaving the A&M system in 1965 did not help matters. As a result of this perception of Woolf, the faculty lost confidence in the president. Woolf knew this and, in April 1968, announced his resignation effective September 1. During his announcement to the faculty and staff, Woolf revealed that he would become "University Professor" of mechanical engineering and "President Emeritus," both honorary titles bestowed by the UT system. In his remarks, Woolf said that his decision had been reached "with deeply conflicting emotions." "On the one hand," he continued, "is a sense of dedication to this school, a desire to serve it, and a reluctance to shirk the responsibilities and the courage required of this office." On the other hand, he explained that after ten years as president, he had "earned the right to a life of lesser responsibilities and more personal freedom for himself and his family."[2]

7.1 By the late 1960s the old and new had merged as the center of campus shifted from Second Street to the newly-created mall in front of the library. Looking from the mall, Carlisle Hall, the tallest building in Arlington when built in 1969, towers above the old gymnasium and Preston Hall's Roundhouse.

7.2 After joining the UT system in 1965, ASC entrusted the development of its graduate programs to Frank Harrison. When President Woolf resigned in 1968, Harrison was named acting president and, later, president of UTA.

After leaving office and returning to the classroom, Woolf could look with pride at his decade-long presidency. During his administration, enrollment had grown from less than 5,000 to approximately 12,000, the annual operating budget had increased from $2.2 million to $11.8 million, the physical plant had increased five times in size, and the school's assets had grown from $8 million to $57 million. Faculty salaries had been increased as well, and the implementation of selective admissions had improved the quality of students on campus. Moreover, graduate programs were begun during Woolf's administration, and the legislature authorized the creation of the Graduate School of Social Work and the Institute of Urban Affairs. Woolf, however, was most proud of taking the school from a junior to a senior college and ultimately to university status. Woolf envisioned the school's next step as becoming a "first-class university," but this step, he warned, would require more resources, more graduate caliber faculty, and higher faculty salaries.[3]

Shortly after Woolf's resignation, Chancellor Ransom appointed Dr. Frank Harrison as acting president of UTA, effective September 1, 1968. Harrison was the consummate UT insider and a man in whom Ransom had the utmost confidence. A couple of months after Harrison's appointment, the UT system launched a nationwide search for Woolf's permanent replacement. Nine months after the search began, the board of regents on June 20, 1969, approved the recommendation of the search committee and removed the word "acting" from Harrison's title.[4]

Harrison had a long and distinguished record as a teacher and administrator prior to his appointment as president of UTA. Born in Dallas on November 21, 1913, he received his B.S. degree in chemistry from Southern Methodist University (SMU) in 1935, studying both at SMU and the University of Texas Medical School in Galveston. After graduation, Harrison moved to Chicago to attend Northwestern University, where he earned M.S. and Ph.D. degrees in 1936 and 1938 respectively. Harrison's specialties were neuroanatomy and neurophysiology. Following graduation at Northwestern, Harrison joined the faculty at the University of Tennessee, where he became professor and chairman of the anatomy department. While at Tennessee, he also designed and directed a medical electronics laboratory. He moved to Dallas in 1952 to join the University of Texas Southwestern Medical School faculty as a professor of anatomy and to complete the requirements for an M.D. degree, which he received in 1956.

After coming to Dallas, Harrison organized the medical electronics laboratory and was named associate dean of the medical school. Two years later,

7.3 In 1969 the UTA library entered the computer era when a new computer punch-card check-out system was put on-line.

he became associate dean of graduate studies at the school. It was while associate graduate dean that Harrison, in 1965, was asked by Chancellor Ransom to organize UTA's graduate program. Two years after this, Harrison assumed the acting presidency of UTA. The UT regents could not have selected an individual with more intimate knowledge of UTA and its faculty, the Dallas-Fort Worth area, and the workings of the system. Chancellor Ransom referred to Harrison as a "top-flight scholar," who would bring to UTA "a keen understanding of the needs of the area the university serves." At the press conference announcing his appointment, Harrison pledged to build strong undergraduate *and* graduate programs, building them together, not developing one to the detriment of the other.[5]

Harrison was a man of his word. During his brief four-year tenure as president, he and his administration worked diligently to add new and needed degree programs to the university. Harrison, either as president or as associate dean of graduate studies at UTA, was instrumental in establishing ten new baccalaureate programs, twenty-four master's programs, and two doctoral programs. Wendell Nedderman, who served as dean of engineering, graduate school administrator, and vice president for academic affairs during Harrison's administration, recalled that prior to 1969 there was a period of debate as to whether or not UTA should be a doctoral granting institution. The debate came to a head in 1968 and 1969, when an out-of-state visitation team, led by Dr. George Town of Iowa State University, came to campus at the invitation of the UT system and the state's coordinating board to evaluate the capability of the School of Engineering for offering doctoral programs. Nedderman remembered that the report summation said, in effect, that "UT-Arlington's School of Engineering is not good enough to offer the doctorate, but it is as good as it is going to be without the doctorate." As a result of the visit, the UT system's support, and the approval of the doctoral program by the coordinating board, UTA started its Ph.D. program in engineering in September 1969. The university awarded its first doctorates in August 1971.[6]

7.4 The high point in UTA swimming came at the 1968 Olympic Games when Doug Russell, a member of the Rebel swim team, won two gold medals. After graduation Russell remained several years as swimming coach.

With the initiation of a doctoral program in engineering came pressure from the UT system for UTA to end its two-year associate degree programs. In September 1969, John J. McKetta, executive vice-chancellor for academic affairs for the system, wrote President Harrison, calling for a phasing out of the program. McKetta suggested that Harrison work with the junior colleges in Dallas and Tarrant counties to accomplish this. At the time, UTA had 412 students enrolled in these technical programs. Once word spread that UTA planned to end its two-year programs, local business leaders, private citizens, and former graduates began petitioning state legislators and the UT chancellor in hopes of saving the programs. Frank C. Erwin, Jr., chairman of the board of regents, responded to the petition drive by calling the technical program a training course "customarily found in vocational education [and] is more similar to vocational education than it is to engineering programs found in our leading colleges and universities." President Harrison began negotiations with TCJC in the spring of 1970 to transfer the programs there. The programs discussed were aeronautical technology, civil technology, electrical technology, and mechanical technology. According to Harrison, UTA's future was focused on "training at the baccalaureate degree and graduate level," not on vocational education. By the fall of 1973, TCJC had full control of the technical programs. The last vestiges of UTA's vocational roots had been severed.[7]

In addition to striving to make UTA a university of excellence, Harrison also worked to place the "UT stamp" on the school. To Harrison, that meant improving communi-

7.5 Upsetting to some, the University of Texas at Arlington's Rebel theme involved not only the singing of "Dixie" and mock slave auctions, but also the mascot, Johnny Reb.

cation with members of the faculty, student body, and community. To this end, Harrison introduced or reorganized a number of committees designed to give the faculty more of a voice in decision making. President Harrison, like Woolf before him, appointed search committees to identify, interview, and recommend individuals for important positions at the university. Unlike the A&M years, the president made copies of the university budget available to faculty and staff, rather than keeping it and the budgeting process a tightly guarded secret. Harrison remembered the atmosphere on campus in this way: ". . . the A&M system was generally run like a military academy. There was a general who was president of A&M itself and running it like a military school; the faculty didn't have much involvement in budgeting, development of programs in general, and Jack Woolf was following that style. . . . This was not the style of the UT system." Harrison's administration went a long way toward removing many of the barriers that had existed between the faculty and previous administrations. In short, UTA became more collegial, open, and democratic under Harrison.[8]

Harrison was president when the Texas legislature created the University of Texas at Dallas (UTD) in Richardson in 1969. In 1967, Gifford Johnson, head of the Southwest Center for Advanced Studies, proposed that the center be given to the UT system and operated as a university, emphasizing the training of students in the sciences and engineering. Regents chairman Frank Erwin and Chancellor Ransom supported the idea. The center had been established in 1961 as a private institution by Texas Instruments (TI) founders Cecil Green, Erik Jonsson, and Eugene McDermott. Their purpose was to build an institution which would provide graduate education for engineers and scientists in the narrow interests of TI, Collins Radio, and other growing electronic businesses in the North Texas area. This was before graduate programs had been added in Arlington.[9]

By the late 1960s, however, the center's founders realized that the institution would be more viable and better positioned for growth if it were given to the UT system and developed as a public university. News of the TI offer hit the newspapers in 1967. While the UTA administration remained neutral on the proposed addition of a sister school in Dallas, the Tarrant County legislative delegation fought UTD's creation. Don Gladden, state representative from Tarrant County, summarized the position of the county delegation when he said the legislators would "fight tooth and toenail" all attempts to create a UT component in Dallas County. In March he argued, "We [the Tarrant County delegation] feel that any graduate school for science and engineering in this area should be located in Arlington. . . ." UTA's supporters joined the fight in Austin. Tom Vandergriff explained the uncomfortable position in which the proposal left him and other supporters: "We were placed in the unique position of having to oppose what we had originally supported, that is expanded higher education in Texas." But, he rationalized, UTA "was just getting its feet on the ground; we didn't deserve to have another branch of the university that close by so soon." In 1969, Tarrant County representative W. C. Sherman predicted "catastrophe" for UTA if another public university was created so close by. [10]

Though the Tarrant County legislators fought the UTD proposal, they were only successful in modifying the provisions of the UTD bill, not defeating it entirely. With the assistance of Governor Preston Smith and following the recommendation of the state's coordinating board, the legislature hammered out a compromise that satisfied both UTA and UTD supporters. The compromise called for the establishment of UTD as a junior, senior, and graduate-level institution, and authorized it to award its first baccalaureate degrees in 1975. Defenders of UTA believed that the compromise bill, leaving the university as the only comprehensive public college in the metroplex, would enable the Arlington school to continue to grow and develop needed programs. [11]

During the Harrison administration and even with the establishment of UTD, the university continued to ride the wave of enrollment growth. Its student population increased from 12,556 in fall 1968 to 14,028 four years later. While these numbers reflect the school's total fall enrollment, graduate student enrollment for the same period increased more dramatically. Indeed, in 1968 the number of graduate students was 301, while four years later that number had grown to 1,008. [12]

The UT regents were generous in their funding for construction, as buildings continued to be added to the campus landscape at a rapid pace. President Harrison's presidency saw seven-story Carlisle Hall completed (1969), Hammond and Trimble Halls opened (1968), the formal opening of the Business-Life Science Building (1970), as well as the opening of University Hall (1970) and E. E. Davis Hall (1971). Additionally, the construction of the $8 million Fine Arts Building was begun in 1972, the year Harrison left UTA.

7.6 The spirit of the Rebel theme not only affected sports, it was also the decorative motif of the student center. Here in the Robert E. Lee Suite even the furniture was covered with portraits of Confederate heroes and slaves working in the fields.

The new buildings added much needed classroom, office, and lab space on campus. The campus comprised 197 acres in 1972 and stretched west to Fielder Road, north to Border, east to Center, and south across Mitchell. The UTA self-study report written in the early 1970s mentioned for the first time that "plans are underway to lower the grade of Cooper Street beginning in the south end near its intersection with New Mitchell and ending at the north end near its intersection with Second Street." Because Cooper Street was a state highway (157), a major north-south traffic artery for Arlington, and a road which essentially divided the campus in half, its depression would involve negotiation and agreement between the State Highway Department, the City of Arlington, and the UT system. Not surprisingly, given the complexity of the negotiations, it would take twenty years before Cooper Street was depressed.[13]

Despite President Harrison's success in expanding physical facilities, degree offerings, and lines of communication, he was plagued throughout most of his administration with perhaps the most divisive and controversial issue that ever hit the campus—the Rebel theme controversy. The controversy centered on the university's use of Old South symbols and motifs and whether these were appropriate for the school. Although the controversy erupted during Harrison's administration, it had been a bone of contention on campus for several years. Its origins can be traced to 1951, when then President E. H. Hereford, hoping to boost school spirit, asked the student body to select a new mascot for the school. Hereford believed that the Blue Riders mascot, adopted in 1949 when the school's name was changed to Arlington State College, was not rallying the students behind its athletic teams. In the first fall assembly of 1951, Hereford presented to the student body Rebels and Cadets as its choices for the new mascot. The students voted to become the ASC Rebels. The new theme won immediate acceptance, and gradually Old South images were used across campus. By 1952, the Confederate battle flag became the official banner for the college and "Dixie" the unofficial

7.7 When student government resolved to abolish the Rebel theme in the spring of 1968, pro-theme advocates rallied in favor of the theme, arguing that it could not be changed without a student referendum.

7.8 As referendum results revealed, student backing of the Rebel theme was overwhelming. Theme supporters established their headquarters in this structure near the present location of Pickard Hall.

school song. Throughout the fifties and early sixties, Confederate symbols were added to band uniforms, cheerleaders' outfits, football jerseys, the school's swimming pool and basketball court, and even furniture and draperies in the student center. The student center also had rooms named after Confederate military leaders, such as Robert E. Lee and Jeb Stuart. Homecoming activities culminated in the election of "Mr. Johnny Reb" and "Miss Dixie Belle," while the week of homecoming was called "Old South Week," when some campus groups held mock slave auctions.[14]

As long as the college remained segregated, the Southern theme was not perceived as a problem. Once the school opened its doors to African Americans, however, it was not long before the theme came under attack as being insensitive and even racist. *The Shorthorn* questioned the appropriateness of the Rebel theme as early as 1962, when it editorialized that it was time to reconsider the college's mascot and Southern traditions. *The Shorthorn* argued that "the whole 'Old South' celebration with its secession and slave auction will no doubt prove to be embarrassing as well as insulting to these students [African American] who certainly deserve as dignified a treatment as any other person enrolled in the college." The editorial concluded that the time was right to change the "old outmoded, needless theme." The newspaper's courageous stand, made the year ASC integrated, had no immediate affect on student attitudes.[15]

The Rebel theme question lay dormant until 1965, the year the college joined the UT system. On April 9, 1965, *The Shorthorn* used the school's move from the A&M to the UT system to advocate breaking "more ties with the past" and "changing . . . the Rebel-Dixie motif." The ASC student government also discussed the issue at length that spring and decided to hold a referendum to gauge opinion on the subject. A month later, the student referendum was held, with 2,429 voting to keep the theme, 448 voting to throw it out, and 222 casting ballots to modify it. The first "significant" student demonstration against the theme occurred five months later on October 29, when twenty-five students, mostly white, staged a peaceful protest in front of the student center just under the flagpole where the Confederate battleflag flew. Led by Ernest McMillan, a sophomore and member of the Student Non-Violent Coordinating Committee, the protesters sang songs and declared the Confederate flag a "symbol of slavery."[16]

The issue receded in importance until an African-American student, James

7.9 Told to select another theme, students cynically suggested that the first animal listed in the dictionary, the Aardvark, be named UTA mascot. Johnny Aardvark made his first appearance in 1968, walking in the homecoming parade and along the sidelines at football games.

7.10 At the start of the 1971 football season, UTA not only had a new mascot, but also a new football stadium when all games moved off campus to Turnpike Stadium, later known as Arlington Stadium.

Frank Wyman, published a moving essay, entitled "The Old Fires," in the fall 1967 issue of the *Arlington Review*, a university publication. Wyman's intent in writing the piece was to show how two different groups could view the same symbols in entirely different ways. Wyman admitted that while some whites viewed the Confederate flag as a symbol of independence, states' rights, and courage to uphold one's beliefs, for people of color it symbolized slavery, racism, oppression, and segregation. He also pointed out that the flag adorned the offices of radical segregationists like George Wallace of Alabama and Lester Maddox of Georgia and was flown proudly at all rallies of the Ku Klux Klan. Based on the flag's use, he wrote, "Supposedly, the attitudes surrounding the flag here at the University are not the same as they are in the previously named places. However, the symbolic representation of the flag is inseparable from it, regardless of where it is flown." For the sake of peaceful co-existence between black and white people, he urged university officials to change the Rebel theme and let "old fires die."[17]

By the spring semester of 1968, *The Shorthorn*, under editor Bruce Meyer, came out in favor of changing the Rebel theme, and a group of seventy African-American students, led by pre-law major Fred Bell, petitioned the student government to act. In March, the student government began meeting to consider both sides of the controversy. After a series of meetings where the issue was hotly debated, the student officials on April 30 approved a resolution that would prohibit the Confederate flag from being flown on campus as of July 1, 1968, and phase out the Rebel theme by July 1, 1969. The vote was twelve in favor of the resolution, five against, and three abstentions. The supporters of the resolution argued that the theme needed to be changed because it was dividing, rather than uniting, the student body. Because elections for new student government representatives had been held before this meeting, supporters of the Rebel theme derisively labelled the government the "Lame Duck Congress." The student government's vote brought tensions to the breaking point and was unpopular with the majority of the student body. In fact, the vote sparked a mass protest where approximately 1,000 students marched around the campus carrying Rebel flags and singing "Dixie." Rebel theme supporters also launched a petition drive, securing 4,000 signatures taking exception to the actions of the government and demanding a student vote on the issue. At this point, President Woolf intervened in the controversy and ruled that while the student government could authorize the removal of the Confederate flag, it could not legislate a change in the theme. That, he ruled, would have to come from a student referendum.[18]

The student referendum Woolf called for took place in November, after he had left the presidency and been replaced by Harrison. The referendum gave students the choice of voting for or against the Rebel theme. Out of a student body of 12,556 students, 3,507 supported the old theme, 952 voted against it, and 38 were undecided. Students were also given a list of thirty-six choices from which to choose a different theme, and the three top vote-getters were Aardvarks with 247, Texans with 176, and Mavericks with 161. With the three-to-one vote in favor of the Old South theme, no changes were made and tempers began to flare. A few weeks after the referendum, someone stripped the Confederate-inspired nameplates from the rooms in the student center and defaced an oil painting depicting Confederate soldiers. Feelings were running deep on campus, and the theme controversy received attention in the national and regional press.[19]

By the spring semester of 1969, opponents of the Rebel theme broadened their protests and addressed a host of other issues of interest to African-American students at UTA. The Collegians for Afro-American Progress (CAP), a student group, presented President Harrison a list of demands, which included the hiring of black professors, establishing a black studies program, providing preparatory courses for students who did not meet entrance requirements, and firing professors the group considered racist. In addition, CAP argued for a change in the Rebel theme and an end to discriminatory housing practices in Arlington. President Harrison rejected the demands, saying the theme would not be changed until the student body voted to do so and, he explained, all the other demands were outside his jurisdiction. Despite his negative response to the CAP demands, Harrison did move to address some of the concerns of African-American students. By 1970, for example, UTA had begun offering courses in African-American history, sociology, and psychology and had initiated a faculty exchange program with Bishop College, a largely black school in Dallas. Moreover, Reby Cary, a black, was hired as associate dean of student life.[20]

Despite Harrison's efforts to placate African-American students and their supporters, the Rebel theme issue refused to die. In August 1969, the Student Congress (formerly named the Student Government) called for another referendum, this one to select an alternate theme to run against the Rebel theme at a future election. The congress set the date for the alternate theme election for December. Before the referendum was held, however, tensions reached the breaking point. On October 17, 1969, a group of seventeen African-American students interrupted a Friday pep rally and attempted to persuade members of Kappa Alpha (KA) fraternity to take down a large Confederate flag. When the KAs refused, a scuffle broke out. Donna Darovich, a student at the time, recalled that a protester came forward and ripped the Rebel flag off of its standard and then "all hell broke loose." "It was my first experience with the mob mentality," she remembered, "somebody grabbed him. Somebody threw a punch. And within seconds people were falling down, people were screaming, punches were being thrown at who knows what." After the fighting was stopped, the students moved into the student center and shouted taunts at each other. A number of Rebel flags were burned in protest. The next day, several Rebel hats were taken from the Student Congress office and burned in a pile in front of the student center. Also on the Saturday following the pep rally melee, a group of African-American students attempted to gain entry into the press box at UTA's football game to address the crowd. After they were denied entrance, they congregated at one end of the field and refused to stand during the playing of "Dixie." Throughout the game they chanted "Go to hell Johnny Reb"

7.11 One of the few construction accidents at UTA occurred in 1970 when, during the construction of University Hall, the freshly-laid concrete roof of the theater collapsed. While the incident attracted much attention, there were no serious injuries.

as other students shouted "Give'em hell Johnny Reb." As a result of these incidents, several students on both sides of the controversy reported receiving threatening phone calls.[21]

In light of the divisive nature of the controversy and its potential for violence, a number of groups began arguing for a change in the Rebel theme. Even before the pep rally fight, the president's Executive Committee had proposed that the theme be eliminated "lock, stock, and barrel." A number of faculty members, led by Donald Weiss of philosophy, encouraged students to do away with the theme on the grounds that it was morally offensive. The Faculty Council also pressed for a change, as did the Texas Intercollegiate Student Association, a statewide organization. Arrayed against this call for change was a group called SOFT, Save Our Flag and Theme, and a majority of the student body. In the tense and racially charged atmosphere on campus, the alternate theme election was held in December. Of the 5,758 students voting, the proposed Texans mascot received 2,330 votes, Mavericks received 2,229, and Apollos 1,199. Because the referendum was indecisive, or at least so said the Student Congress, a runoff election was held in February 1970 between Texans and Mavericks. Obviously put off and frustrated by the lingering controversy, most students avoided the runoff. Nevertheless, the Maverick theme did win 318 votes against the Texans' 174.[22]

A month after the runoff election, the UT regents, hoping to calm matters on campus, ruled that the Texas state flag would be the official flag of each component in the system. The Confederate battle flag had not officially flown at the student center since June 31, 1968, and this ruling ensured that it would never fly on campus and symbolize UTA again. With the problem of the flag solved, students participated in yet another referendum, this one pitting the Rebel theme against the Maverick theme. The students voted on March 23-25, 1970, and once again the Rebel theme was the clear preference, but its margin of victory had diminished. The Southern theme received 2,198 votes, while Mavericks garnered 1,755, a 56-44 percent split. President Harrison voiced his intention to follow a democratic policy and not interfere with the rights of students as citizens, as long as order was maintained on campus.[23]

Harrison did his best to maintain order on campus and defuse potentially violent situations. Early in the fall of 1970, he addressed the marching band, urging it not to play "Dixie" at football games. He appealed to the band members'

7.12 Since Greek organizations came to campus in the mid-1960s, Greek Week and the Winter Olympics have been celebrated annually. Here various campus groups participate in the Greek-sponsored bed races down Second Street.

7.13 Although some of UTA's elevators may seem unreliable, this cadet is not looking for an alternative way to the ground, but participating in an descent exercise on the side of Carlisle Hall.

emotions, explaining that while a Southerner himself, he realized that the song humiliated certain students and produced divisiveness rather than unity. The band followed his wishes. Shortly after this, the Confederate flag was removed from band uniforms. President Harrison also met with student groups on both sides of the controversy, and these meetings were often confrontational. In these meetings, Harrison was always cool, rational, and firm. The best efforts of the administration and faculty did not quell the debate on or off campus. In fact, local residents made their feelings on the Rebel theme known too. Harrison received a number of letters from Arlington citizens supporting the theme, and the local newspapers published several "Letters to the Editor" on the controversy. In November 1970, the board of directors of the UTA Ex-Students Association called for a return of "Dixie" as the school's fight song, rationalizing that it would spark increased school spirit. The vote, a narrow six to five, with one abstention, reflected a board evenly split on the issue. The board also appealed to the UT regents to fully restore the Rebel symbols and motifs on campus.[24]

The regents considered the Rebel theme question during their meeting at Southwestern Medical School in Dallas on January 29, 1971. Fed up with the problems the controversy had caused and the harm it had done to the university's image and convinced the issue would not go away unless a change was made, the regents voted seven to two to abolish the Rebel theme by summer. Chancellor Charles A. LeMaistre made the motion calling for the theme's abolition. Chancellor LeMaistre argued that the theme had "adversely affected the morale" at UTA and had been a continuing cause of "discord and contention." He went on to say that "the distinguished and honored period of Texas heritage is not the issue—the abuse of it and the misuse of that heritage for divisive purposes is intolerable." Among those who attended the meeting from UTA and opposed the theme were President Harrison; Hugh Moore, Student Congress president; Chena Gilstrap, UTA's athletic director; and Dan Sloan, editor of *The Shorthorn*. Supporters of the theme attending from campus were Jim Jeffries, board member of the alumni association; Rebel Rouser president Tom Wheeler; history professor Martin Hall; and Thurman Jasper, math professor and sponsor of the Students for Representative Government. After the vote, the regents directed President Harrison "to hold, as soon as possible, such consultations and/or other elections necessary to permit the students to select and recommend a new theme other than the Rebel theme for use after June 1, 1971." Looking back on the controversy in 1976, Harrison justified his change of position by saying, "We were not talking about Southern heritage, we were not talking about the Confederacy, we were talking about a campus, and it [the Rebel theme] was divisive. . . ."[25]

Response to the regents' vote was immediate and, in many cases, hostile. Harrison was the target of much of the criticism for supporting the students' right to decide and then opposing the theme before the regents. The *Rebel Bugler (Extra)* accused him of accepting a bribe to change his stand and chastised him for going against the student referendum held in March 1970. Another newspaper, the *Roaring Reb*, attacked the president for lying to the student body and suggested that he resign. A number of angry letter writers saw the regents' action as a "blow to Southern Aristocracy" and "unnecessary." President Harrison did not dwell on the criticism, but rather moved to call another student election to end the controversy once and for all. Scheduled for April 26-28, 1971, the referendum was to decide UTA's new theme. The results of the election proved indecisive, with Mavericks receiving

7.14 President Nedderman and his administrative team directed the university for nearly two decades. Participating in a 1977 question and answer session are (from left to right) W. A. Baker, vice president for academic affairs; President Nedderman; Wayne Duke, vice president for student affairs; and Dudley Wetsel, vice president for business affairs.

460 votes, Toros 408, Rangers 370, and Hawks 361. Harrison called for a runoff at the end of the spring semester and, in the runoff, Mavericks garnered 1,863 votes and Toros 1,431. On June 4, President Harrison reported to the board of regents that the student body supported Maverick as the new theme. The adoption of the Maverick theme ended the Rebel theme controversy, but left large numbers of students with hard feelings, particularly the Rebel supporters. Even today, twenty-four years after the controversy, many former students remain critical of Harrison.[26]

The end of the Rebel theme controversy occurred at the same time that the Harrison administration was attempting to introduce affirmative action programs to campus. In 1970, the U. S. Department of Health, Education, and Welfare (HEW) pointed out to university officials that UTA's faculty and staff were too homogenous a group, with less than 1 percent being minority. Indeed, of the 1,032 employees of the college at the time, only 5 were African American and 4 had Spanish surnames. HEW urged the university to follow the Department of Labor's Executive Order Number 4, which required all institutions to have clearly articulated affirmative action programs in place in order to qualify for federal funds. The following year, HEW concluded that UTA was still having a problem with minority and female hiring and gave the university a February 5, 1972, deadline to bring its recruitment and hiring practices into compliance with federal guidelines. This the school did. Despite the implementation of an affirmative action program in the early 1970s, the number of minorities on the full-time faculty and staff as recently as 1993 remained embarrassingly small.[27]

The first few years of the 1970s also saw a number of programs, services, and organizations created on campus aimed at attracting minority students and retaining those enrolled in school. In 1972, the Minority Student Advocacy Caucus was organized to recruit minorities into UTA's graduate programs, and the library opened its Minorities Cultural Center (MCC), which collected library resources focusing on African Americans, Hispanics, and Native Americans. As Reby Cary said at the dedication of the MCC, "The basic purpose of the center is to bring about an understanding of the different races of people and their problems and to point out the cultural contributions of their groups. . . ." Cary expressed hope that initiatives like the creation of the MCC and the removal of the Rebel theme would help alter UTA's "lily-white" reputation among people of color.[28]

Enrollment figures indicate that the university's new initiatives worked to some degree. In 1970, for example, there were only 176 African-American and 157 Hispanic students enrolled at UTA out of a total student population of 14,028. By 1979, however, there were 1,065 black students and 594 Spanish-surnamed students out of a total enrollment of 19,138. Minority students also became more involved in campus life and organizations, and, as a result, a number of "firsts" occurred in the 1970s. Dickie Fears became UTA's first African-American cheerleader in 1970 and Alpha Phi Alpha the university's first black fraternity. In 1971, Alpha Kappa Alpha, an African-American sorority, was organized. Royce West was the first elected African-American president of the Student Congress in 1974, and, three years later, Penny Willrich was the first black woman elected to the post. In 1980, Wanda Holiday and Rodney Lewis were the first African-American homecoming royalty. Also during the seventies, Hispanic students became more active on campus, and the Association of Mexican-American Students (AMAS) sponsored a number of programs and activities celebrating Hispanic culture and history.[29]

Many of the gains made by minority students came as a result of the Harrison administration's modest attempts to diversify the campus but, ironically, these occurred after Harrison himself had left UTA. In the fall of 1972, Harrison resigned from the university to accept the presidency of the UT system's Health Science Center in San Antonio. Dr. Harrison explained his motivation for leaving UTA in a 1991 interview: ". . . I would have been perfectly happy to stay here the rest of my life. It was getting back to the medical center concept of putting all these schools together, developing a graduate program down there, it was just attractive to me." Harrison had come to UTA from a medical school, and it is not surprising that he left the university—a general academic institution—for the opportunity to lead a new and growing medical center during its formative years. On November 4, 1972, Wendell Nedderman, Harrison's vice president for academic affairs, was named acting president.[30]

Nedderman, a man whom Harrison characterized as "personable, likable, competent, [and] trusted by the faculty," was a popular choice to serve as acting president. In addition to being genuinely liked and admired by staff and faculty, Nedderman was a straight-talking, unpretentious Midwesterner, whose tenure at the school stretched back to September 1, 1959, when he joined the university as its first dean of engineering. Since that time, Nedderman had held a number of administrative positions on campus, many concurrently. He served as engineering dean from 1959-1969; graduate school administrator, 1967-1969; vice-president for research and graduate affairs, 1967-1968; and vice-president for academic affairs, 1968-1972. In short, Nedderman had intimate knowledge of the workings of the university and was a zealous booster of its potential.[31]

In many ways, Nedderman's background prepared him well for the rigors of administering a large public university. Born on October 31, 1921, in a small Iowa town, he attended a one-room school house as a young boy. In 1939, he graduated as valedictorian of his high school (one of twenty-six graduates) and attended one year of junior college before entering Iowa State University. He received his B.S. in civil engineering in March 1943 and entered the U. S. Naval Academy's Reserve Midshipman's School under the V-7 program. After four-months training, he was commissioned as an ensign and assigned to a destroyer, the *USS Patterson*, during WWII. On the *Patterson*, he logged more than 150,000 miles, seeing action in the Marianas, Philippines, Iwo Jima, and Okinawa. He was awarded eight battle stars and three theatre campaign ribbons for his war service. After the war, a former professor told him about the engineering program at Texas A&M and, in 1947, he joined the College Station faculty as an instructor and also began work on a master's degree. He graduated in 1949. He left Texas A&M briefly to return to Iowa State for his Ph.D., a degree he earned in 1951. He returned to A&M that same year as an assistant professor. By 1959, the year Jack Woolf hired him to administer ASC's College of Engineering, Nedderman was professor of civil engineering at Texas A&M. Nedderman accepted Woolf's offer because he viewed coming to a newly created four-year college as "A pioneer experience very few would have." He relished the opportunity "to get in on the ground floor" of a developing school and was "intrigued by the potential." He was thirty-eight when he and his wife, Betty, moved to Arlington in 1959.[32]

For thirteen years Nedderman understudied for the presidency, first under Woolf, then Harrison. When he was asked by the chancellor to serve as UTA's acting chief administrative officer, he was ready. He brought with him a philosophy of running the school and dealing with people which was molded by his family and his down-to-earth personality. His honest, decent, "square-shooting" style endeared him to people and paved the way for a long tenure as president. Upon becoming acting president, he vowed not to be a caretaker, but rather to act

7.15 When UTA lost its dedicated source of building funds in 1979, the axe fell on the planned $14 million Special Events Center. The loss of funding for this structure was not only a disappointment for President Nedderman, but it also left a lasting void in the facilities at UTA.

as if "I'm going to be president for the next twenty years." Nedderman's statement proved prophetic because on February 2, 1974, he became president of UTA, a position he held until his retirement on July 13, 1992. Counting the time he served as acting president, Nedderman indeed led the school for twenty years.[33]

When Nedderman was selected as acting president in 1972, UTA had 14,000 students, an $18.7 million budget, and a reputation as a commuter college. Nedderman brought with him an unshakable faith in the university and a fervent desire to build on each of its three segments: people, programs, and facilities. Like his predecessors, Nedderman and his administration oversaw and managed a rapid increase in the student population. During his tenure as president, enrollment climbed from 14,028 in the fall semester of 1972 to 25,135 in fall of 1991, the last fall semester he occupied the president's chair. In fact, the 1991 fall enrollment was the largest in UTA history. Graduate student enrollment increased even more dramatically, growing from 936 in 1972 to more than 4,200 nineteen years later.[34]

7.16 After having been off campus for nearly ten years, football returned in the fall of 1980 to the newly-completed Maverick Stadium.

Driving the increase in the student population was the growth and economic vitality of the Dallas-Fort Worth area, the coming of age of Baby Boomers, the relatively low cost of tuition and fees at the university, the growth of junior colleges in the area which served as pipelines into UTA's advanced and graduate courses, and the expansion of the university's "role and scope." To President Nedderman, "role and scope" meant the range of degree programs, especially at the graduate level, that the university offered. During his presidency, UTA added to its inventory seventeen doctoral programs, twenty-three master's programs, and twenty new bachelor's degrees. Somewhat modestly he admitted, "I think this has had an uplifting effect on the entire university." Moreover, his administration pushed successfully for the creation of a School of Architecture, a School of Nursing, and a Center for Professional Teacher Education.[35]

For the most part, the degrees added during the Nedderman years—particularly the doctoral programs—were in the sciences and the professional schools, such as engineering and business. Political and practical reasons steered graduate development in this direction. Politically, all new degree programs had to be approved by the state coordinating board, which looked closely at whether proposed programs competed with similar ones offered at other universities in the region. Student demand for graduate programs also played a role in the board's deliberations. Practically, the coordinating board was more willing to approve programs in disciplines where the university had achieved some level of success and notoriety. At UTA, this meant engineering, science, and business. W. A. Baker, vice president for academic affairs from 1972-1993, explained that the reason for doctoral programs in the professional schools "was not so much a philosophical one where someone decided that was more desirable than liberal arts programs, it was just a practical fact that there is not anyone beating down the doors for new programs in the liberal arts." Not surprisingly, then, the university in 1995 offered only one Ph.D. program in the liberal arts, and this one an interdisciplinary doctorate in humanities.[36]

With the development of more graduate programs came greater emphasis on the part of faculty members to conduct research and publish their findings. As a result of this so-called "publish or perish" pressure and the fact that research activity became an important part of tenure and promotion decisions, the nature of the university's faculty changed. Before graduate programs were introduced on campus, faculty members were primarily teachers who were not expected or encouraged to do research. After their introduction, however, faculty were hired with the expectation that they engage in active research programs and train students to do the same. Research and publishing activity increased on campus as a result. An indication of this increase was the amount of research funding the university received from outside sources, such as government agencies, foundations, and corporations. In 1972, Nedderman's first year in office, UTA faculty received approximately $200,000 in outside funds for sponsored projects. By the time Nedderman retired in 1992, that amount had grown to $12.7 million, a dramatic increase. As Vice President Baker explained, "Your funding always lags behind your status, and your reputation lags behind your ability, so it takes a while to develop the programs to develop the reputation that brings the fund-

7.17 More than ten major building additions were completed during President Nedderman's twenty-year tenure at UTA. The building activity climaxed with the addition, in 1986, of a new engineering building now appropriately named Nedderman Hall.

ing." Baker credited the faculty, not the administration, in aggressively seeking outside grants, saying, "Research funding comes primarily through the efforts of faculty. Faculty write proposals and they get them funded. The administration can't get research funding for the faculty; the faculty has to do that. . . ."[37]

The rapid student growth during the decades of the seventies and eighties, combined with the expansion of graduate programs and accompanying research, created a continual demand for space and facilities on campus. President Nedderman and his administration lobbied hard for new building and renovation money during this period and had much success. During his presidency, the physical plant inventory grew by twenty new buildings (or major additions) totaling approximately 1.6 million gross square feet of space. The total cost for this new construction was $158.45 million. A significant addition to the college's physical plant occurred in 1987 with the establishment of UTA's River Bend campus in east Fort Worth. There, a 48,000 square foot

7.18 Having played only five years in its new stadium, football, which had been played in Arlington consistently since the founding of Grubbs Vocational College in 1917, was eliminated by President Nedderman due to poor game attendance and resulting financial problems.

building was constructed on eighteen acres of land to house the Automation and Robotics Research Institute. This was the result of a $10 million capital fund drive spearheaded jointly by the Fort Worth Chamber of Commerce and UTA. Also during Nedderman's presidency, the university received an additional $14.94 million for both major and minor renovations to existing buildings, while $18.35 million was appropriated for land acquisition and landscaping. Despite this impressive record of growth, President Nedderman did not get everything he wanted, and what he did get took "scrambling, arguing, debating, and politicking." In fact, one of the major disappointments of his presidency was the scuttling of a special events center which had been approved for construction by the regents in 1977. The center was to seat 10,000 people for basketball, volleyball, and special events, and cost $14 million. Its funding was to come from the state's ad valorem tax, which had been UTA's major source of construction funds since the mid-sixties.[38]

Unfortunately for UTA and sixteen other colleges in the state that depended on the tax for revenue, the Texas legislature, in response to a lawsuit by Representative Wayne Peveto of Orange, virtually eliminated the tax in 1979. Not only did the legislature abolish the tax, but it failed to provide another source of building funds for these schools. With a dedicated source of funding gone, UTA placed the special events center, a continuing education center, and other construction projects on hold. In 1982, however, UTA did receive a special appropriation of $25 million from the legislature to build a thermal energy building and the Architecture Building. For the next few years, the legislature struggled to devise a plan which would provide funding to colleges like UTA, and President Nedderman, Vice President Baker, and other university officials and supporters worked in Austin for a solution to the problem. By 1981, UTA administrators supported the push in the legislature to make funds generated by the Permanent University Fund (PUF) available to all components of the University of Texas and Texas A&M systems. The Texas constitution of 1876 had established the fund to support and maintain "a university of the first class." It was endowed in the nineteenth century with two million acres of land, mostly in West Texas. The fund, however, assumed paramount importance in 1923, when oil was discovered on this land. By the early 1980s, the book value of PUF was more than $1.3 billion, making it the second largest university endowment in the country behind Harvard's. PUF generated, at the time, $100 million a year in interest, and it was to this money, called the Available University Fund, that UTA and other UT and A&M component schools wanted access. President Nedderman, in 1981, called this funding issue "the most critical for UTA since its elevation to senior college status."[39]

The legislature did pass a bill calling for a statewide vote on PUF and college funding in general. Proposition 2—as the amendment was called—was presented to Texas voters on November 6, 1984. It called for making PUF monies available to the fourteen schools in the UT system and the nine schools in the A&M system

7.19 With the deficit funding of football eliminated, UTA was more able to fund women's sports like softball, as required by Title IX.

7.20 Since the end of football, the UTA track team has won four conference championships.

for purposes of new construction, renovation, capital equipment, and land acquisition. It also would create a separate construction fund for twenty-six state-supported schools outside of the two large systems. Despite the attractiveness of the proposition, it did have its drawbacks, the most important being that any money coming from either PUF or the fund for the other schools could only be used for classroom and research facilities, not for auxiliary buildings, dormitories, and athletic projects. Moreover, the amendment did not alter the roles of Texas A&M and the University of Texas at Austin as the flagship institutions in their respective systems. They were to remain the only schools that could use PUF monies to augment their operating budgets. The amendment's shortcomings, however, did not outweigh its benefits to UTA, and President Nedderman and others on campus breathed a sigh of relief at its passage. Once the amendment passed, construction on campus resumed, but the special events center never was built. It was a casualty of construction and funding priorities which emphasized academic needs over all others.[40]

Construction funding was just one of many problems Nedderman faced while president. His personality and straight-forward style made him realize early that a "certain degree of stress is normal" in a job like his, and one should "accept it and not worry about it." He also subscribed to what he called the "pendulum theory," a lesson probably learned in the halls of academe. According to his theory, "if things are going badly, just hang in there and they'll get better. And if things are going well, don't get smug because they will get worse."[41]

Things did indeed get worse for the UTA president in 1985, a year, more than any other during his administration, marred by controversy. The first controversy to hit was centered on X-rated films and whether they should be shown on campus. The dispute arose in late January, when Greg Sullivan, president of the Baptist Student Union, organized a petition drive protesting the showing of "pornography" on campus. Sullivan's drive was in response to the showing of the X-rated film *Emmanuelle: The Joys of a Woman*. More than 600 people attended the two showings of the film. The film's selection was made by the UTA Film Council, a student group, and approved by staff in the university's student affairs office. With *The Story of O*, another X-rated film, scheduled for the end of March, Sullivan took action in an attempt to persuade administrators to cancel its showing. Sullivan argued that "the campus is our neighborhood and we feel showing X-rated films decreases the quality of our neighborhood." University officials defended the film's showing, countering that they had been shown before without protest and that the college's guidelines allowed "erotic" films be played on campus. Wayne Duke, vice president for student affairs, explained that "the movies that are in question make up less than 3 percent of all the films we've shown in the past seven years."[42]

The issue, no doubt, would have died a natural death if not for the efforts of two state legislators. But joining Sullivan in his protest were State Senator Robert McFarland and Representative Jan McKenna, two Arlington legislators. Both expressed outrage that such films were being shown on the campus of a state-supported university, and both threatened action if something were not done about it. Senator McFarland argued, "I'm not trying to suggest a form of censorship on the movie fare of UTA students. If the students want to go off campus for a mass orgy or hold an X-rated film festival off campus—that's fine with me. But I object to X-rated films being shown at state facilities on state land that are maintained by the taxpayers' money." Both legislators made it clear that they would take "whatever action necessary," including the withholding of state funds, to prevent such films from being shown on state college campuses. Pushed to the wall by the Arlington legislators, President Nedderman agreed that the university would draft a new policy on campus films later in the spring, vowing "I won't be put in a position to defend X-rated films in the future."[43]

The new policy was announced in early April, and it banned X-rated films with "strong sexual content" from being shown on the UTA campus, unless the films were used as part of a "legitimate academic or educational program." The policy satisfied McFarland and McKenna's concerns, but it raised the ire of the Fort Worth chapter of the ACLU, which viewed it as "an arbitrary kind of standard." Mamie Bush, president of the UTA Student Congress, stated that the Film Council would be "upset about this, along with a lot of other students," but expressed empathy for Nedderman who, she said, "made the best decision he could, given the university as a whole." Bush's prediction proved right. A few weeks after the announcement of the policy, *The Shorthorn* reported the results of a poll which showed 87 percent of the student body disagreed with the policy and President Nedderman's action. Most saw the ban as an infringement on their first amendment rights and censorship on the part of the administration.[44]

President Nedderman weathered the X-rated film controversy early in 1985, but faced an even greater one seven months later. This one, however, was largely of his own doing and, as he admitted afterwards, resulted from "the toughest decision I've ever had to make." The decision was to eliminate the university's football program. Nedderman made the fateful announcement on November 25, 1985, only two days after the close of the football season. The decision to abolish football at UTA was not hastily made, however. Rather, it was a decision Nedderman arrived at after thirteen years of "agonizing" over the program and doing everything in his power to save it.[45]

In making the announcement to end football, President Nedderman pointed to three reasons for his decision. The first was an annual deficit of close to a million dollars for the football program. He explained that with "funding of over $800,000 from student service fees, in addition to income from ticket sales, guarantees, and the Maverick Club [booster organization], we face a deficit of approximately $950,000." This deficit had to be covered by university auxiliary enterprise income, such as profits from the bookstore and by other locally generated sources. This was "flexible money," according to the president, which *could* be used to further the university's primary mission of teaching and research, but instead was supporting a financially weak football program. The second reason for ending football was "a matter of

7.21 In 1987, when the Select Committee on Higher Education suggested that UTA's role and scope statement emphasize teaching rather than research, concerned students gathered in front of the library to hear President Nedderman speak on the proposal.

attendance." Attendance at UTA home games had been declining since Maverick Stadium opened in 1980. In fact, one of the primary reasons for building the new 12,000-seat stadium was to boost attendance at the games in hopes of strengthening the football program. Unfortunately it did not work. Average annual attendance at the stadium in 1980 was 7,950, five years later it had dropped to 5,600. Even though UTA was by far the largest institution in the Southland Conference, its average annual attendance at home games was less than *half* that of the other colleges. In explaining his reasoning to the Faculty Senate in late November, President Nedderman said that "the thing that really hurts is when one looks across the east side [of the stadium] and the band, which is required to attend moves out, one sees only two or three or four hundred students out of a student body of 23,100."[46]

The final reason Nedderman gave for ending football was the negative impact its deficits were having on other sports at UTA. All the other fourteen sports at the university suffered because football siphoned off half of the total athletic budget. Nedderman bluntly admitted that "we have a broad array of underfunded programs in our total athletic program." His intent, by eliminating football, was to narrow the scope of the athletic program to something more affordable and to sports "in which we can expect to consistently excel." Nedderman agreed to honor Coach Chuck Curtis' contract and to extend aid to football scholarship holders through each student's fourth consecutive year of academic work at UTA.[47]

Nedderman's surprise announcement hit like a bombshell. Jack Davis, president of the 900-member athletic booster organization, the Maverick Club, expressed dismay at the decision and called it reversible, "especially if there is an outpouring of support for the football program from the community." Community leaders Tom Cravens and Tom Vandergriff, the announcer of UTA games and a major supporter of the college, appealed to the president to change his mind. Business leaders and the Maverick Club mobilized in an attempt to raise $800,000 in pledges for UTA football. When asked at the press conference following his announcement what could change his mind, Nedderman responded, "Somebody would have to come up with a million dollars a year for an indefinite period." For

7.22 In March of 1974, after a generous donation by Jenkins and Virginia Garrett, the library's Special Collections Division formally opened. At the opening were Jenkins Garrett (left) and Harry Ransom (right), chancellor of the UT system.

two weeks after his announcement, as controversy swirled around him, Nedderman cloaked himself in silence and refused to talk to the press. He broke his silence on December 9 at another press conference, when he reaffirmed his earlier decision and appealed to the Maverick Club and its members to "rally behind our remaining sports [and] help us to fund them fully." He went on, "To those alumni who say, in the emotion of the moment, that they will withdraw *all* support to their university without football, I beg you reconsider. Surely *your* university transcends football." Nedderman closed his remarks with an olive branch offered to his critics, saying, "Let us all join together. The past is the past. A great future for our university lies ahead."[48]

Nedderman's decision about football was not met with hostility in all quarters, however. On the contrary, the president received at least twice as many calls and letters supporting his decision as opposing it. The faculty also came out strongly in favor of his courageous stand. The state commissioner of higher education commended Nedderman for placing academics first. Student response was largely apathetic. Allan Saxe, a political science professor and newspaper columnist, observed at the time, "If you polled the student body at UTA today, I have a feeling that 70 percent would say they are not

7.23 In an effort to make UTA more accessible to the disabled, President Nedderman and other administrators participated in a Handicapped Administrators Day on March 21, 1974. Regarding the experience Nedderman said, "I gained a new perspective from the vantage point of a wheelchair."

heartbroken over dropping football. Ten percent are heartbroken, and the remaining 20 percent did not know UTA even had a team." Indeed, in the mid-1970s, according to Saxe, the student body was polled on the topic of football and voted to drop it. Nedderman, at that time, drew criticism for continuing the program![49]

Five years after the football program was dropped, *The Dallas Morning News* reported that "nearly every UTA athletic program, now funded comparably with its competition, has achieved or is nearing success unparalleled in the school's history." The paper cited as evidence the women's softball team winning the conference championship in 1988, the men's track team winning the conference indoor championship in 1988 and 1989, the baseball team winning its first title in 1990, and the women's volleyball team's string of fifty-four consecutive conference victories as of 1990. Time seemed to vindicate President Nedderman and his draconian cut of football.[50]

In December 1986, another controversy bubbled to the surface on campus, getting the attention of the faculty, students, and community. This one occurred when the Select Committee on Higher Education, a statewide group appointed by Governor Mark White to eliminate program duplication at the state's thirty-seven public colleges, proposed a role and scope statement for UTA that many people found objectionable. The committee recommended that the university be characterized as a "comprehensive university" with an emphasis on teaching, not research. Faculty and students were shocked by the proposal and feared such a statement, if adopted by the legislature, could limit or eliminate future research and doctoral programs, preventing the university from developing into a research institution of national significance. The campus community was further stung by the Select Committee's characterization of the University of North Texas, Texas Tech, and the University of Houston as emerging national universities with emphases on research. Most people at UTA considered these to be peer institutions. From the faculty's perspective, the committee had failed to consider UTA's emergence as a research-level institution and placed the blame on the Nedderman administration for not doing enough to communicate this message to the committee in particular and the public in general. Stanley Palmer, at the time chairman of the history department, summarized faculty suspicions when he commented, "Whatever the facts, there's a strong feeling the administration didn't do what was needed. Right now there's a certain amount of distrust and the burden is on them to restore that trust if possible."[51]

The committee's recommendation clearly caught the Nedderman administration off-guard. But once the proposed role and scope statement was made public, President Nedderman swung into action. At first, he worked behind the scenes with the UT system administration to try to get the Select Committee to change UTA's statement to one recognizing the university's research role. When the

7.24 Jane Fonda's visit to campus in 1971 not only sparked debate about the U.S. role in Southeast Asia, but it also symbolized the more permissive atmosphere that developed after the school's break with the tightly controlled Texas A&M system.

committee refused to do this, Nedderman and the faculty mobilized student and community support to bring pressure on the committee through the Texas legislature. State Senator Bob McFarland took the lead in the legislature, vowing to block the adoption of the Select Committee's recommendations if UTA's statement were not changed. Senator McFarland said bluntly, "This is an over my dead body situation." Lending political support to the university were the Arlington City Council, Fort Worth mayor Bob Bolen, State Representative Kent Grusendorf, and board of regents chairman Jess Hay. Nedderman called an emergency meeting of the faculty and urged faculty members to write letters to legislators. The Faculty Senate and Student Congress also came out strongly in favor of amending the committee's recommendation. On February 11, 1987, President Nedderman, threatening a "massive legislative effort," addressed 3,000 students and faculty at a rally on the subject in front of the library.[52]

The outpouring of support for the university worked. On February 18, Larry Temple, chairman of the Select Committee, announced that UTA's role and scope statement had been upgraded by the committee. Temple revealed that the new statement would read, in part, "The institution would have the responsibility for achieving excellence in all academic areas—teaching, research, and public service. Research endeavors benefitting the academic strength and national perspectives of the institution and/or addressing the economic needs of the Dallas-Fort Worth metroplex would be encouraged." Nedderman expressed satisfaction at the new role statement as did the majority of the university community. Senator McFarland commented after Temple made the announcement that he had received hundreds of letters and phone calls. "This kind of concern," he said, "is refreshing because it shows me that there are people out there willing to get involved and support UTA." Temple explained that the Select Committee's initial recommendation for UTA had been misunderstood as being "limiting," but it was not intended to be. He expressed relief that the misunderstanding was over, and he recognized the university as a "premiere research institution."[53]

Despite the affirmation of UTA's research mission, many members of the faculty believed that Nedderman and his administration were not aggressive

7.25 Even though Iranian students represented a large minority portion of UTA's student body, many students protested against Iranians and even advocated deportation during the Iranian hostage situation in 1979 and 1980.

enough in lobbying for the university in Austin. By the early 1990s, there was a general feeling on the part of many faculty that President Nedderman and his administrative team had been in their positions too long and were resistant to change. Moreover, some believed that the Nedderman administration's management style left too much power in the hands of the college deans. As a result, Nedderman's critics argued that some of the colleges progressed faster than others during his tenure as president. Though most within the university community admired and liked Nedderman, they believed it was time for new blood and new vision in the administration.

One of the reasons Nedderman served as president for twenty years was his genuine fondness for the students. Throughout his presidency, he maintained an open-door policy toward students. If a student wanted to meet with him for any reason, the student was always welcome, and Nedderman made himself available. Students appreciated the president's accessibility and openness. Nedderman characterized UTA students as a "working-class student body," one that was "goal oriented [and] who knew what they wanted and were willing to work for it." Nedderman himself had these attributes, and he admired them in students. Like the ASC students before them, UTA students were older, had jobs, and took fewer courses than their counterparts at other colleges. In addition, with only a minimal number of dormitory rooms on campus, the overwhelming majority of students lived off campus. These student characteristics—age and location of residence—helped to shape the nature of student life throughout the UTA years. According to student surveys, most students neither participated in university-sponsored activities nor joined campus organizations. While some faculty characterized the atmosphere on campus as a "a hotbed of apathy," that was not

7.26 **When the Pulitzer Prize-winning author of** *Roots*, **Alex Haley, spoke at Texas Hall in 1980, Ku Klux Klan members demonstrated outside.**

always the case, as the Rebel theme and X-rated film controversies proved. Though UTA was never a center of violent protests in the 1960s and 1970s, students did march in both protest and support of U. S. involvement in the Vietnam War. Jane Fonda, actress and critic of the American policy toward Vietnam, brought her protest movement to campus in December 1970. In a speech to more than 1,000 students at Texas Hall, she called for an end to the war and to what she termed "misrepresentations" about it from the White House. While *The Dallas Morning News* criticized Fonda as an "apostle of socialism," her visit to UTA sparked a healthy debate on campus on the country's proper role in Southeast Asia.[54]

Vietnam was not the only subject to spark protest. In 1979, for example, 100 students of the American Arab Society and the Organization of Arab Students gathered on the library mall to condemn President Jimmy Carter's Middle East policy. A few months later, UTA students gathered again, this time to protest the construction of the Comanche Peak Nuclear Power Plant in Glen Rose, Texas. And in November 1979, more than 100 anti-Iranian student demonstrators marched up and down Cooper Street, calling for retaliation against Iran for taking American citizens hostage earlier in the year. In 1980, a speech by Pulitzer Prize-winning author Alex Haley sparked a demonstration on campus by the Ku Klux Klan (KKK), which saw Haley's book *Roots* as a "distortion of history." The KKK's presence on campus quickly attracted a group of students who staged a counter-protest.[55]

During the UTA years, a number of national celebrities and political leaders came to campus. These have included Gerald Ford, minority leader of the U. S.

7.27 Bringing thousands of people to campus in September 1975, the Urban Survival Fair was jointly sponsored by UTA and local radio station, KZEW, in order to educate people regarding urban service agencies.

House of Representatives, who spoke in 1968; irreverent counterculture comedians Cheech and Chong, who performed in 1977; consumer advocate Ralph Nader, who spoke that same year; and Geraldine Ferraro, the vice presidential nominee for the Democratic party, who campaigned on campus in 1984. Country music star Willie Nelson performed a benefit show for the athletic department in 1975. The single largest event in UTA history, however, was the "Urban Survival Fair" held on campus in September 1975. Sponsored by radio station KZEW of Dallas and the university's Institute of Urban Studies, the weekend fair attracted 65-70,000 people to campus. For those who attended, there was free music by the

Nitty Gritty Dirt Band as well as eighty-five booths, where social service, educational, and art organizations distributed information. The *Arlington Citizen-Journal* observed that the fair was "a consumer's paradise with a potpourri of information available on everything from 'how to avoid auto repair rip-offs,' to 'how to file and win a lawsuit—cheap.'" President Nedderman commented that the fair was an "example of UTA's determination to be a worthwhile contributor to the Dallas/Fort Worth community." The 1976 school annual stated about the fair that "while a hundred student volunteers helped the campus police protect the grass underfoot, nobody paid serious attention to the grass that was being puffed in pipes."[56]

Also in the 1970s, UTA began a concerted effort to better meet the needs of physically

7.28 During the 1984 presidential campaign, Democratic vice-presidential candidate Geraldine Ferraro spoke to a large group of students on campus.

challenged students. Prompted by federal laws requiring accommodations for the handicapped, an active Handicapped Student Association (HSA), and an administration determined to remove as many barriers as possible because it was the "right thing to do," the university expended great effort and considerable money to develop a "model institution for handicapped students." In 1973, Jim Hayes, who was the administrative liaison with the HSA, wrote to Wayne Duke, then dean of student life, saying, "There is a real need for a 'totally equipped' campus because the number of handicapped students is on the rise. . . ." Hayes and others realized that such a campus would provide opportunities to the disabled which were never before possible because of the severity of their particular handicap. By the mid-seventies, UTA was recognized as one of the leading institutions in the state for removing barriers to the physically challenged and for employing the disabled. These efforts did not stop in the seventies. In the 1990s, the university has continued its effort to make academic life more accessible to disabled students. In 1994, Hayes, now director of the Office for Students with Disabilities, said after the UTA Movin' Mavs wheelchair basketball team won its fourth consecutive national title,

"I work at probably the greatest university in the world when it comes to a real commitment to the advancement of disabled students. Based on the national picture, UTA has the premiere program from a funding and policy standpoint."[57]

In fact, it has been the Movin' Mavs who have given the university the positive national attention it desires. The Mavs began intercollegiate play in 1989, posting a 36-3 overall record from 1989-1994 and a 12-2 mark in tournaments. As recognition of the team's third

7.29 When UTA opened its Automation and Robotics Research Institute in the Riverbend development of Fort Worth in 1987, it marked UTA's first satellite campus since the old aeronautics program was discontinued.

consecutive national championship, the players and other university representatives were invited to the White House in 1994 to meet with and be congratulated by President Bill Clinton. The Movin' Mavs personify the commitment UTA has made to the disabled. The university remains the only school nationwide to offer full scholarships to five of eleven basketball players.[58]

The Movin' Mavs were not the only UTA sports team to achieve success. Though sports have never been a central focus of student life at the university, they have been important to a segment of the student population. UTA is an NCAA Division I affiliate of the Southland Conference, fielding seven women's teams and seven men's. The women's teams are in volleyball, basketball, softball, indoor track, outdoor track, tennis, and cross country, while the men compete in cross country, indoor track, outdoor track, golf, baseball, basketball, and tennis. More than two hundred students a year participate in organized sports. A number of UTA's teams have successfully competed in the conference. During the Nedderman years, the baseball team won the conference championship in 1990 and 1992; men's indoor track in 1990, 1991, and 1992; men's outdoor track won in 1989, 1990, 1991, and 1992; the women's softball team was champion in 1986 and 1989; the women's volleyball team was a powerhouse throughout the 1980s and early 1990s, winning conference championships in 1982, 1985, 1986, 1987, 1988, 1989 (making it to the Final Four national tournament), 1990, and 1992; women's cross country won in 1986; and the women's outdoor track team won in 1991. The Nedderman administration began UTA's women's sports program in 1973, placing, for the first time, a line item in the budget for women's athletics.[59]

The increasing importance of women's sports reflected, in a small way, one of the many demographic changes in students that occurred during Nedderman's tenure in office. From 1972 to 1992, the number of women on campus increased dramatically, changing the men to women ratio from approximately 2 to 1 in the early seventies to closer to 1 to 1 in the early nineties. Also, as mentioned above, the number of minority students increased, with African-American students going from 2.6 percent (367 students) of the student population in 1972 to 7.2 percent (1,801 students) in 1992. Hispanic students also increased during this same period from 1.9 percent (277 students) of the student body to 6.3 percent (1,571 students) twenty years later. The most dramatic demographic trend during this period was the explosion in the number of Asian/Pacific Islanders on campus. In 1972, less than 1 percent (48 students) of UTA's students were Asian or Southeast Asian, while in 1992, 8.5 percent (2,118 students) were. Also, by the end of Nedderman's presidency in 1992, almost half of the student body (47.6 percent) was twenty-five years old or older. Student surveys conducted over the twenty-year period consistently showed that UTA's location was the main reason for students selecting the university. Other reasons cited by students were the school's low tuition and its academic reputation.[60]

In 1991, President Nedderman, nearing his seventieth birthday, announced his intention to retire at year's end. Nedderman had served as president for nineteen years and now intended to spend more time with his family and pursue his favorite hobbies, such as fishing. He also planned to teach part-time in the civil engineering department. When asked at the time the reason for his retirement, his answer was a simple, "It's just time to do so." Despite Nedderman's plan to step down by the end of 1991, Hans Mark, the chancellor of the UT system, asked him to serve as president until a replacement could be appointed. This he did, serving until July 13, 1992. When Nedderman retired, he had been president for nearly twenty years, longer than any of his counterparts in the UT system and in all of the public universities in the North Texas region.[61]

Nedderman's years as

7.30 Begun during the 1970s, International Day has grown into a week-long celebration of UTA's unique cultural mix.

7.31 **Attending UTA in the early 1980s, Lou Diamond Phillips (pictured on the right) acted in several campus productions before moving on to the big screen.**

president were characterized by an atmosphere of open communication, a free flow of information, and teamwork. One of the key factors in his success was the administrative team he assembled and its remarkable longevity. Of the four vice presidents serving at the time of his retirement, only Peter Van't Slot, vice president for development and university relations, was a relative "newcomer," joining the team in 1984. The others—Baker, vice president for academic affairs; Duke, vice president for student affairs; and Dudley Wetsel, vice president for business affairs—had worked with him since 1972. Another integral member of the team was Elwood Preiss, who served as executive assistant to the president throughout Nedderman's presidency.[62]

Like Woolf and Harrison before him, Nedderman was president during a period of dramatic enrollment growth, feverish building activity, and rapid program development. These three areas consumed most of his effort and energy during his tenure. His focus was an inward one, trying to ensure that UTA had the space, facilities, faculty, and undergraduate and graduate programs to attract and educate a growing student population. This he did well. Moreover, Nedderman enjoyed the trust and the support of three UT system administrations and the board of regents for two decades—no easy feat. Critics would say he was well liked in Austin because he did not make waves for the system, but the reality was that Nedderman was an effective advocate for UTA and a skillful political player. He admitted later that he learned from President Harrison always to be well prepared before making presentations to the regents and to discuss university-related issues and address concerns with individual regents before meetings, if possible. This method worked for him.[63]

Nedderman did not achieve all of the goals he set for himself and his administration. Perhaps the most elusive was his fervent desire to change UTA's image as a commuter school to that of an urban research university. He rationalized that the commuter image would change in time, as UTA graduates moved into positions of authority, influence, and power. He envisioned a day when the university would be "so darn big and so darn good, we can't be ignored." This did not happen during his administration, however. In fact, the controversy over UTA's mission statement in 1987 centered largely on this issue of image and the growing concern on the part of the faculty and others that Nedderman was not doing enough to change it. Additionally, although Nedderman started the university's development office in 1974, many people on campus believed that his administration was not aggressive enough in raising money from outside the UT system and building bridges to the community. Vice President Baker characterized UTA's efforts in this area as not well organized. Vice President Duke echoed this sentiment when he commented that the university's efforts in building support among alumni were inadequate. Moreover, the Nedderman administration's record in recruiting minorities to faculty and administrative positions was, at best, spotty. Whatever the shortcomings of President Nedderman, however, he was totally committed to the university, its development, and its students, and was a zealous advocate for all three.[64]

7.32 Noted as a hazard as early as the mid-1960s, the Cooper Street crossing problem was finally solved in 1990, when the street was partially depressed and three walkways were constructed over it.

When President Nedderman retired, he realized that UTA's period of rapid program, enrollment, and facility growth was slowing and that his successor would have vastly different challenges than he did. When Ellen Temple, a regent from Lufkin, asked in 1991 the one piece of advice he would give the next UTA president, Nedderman responded, ". . . be sure to listen . . . I think it is very important to make a conscious effort to listen to what faculty are saying, what staff are saying, what students are saying." For twenty years, Nedderman listened, kept the lines of communication open, and acted in what he considered the best interests of the university. To him, UTA was a "positive slope institution," always improving.[65]

Point-Counterpoint

During the Rebel theme controversy, much ink was spilled, rationalizing and justifying both sides in the debate over UTA's school symbol. In the November 25, 1968, issue of *The Shorthorn*, which was published prior to the first student referendum on the question, student editor, Donna Darovich, and Student Congress president, Jeff Hensley, presented their views on the subject. Their editorials, which were later shortened and included in the 1969 UTA annual, are reprinted below. Their views represent the two sides of the theme issue and were passionately debated during the Rebel controversy.

DONNA DAROVICH

This university is sick to death. Sick of being branded a racist, bigoted, hate-infested institution all because of a single issue.

There is the anti-theme side. These are the students, black and white, who claim the Rebel theme is offensive.

Surely the theme should have been considered by these students before they decided upon UT Arlington and if they found it undesirable and a threat to their well-being, they should have reconsidered their choice of universities.

It is our belief that a great portion of these students did not decide until very recently that this university's theme offended them, mainly because they were told they should be offended, whether they were or not. Many, many students who could care less were beguiled or forced to take a stand which they did not necessarily agree with.

It is the white students, the self-appointed moralists who needed a band-wagon to jump on, who have made the most noise.

The Civil War has quite wrongfully been placed in the center of this issue. It has been almost 104 years since the Civil War. The injustices of that war cannot be forgotten and they shouldn't be. They should be remembered as should any distasteful history so that the same mistakes might not be made again. What happened 104 years ago is neither the fault nor the responsibility of the students at UT Arlington, and when those students wave their flags, prejudice and the Civil War are not what they are upholding. You can't change the past by changing the present.

JEFF HENSLEY

Let's go back to the early part of last spring semester when the issue of the theme's offensiveness was first raised by a small group of Negroes and whites. At this time my reaction was very much the same as the one I have witnessed in many other people over the last nine or ten months. I felt that a group representing a minority

7.33 In July 1968, the flag of UTA, the Stars and Bars, was permanently removed from its pole in front of the student center. The Rebel theme controversy and this action provoked the strongest student reaction since the school joined the UT system.

was raising altogether too much trouble over a small point.

One word can be used to sum up my initial attitude: closed. But, gradually as I listened to the arguments against the flag and theme, I opened by mind. I became convinced the Confederate theme was sufficiently offensive to significant numbers of students to justify removal.

The most important consideration is the personal offense which the Confederate theme inflicts on the Negro student. Imagine yourself a Negro student, entering the Robert E. Lee Suite of the student center for the first time. As a Negro, what would be your reaction to the lovely couches in the suite? The ones with the portraits of Jackson and Lee in the upholstery. Look closer. In between the portraits of these fine gentlemen is another picture, one not so pretty. It's a Negro slave hoeing cotton in the field.

Okay, so perhaps 80 percent of us white students agree that no ill feeling is intended in the Confederate theme. What does that assurance mean to the black man when he thinks about the theme?

Does it mean he can laugh off the fact that white students with black shoe polish on their faces were sold in slave auctions during the Old South celebrations as recently as four years ago?

Does this phrase bring to him a mental image of his great-great-grandfather pulling a bag of cotton between the rows? What do you think?

CHAPTER EIGHT

Change Is Hard

On April 10, 1992, the UTA community met its newly-appointed president, Dr. Ryan C. Amacher, in a ceremony held in the student center. Sharing the stage with Amacher were his wife, Susan; President Nedderman; Hans Mark, chancellor of the UT system; James Duncan, the system's vice chancellor for academic affairs; Nathan Robinett, a community representative to the presidential search committee; and Royce West, a former UTA Student Congress president and spokesman for regent Zan Holmes. More than 400 faculty, staff, students, and university supporters attended the ceremony, anxious to get a glimpse of the individual the regents hoped would lead the university into the twenty-first century. At the ceremony, Amacher admitted excitement over his selection and spoke briefly on two trends that were affecting higher education—scarce resources and the changing demographics of students. Amacher pledged himself to aggressively market the university and to actively recruit minority students, staff, and faculty.[1]

The latter issue, recruitment of minorities, had become a *cause célèbre* during the presidential search process. A vocal group of African-American leaders had criticized the UT system for appointing a search committee without black representation on it. While the committee did include two women and a Hispanic, it failed to select an individual of color as a finalist in the search process. As a result, a coalition of black leaders called for the addition of an African American to the committee and a ninety-day extension of UTA's presidential search. While the UT regents refused the coalition's requests, they did agree to amend the rules governing the constitution of future presidential search committees, increasing the size of the committee by three. Two of these appointments would be made from university staff, not faculty, in response to criticism that the search process excluded staff, and the other one would be chosen from outside the university. The regents also agreed to consider racial integration when naming committee members.[2]

Shortly after the announcement that Amacher was the next UTA president, Darren Reagan, president of the Black State Employees Association of Texas, told *The Dallas Morning News* that the new president "needs to come in and provide strong, innovative and risk-taking leadership—something that's uncommon in the current UT system leadership." Citing statistics showing that only 1 percent of the university's faculty and 7 percent of its students were African American,

8.1 Since Arlington College began producing graduates in the last years of the nineteenth century, graduation has always been a time of accomplished joy in Arlington.

Reagan implored Amacher to "demonstrate a leadership of inclusion of all ethnic groups, particularly African Americans, and to be sensitive and responsive to our concerns." It was to Reagan and other minorities that Amacher said, during the April ceremony of introduction, "I urge you to be cynical. All I ask for is a chance. I'm anxious to work with the minority community." Amacher got his opportunity to replace words with action when he assumed the presidency in July.[3]

8.2 Sam Maverick is the last in a long list of school mascots, including the Grubbworms, Hornets, Junior Aggies, Blue Riders, and Rebels.

At the time of his appointment, Amacher was forty-six and on the administrative fast track. Born on November 9, 1945, in Marshfield, Wisconsin, Amacher received his bachelor's in economics from Ripon College in 1967 and his doctorate four years later from the University of Virginia. After earning his Ph.D., he rose rapidly through the academic ranks. He taught at the University of Oklahoma from 1972 to 1974, and then, after a yearlong stint with the U.S. Treasury, he joined the faculty at Arizona State University (ASU) in 1975. At ASU, he became chair of the department of economics in 1977, a position he held until he was appointed dean of the College of Commerce and Industry at Clemson University in 1981. While at Clemson, Amacher honed his skills as an administrator and built a reputation as a capable fundraiser. Jim Sheriff, a colleague of Amacher's at Clemson, said about him, "He had tremendous rapport with community leaders and leaders of various business and civic organizations and the entire state of South Carolina." It was his talent for fundraising and enthusiasm for outreach and marketing that most impressed the search committee and the regents.[4]

When Amacher became president of UTA in the summer of 1992, he devoted his first few months to meeting students, faculty, staff, and community leaders. He viewed these meetings as an opportunity to learn more about the university. They were essential to him because the information and impressions he gained helped to shape his agenda for the school. What he gleaned most from these meetings was that people viewed him as an agent of change and most wanted—indeed welcomed—change. After spending twenty years under the same administration, the campus community *seemed* ripe for new initiatives, new directions, and a new style of leadership.[5]

President Amacher committed himself and his administration to change, and controversy soon resulted. Unlike Nedderman, who focused his attention on adding buildings, degree programs, and faculty to keep pace with a growing student enrollment, Amacher hoped to focus on external relations and development in an attempt to garner increased financial and political support for the university and to boost the school's image. Amacher, however, had not anticipated a drop in enrollment which, because of the way the state allocated money to universities, could lead to decreased appropriations. President Amacher had the misfortune to be in office when the university's enrollment dropped approximately 8 percent over three successive fall semesters. Indeed, the fall 1992 enrollment was 24,727, down 408 from the fall before, and, by fall 1994, the student population had dipped to 23,280. Faced with this decline, Amacher worked to initiate plans to aggressively recruit students and to block any university policy changes which would, in his judgment, adversely affect enrollment. In the fall semester of 1992, Amacher quashed a plan supported by Vice President Baker and many faculty members and deans to raise admission standards to improve the quality of students at UTA. President Amacher blocked the plan because he thought it would lead to further decreases in enrollment and would affect minority recruitment. To him it was a dollars and cents issue: raise standards, lose students, and, as a result, absorb budget cuts. As he said in early 1993, "I'm for higher standards, but I will never be convinced by the argument that raising admissions will draw more students."[6]

A firestorm of debate swirled around the admission standards issue, but the new president held firm to his decision. While the debate raged on campus, W. A. Baker, Nedderman's vice president for academic affairs and a proponent of higher standards, announced his intention to return to teaching in January 1993. Other administrators, including deans and vice presidents, also stepped down, allowing President Amacher to build an administrative team which supported his goals and was comfortable with his management style. Perhaps the most important addition to the Amacher administration was Dr. Dalmas Taylor, who assumed the newly created position of provost on August 20, 1993. Taylor, fifty-nine years old at the time, came to UTA to administer the internal operations of the university. He held a Ph.D. in psychology from the University of Delaware and had served in administration at various colleges and universities since the late-1960s. Upon his appointment, he became the highest ranking African American on campus. Taylor, a calm and reflective man, complemented the more emotional and demonstrative Amacher and embraced the president's agenda.[7]

The enrollment decline and its expected adverse impact on the budget convinced the president that better marketing and aggressive recruitment were essential to attract more students to campus. One way to better market the university, Amacher concluded, was to invest more resources in the athletic program. By doing this, he wanted to make UTA's sports teams more competitive and bring the university into full compliance with Title IX, which called for equity between women's and men's sports. In October 1992, Amacher hired a former Clemson colleague, B. J. Skeleton, to be UTA's athletic director and charged him with the job of bringing the university "to national prominence." For the first time in the school's history, an administration was willing to invest significantly in athletics and make sports a priority. By 1994, the president had increased the athletic department's budget to $2.9 million a year, an increase of $500,000. This increase allowed Skeleton to add more coaches and trainers and to adjust salaries in the department. The university also made major improvements to its sports facilities, including the track, weight training room, baseball stadium, tennis courts, and offices. President Amacher characterized his emphasis on sports as an experiment which, if successful, would focus attention on the school and raise its visibility. Higher visibility, in turn, would attract

8.3 The long-lasting tradition of military science has endured on campus since its establishment during the Carlisle Military Academy period.

more students, more alumni support, and more resources. Convinced that "real universities do athletics," he hoped the sports program would eventually help to "enhance academic programs across the campus." Others on campus characterized Amacher's investment in sports as a costly gamble destined to lose.[8]

Amacher believed that a successful sports program would help build a sense of community around the school and energize campus life, both important factors in attracting more students. Also needed to help boost recruitment was more housing

8.4 Viewed as one of the school's unique assets, UTA's non-traditional students make up a growing portion of the student body.

on campus. When Amacher became president, the university had four dormitories and owned seventeen apartment complexes. These facilities housed 2,000 students, but frequently there was a long waiting list for students wanting campus housing. President Nedderman identified this as a problem in the 1980s, but high interest rates and the fact that student housing had to be funded through auxiliary rather than state-appropriated funds prevented his administration from adding more housing during the eighties. In 1985, President Nedderman did receive the regents' approval to work with a private developer to plan and build more housing. The university, however, was unable to find a developer willing to take the risk to build in this inflationary period. Five years later, UTA purchased a tract of land on the southwest corner of Cooper and Mitchell streets for future use. It was President Amacher who later took advantage of the groundwork laid by Nedderman. In 1993, UTA entered into an agreement with Century Property Management Company of Houston to build the Centennial Court Apartments on

the Cooper and Mitchell streets tract. In the agreement, Century agreed to lease the land from the university, fund the apartments' construction, manage the apartments, and split any profits with the university. After thirty years, the apartments would become the property of the university. The apartments opened in the fall of 1994 and became home for more than 500 students. In August 1995, Century completed the second phase of the project, adding space for an additional 456 students. This cooperation between a public institution and private business appears to be a "win-win" situation for both.[9]

President Amacher also worked closely with the City of Arlington in developing plans for a possible 19,000-seat multipurpose facility which could host university-wide programs and sports events as well as be the

8.5 Arriving on campus in the summer of 1992, President Amacher attempted to establish good rapport with students by participating in campus activities.

8.6 Although the UTA physical plant is relatively compact, one of the goals of administration has always been to maintain an aesthetically-pleasing campus.

home of the National Hockey League's Dallas Stars and the Dallas Mavericks professional basketball team. Although planning, as of this writing, is still in its preliminary stages and the viability of such a joint venture has yet to be determined, Amacher saw such a facility as vital to UTA's future development. Not only would a state-of-the-art arena make it easier for the university to attract quality athletes, it would also make it possible to move the university's unified commencement ceremony to a site on or near campus. When the Amacher administration went to a single graduation ceremony in May 1994, rather than separate ceremonies held in each of the university's nine colleges and schools, a groundswell of protest arose from some students and faculty, who complained that a single event would be long, impersonal, and inconvenient because of its location at the Tarrant County Convention Center in downtown Fort Worth. A multi-purpose arena in Arlington would help to blunt some of these criticisms.[10]

While President Amacher and his administration were working on recruitment as a way to increase the student population and stabilize funding, they also began laying the foundation for a more active development program. As mentioned in the previous chapter, fundraising and development were never high priorities for President Nedderman, but they were for Amacher. Shortly after coming to UTA, President Amacher moved his and other administrative offices from Davis Hall to College Hall, and spent more than $186,000 renovating the new space. Amacher justified the move by saying that the old office was dark and small, and he wanted to be closer to the center of campus activity. He also authorized the spending of more than $218,000 to remodel unused space in the student center, turning it into an upscale dining and meeting facility ideal for entertaining donors and potential donors. And entertain them he did, hosting parties and recognition dinners on campus. Although these types of development functions are common at colleges across the country, many people on campus objected to them because they saw such spending as misdirected and unwise, especially during tight budgetary times. President Amacher defended his decisions, saying, "One way people buy into universities is you invite them to a lot of functions and social gatherings." In short, the president saw UTA's entertaining as investments in the university's future. The president, in January 1995, hired a new vice president for development and university relations to plan and launch a major fundraising campaign. Frederick J. Bennett, the new vice president, hoped to have the president spend half of his time on development activities.[11]

Although many people on campus believed that the president's intentions were good, he came under increasingly vitriolic criticism from faculty and students. His detractors pointed to a long list of grievances they had with him and his administration. Among these were extravagant spending practices, misdirected priorities which seemed to favor sports over academics, centralizing decision-making in the provost's office and "micro-managing" colleges and departments, "cronyism" in his hiring practices, an unwillingness to tolerate opposition, and an insensitivity to the wants and needs of students and faculty. The debate over campus policies turned ugly and personal when, in the span of an eighteen-month period, the president's home was vandalized four times. The administration was not without its supporters, however. Those who defended the president and provost credited the administration with making a sincere commitment to diversify the faculty and student body, raising the visibility of the university, establishing solid ties with local leaders and alumni, and trying to build a sense of community and pride on campus. By the fall semester of 1994, the university was divided into two warring camps, and President Amacher and Provost Taylor seemed incapable of unifying the campus. When a number of the administration's supporters argued that racism was, in part, responsible for some of the opposition to Amacher and Taylor, faculty members criticized the two for not jumping to the faculty's defense quickly enough. By December 1994, tensions on campus were strained to the breaking point.[12]

Local media exacerbated the divisions on campus by seemingly reporting every criticism, innuendo, and charge and counter-charge that bubbled to the surface.

8.7 Although called progressive by some, the policies of the Amacher administration sparked a campus-wide debate that divided the university.

8.8 Participating in the annual administration-student switch, Provost Dalmas Taylor assumes the role of student for a day.

The most damaging piece published on the Amacher administration appeared in the *Dallas Observer* in early 1995. Entitled "Fast Times at UTA," the nine-page exposé repeated—and seemed to give credence to—the criticisms levelled at Amacher at both Clemson and Arlington. The article concluded that the university, because of the president's management style and questionable spending practices, was like a wagon "going down the street with all the wheels coming off it." While the president labelled the *Observer* piece as slanted and one-sided, the article and others like it in the *Fort Worth Star-Telegram* and *The Shorthorn* prompted University of Texas system chancellor William H. Cunningham, on January 25, to call for a far-reaching management audit of UTA. Chancellor Cunningham hoped to defuse the growing controversy by dispatching an audit team to Arlington to gather the facts on the administration's spending and management practices. Cunningham characterized his action as "routine" when questions about financial and management issues were raised at a UT component. Amacher welcomed the audit, expressing confidence that he had done nothing "amoral or illegal or inappropriate." He expected that the audit, which would take three to four months to complete, would exonerate him and quiet campus unrest.[13]

Amacher's critics on the faculty, however, were unwilling to wait for the audit's completion. On February 1, 1995, the university's Faculty Senate, a forty-two member deliberative body that represents each academic department, considered circulating a petition that, if signed by 10 percent of the estimated 565 full-time faculty members, would compel the president to call a faculty meeting no later than March 8 to address campus concerns. After the called meeting, faculty would then decide whether to proceed with a confidence vote on the president and provost. Hoping to derail any confidence vote until the audit was completed, President Amacher appealed to the senators to wait. Referring to the *Dallas Observer* article and the growing crescendo of criticism against him, the president told the senate, "I've been assassinated unfairly by what is no other fashion than a conspiracy." He also pointed to the timing of such a vote as being especially harmful to the university, coming as it would in the middle of a legislative session. He concluded his remarks, saying, "If I were fired . . . if you love UTA . . . this place is going to be dead in the water during the legislative session. It's going to be dead in the water with the alums. It's going to be dead in the water in development. Then you are going to get someone just like me." The Faculty Senate ignored the president's plea and voted 28 to 13 to circulate the petition. The first step toward a confidence vote had been made.[14]

The president and provost's supporters on and off campus accused the Faculty

8.9 A leading figure in the Chicano movement, José Angel Gutíerrez not only teaches political science, but also heads up UTA's Center for Mexican American Studies.

Senate of "rushing to judgment" before the evidence accumulated by the management audit was in. The administration's detractors, however, argued that the confidence vote was not about finances and spending practices, but rather about the "direction of the university." As English faculty member, senator, and administration critic Laurin Porter explained, "The audit will examine the style, we want the content." Two days after the February 1 vote in the senate, a petition was circulated to the faculty for a two-week period. On February 17, the Faculty Senate revealed that 256 faculty members, or 45 percent of those eligible, had signed the petition, forcing the president to call a faculty meeting to answer a wide range of questions. The meeting was scheduled for March 8, and John Beehler, chairman of the senate, asked that by March 1 the faculty submit questions to him for the president and provost to address. Beehler planned to screen the questions for duplication and send them to Amacher and Taylor several days before the meeting.[15]

On March 6, 1995, a frustrated and fed-up President Amacher shocked the campus by announcing his resignation, effective "no later than September 1." In his letter of resignation to Vice Chancellor James P. Duncan, Amacher said it was time "to put an end to the circus atmosphere that has developed on campus." Realizing that the divisions at the school would not disappear as long as he was in office, Amacher resigned in hopes of initiating the healing process at the university. Within hours of the president's surprising announcement, African-American community leaders, black students, and a small group of faculty began pressuring for Provost Taylor to be named interim president. Lee Alcorn, president of the Dallas chapter of the NAACP, and Darren Reagen of the Black State Employees Association threatened "civil unrest" should the provost be overlooked for the interim office. They argued that underlying the opposition to Taylor was a racist attitude prevalent in some quarters on campus. Alcorn claimed, "I don't know a white man anywhere who likes to take direction from a black male." The provost also began quietly lobbying faculty members for their support of his appointment to the position.[16]

Amacher's resignation allowed him to avoid facing the faculty on March 8. The Faculty Senate, however, decided to proceed with the called meeting, which would now focus only on the provost. The meeting was held two days after the president's resignation and during a demonstration by fifty African-American supporters on behalf of the provost. During the meeting, Taylor faced approximately 500 faculty and, for close to three hours, answered questions on racism at UTA, his management style, the alleged growth of his office staff, and a host of other issues. The meeting was tense, with a number of his responses prompting catcalls from the faculty. After Taylor answered the faculty's questions, he left the room, and the faculty voted overwhelmingly to push ahead with a confidence vote on him. While some admired the provost's bravery in meeting with a generally hostile faculty, most agreed that few minds were changed during the session. Peter Rosen, dean of the college of science, perhaps best summarized the provost's performance: "I didn't get a sense that [Taylor] moved people to his side of the fence. He seemed to say the same things we had been hearing before."[17]

On the day after the meeting, ballots on Provost Taylor were mailed to 578 faculty. The Arlington accounting firm of Thomas Hendrix and Associates tabulated the votes and released the results on March 27. The results of the confidence vote were decisive: 452 faculty members voted no confidence in the provost, 44 voted in his favor, 13 abstained, and 69 did not return ballots. The resounding vote of no confidence, especially the 9 to 1 margin against Taylor, surprised even the administration's most vocal critics. Opposition to the policies and practices of the Amacher administration was even more widespread than most people had thought. Not surprisingly, different people interpreted the vote in different ways. Faculty Senate chairman Beehler admitted that the vote "is not something the faculty enjoyed being involved in." And to the provost's supporters, he said, "The faculty here at UTA resent any implication that the results of this vote of confidence are in any way related to race." Tasha Kendricks, an African-American pre-med major, disagreed, seeing the vote as a "witch hunt and public lynching of an African American." Student Congress president Reace Alvarenga advised the provost to "take a look at the numbers and take them to heart." The provost refused comment after the vote. The election results were sent to the chancellor of the UT system, the regents, and the UTA president.[18]

By the time the vote was tabulated, Chancellor Cunningham and Vice Chancellor Duncan had already selected Robert E. Witt, dean of the College and Graduate School of Business at the University of Texas at Austin, as UTA's interim president. Cunningham introduced Witt to the campus community in a news conference on March 24, saying the interim president would serve for at least two years, beginning on June 1, 1995. In his introduction, the chancellor characterized Witt as a "fair, thoughtful, creative administrator" and "an academic leader of extraordinary skill and extremely broad experience." Cunningham knew Witt well, having worked closely with him at UT-Austin. He selected Witt because the business school dean had the academic background, administrative experience, and calm, soft-spoken demeanor to unite the UTA campus. Witt had the added advantage of being an outsider, someone untainted by the controversies which had rocked the Arlington campus.

8.10 Begun in the 1970s under the direction of Jim Hayes (top center), the wheelchair basketball team has won four national championships and met with President Bill Clinton.

8.11 When President Amacher announced his resignation in March 1995, many African-American students led a march expressing their support of Provost Taylor as UTA interim president.

Chancellor Cunningham rationalized not selecting Taylor, explaining, "There was simply too much bitterness on this campus. We felt we needed to get someone [from] off this campus to begin to heal that process."[19]

Witt seemed a good choice to soften the hard feelings on campus. Born in Bridgeport, Connecticut, on September 16, 1940, he received his B.A. in economics from Bates College in 1962; his M.A. from the Amos Tuck School, Dartmouth College, in 1964; and his Ph.D. in business administration from Pennsylvania State University in 1968. He had spent most of his professional career at UT-Austin, where he was hired in 1968 as an assistant professor in the marketing department. He quickly rose through the academic ranks, becoming an associate professor in 1971 and professor four years later. He chaired the marketing department from 1973-1983, before being appointed associate dean for academic affairs in the business school in September 1983. He was made acting dean two years later and, in April 1986, permanent dean. Witt's colleagues at UT-Austin praised him as a quiet, industrious, consensus builder and a man of "high integrity." Reuben R. McDaniel, Jr., a professor of management in Austin, said, "Witt's a fun and pleasant person to know, but he's not a big party guy. He's not going to shake every hand in Dallas. He didn't take the job to throw a party but to run the school." Mark Yudoff, Witt's supervisor at Austin and the UT provost, said the dean was an "administrator's administrator," an individual who is "very unflappable, very careful." "He interacts well with faculty and students," Yudoff went on, "and he doesn't rile people." These were the qualities that prompted Cunningham to appoint Witt.[20]

In the news conference where Witt was introduced to the university community, he voiced his pleasure at being appointed interim president and promised to work to create an atmosphere on campus "characterized by a mutual respect and trust, [and] by openness and strong lines of communication that are used on a very regular basis and not just when challenges occur." When asked if he believed he could heal the tension among African-American students who had worked for Provost Taylor's appointment, he replied, "If I didn't believe I could, I wouldn't accept this position." Witt's charge while interim president came from Chancellor Cunningham and was clear and emphatic. "Dr. Witt's first and primary responsibility," said the chancellor, "will be the internal administration of this institution." In other words, Witt was to quiet campus unrest, unite various factions in support of a shared vision for the university, and end the rancor between the administration and the faculty—a tall order by anyone's standards. The chancellor gave Witt wide latitude to carry out his charge, including the freedom to reshape his administrative team. To faculty, students, and the outside community, Chancellor Cunningham warned that "we need not rehash past conflicts or attempt to assign guilt or blame for the difficult time. We do need to set aside the tension and stress that have become all too prevalent and paralyzing. There is nothing to be gained by picking over old bones or recounting tales of old feuds."[21]

Dr. Witt moved quickly to build his own team. On May 22, 1995, he announced that Provost Taylor had been placed on administrative leave for the summer and his place would be taken, on an interim basis, by Dr. George C. Wright, a former colleague of Witt's at UT-Austin and, at the time of the announcement, director of the Afro-American Studies Program and vice provost at Duke University. Witt also announced other changes in the provost's office, replacing Taylor's team with one of his own. These changes came less than a week after the UT system revealed the results of the management audit of the Amacher administration. The audit concluded that "the widespread opposition and associated problems experienced by the President and the Provost stemmed primarily from their failure to consider adequately basic decision factors or to employ an appropriate decision process methodology." While the audit did not find any illegalities, it did place the blame for the campus turmoil squarely on President Amacher and Provost Taylor. It was not surprising then that Witt, hoping to distance himself from the Amacher administration, said in announcing Wright's appointment that "we needed a clean break with the past." The audit results were not wasted on Wright either who, at the news conference for his appointment, commented, "Sometimes people are too quick to try to make dramatic change instead of first understanding these are people who have invested a lot of their careers in a place, and that you ought to at least hear them out."[22]

The problems facing Drs. Witt, Wright, and their administrative team are many. On the local level they must deal with racial tension on campus and a growing concern among some minority groups that UTA has not embraced diversity. Moreover, the Witt administration must convince students, faculty, and staff that it welcomes—even solicits—their input in the decision-

8.12 Since coming to UTA in the late 1960s, the outspoken political science professor, Allan Saxe, has donated art treasures to the student center and provided scholarships for students. His latest gift was the remodeling of the UTA baseball field in 1994, which was renamed Allan Saxe Stadium in his honor.

8.13 Accompanied by UT Chancellor William Cunningham (left), Robert Witt (right) was named interim president of UTA in the spring of 1995.

making process. President Witt must also work to repair the university's tarnished reputation, a result of two years of negative publicity. He must deal openly and honestly with the press, rather than viewing the press as adversaries. Finally, he should follow Amacher's lead in establishing strong and close ties with legislators, alumni, and community leaders.

Beyond these local challenges, Dr. Witt faces many of the same issues as other college presidents in the late twentieth century: adapting to changing student demographics and declining enrollments; diversifying faculty, staff, students, and the curriculum; preparing students for a culturally diverse and highly automated world; upgrading facilities and improving the campus computing infrastructure; increasing salaries; decreasing state support; encouraging increased research efforts and improved teaching; making outreach and service an integral part of faculty and staff responsibilities; and delivering quality services to students. Witt confronted these issues head-on when he assumed the presidency on June 1.

But in addition to problems, President Witt will find numerous opportunities at UTA, including a campus community that cares deeply about the university and wants to put the acrimony of the Amacher years behind it. Moreover, most on campus embrace the goal, articulated by Provost Taylor in October 1993, to develop the university into "an internationally prominent institution in areas of research and scholarship" and a recognized leader in "providing service to the metroplex [by] bringing faculty skills and talent to points of application in our local environment." Witt has yet to reveal his vision for the school, but when he does it is sure to include UTA's continued development in the traditional areas of teaching, research, and service. Also, the impetus to become a research university, which began in the Nedderman years and gained momentum during Amacher's administration, is strong and getting stronger with each outside grant faculty members receive and each graduate program added to the college's inventory.[23]

8.14 Although UTA no longer competes in football, the Department of Intercollegiate Athletics has made progressive strides in the areas of track, basketball, baseball, and softball. Here a member of the Lady Mavericks track team surges ahead of competitors from Baylor and the University of Oklahoma.

Today, UTA is considered a Doctoral University I, according to the Carnegie Foundation's classification scheme. Although the classification is not a qualitative judgment, it places the university at the same level as the College of William and Mary, Marquette University, and the University of Louisville because they, like Arlington, confer at least forty doctorates a year in five or more disciplines and offer a broad array of baccalaureate programs. Most faculty and administrators believe it inevitable that the university will eventually become a Research I institution, the same rank as the University of Texas at Austin and Texas A&M University. To make this move, UTA must award fifty doctorates a year and receive $40 million annually in research money and grants. In the 1993-1994 school year, the university awarded 85 doctoral degrees and 1,081 masters. The school's inventory of graduate programs includes 60 master's and 19 doctoral programs. Research funding on campus currently falls between $9 to $12 million annually, and the trend is toward increased extramural funding.[23]

If the past is any indication of the future, UTA, in the long term, can expect continued growth and program development in its drive to become an urban research university of note. Although the challenges are great, so is the university's momentum, built up over the past one hundred years. UTA's location, perhaps more than any other factor, has served to shape and define the school. In 1895, when Arlington was a town struggling for growth, identity, and viability, the college struggled along with it. When the school became a state-supported institution and a part of Texas A&M in 1917, it developed a mechanical and agricultural curriculum relevant to the surrounding region. But as Dallas and Fort Worth rapidly grew and urbanized, the college changed along with them, dropping its agricultural courses and adding new ones in fields such as engineering, science, and business, all relevant and in demand in a metropolitan area where manufacturing and service industries were becoming increasingly important. Today, as the so-called metroplex strives for national—indeed international—prominence in many areas (high tech industries, telecommunications, arts), so too does UTA. As a part of the University of Texas system and a dynamic urban region, the university is positioned to make great strides in the next century. While "change is hard," as President Amacher was fond of saying, it is—and always has been—a constant companion of the Arlington school. But with a clear understanding of the university's history and a clear vision of its future, the University of Texas at Arlington stands ready to achieve national prominence in the twenty-first century.

8.15 The Carlisle Military Academy campus c. 1911 and the present UTA campus reveal the growth in the school's physical plant that originally served 100 students. Today's campus has accommodated as many as 25,000 students.

Legend and Lore

Rumors and legends are ubiquitous on college campuses, and UTA is no exception. One of the more enduring—and certainly the most frequently repeated—legends at the university is one about a white elephant being buried somewhere on campus. A number of people mentioned the elephant story to the author and his research assistant, but few knew the details. Hoping to uncover more about the elephant, Chris Ohan, a graduate assistant researching the school's history, began looking for a source which could verify or discredit the story. He found such a source in John D. Boon, a retired professor emeritus living in Virginia. Boon taught geology at the college from 1942 to 1980 and was an eyewitness to the elephant's burial and subsequent exhumation. In a letter written in January 1995, Boon said this about the so-called buried elephant:

A part of the materials necessary to doing work with vertebrate paleontology is a collection of recent skeletal elements for comparative materials. Vertebrate fossils seldom occur in more than a fragmented and disarticulated bone scrap. This scrap can be identified and described by comparison with living forms.

Dr. C. L. McNulty, our paleontology professor, needed to build a collection of living vertebrate skeletal elements.

As a part of this collection we, along with the biology department, bought an elephant from the Fort Worth Rendering Company. The elephant had died at the Fort Worth Zoo; this animal had been purchased by the children

8.16 While the buried elephants have become a campus mystery, these photographs reveal the excavation as nothing more than a geology project.

of the Fort Worth schools from their nickels and dimes collections. I think that the elephant was named "Queen Tut."

We bought the skeletal elements of the elephant from the rendering company for $24; this amount was paid by the biologists. In order to clean the bones of marrow and bits of flesh we buried them. A large hole was dug in what is now the southeast corner of the stadium parking lot on campus. The cost of the digging was paid by the geologists; the cost was $25. Incidentally, the hole was at least twice as large as necessary. None of us knew how large a hole that would be necessary to bury the skeleton of an adult elephant. Several years later the skeletal bones were exhumed and added to the comparative collections in the geology department.

As a witness to the burial and exhumation I can verify that this "white" elephant, if still on campus, is a part of the collections of the geology department, and is not legendary.

A second elephant skeleton was purchased but never buried. The bones were cured on the roof of the science building.

Opening Ceremonies

AUGUST 30, 1995

8.17 UTA began its Centennial with a bang on August 30, 1995, with a parade, speakers, the unveiling of a historical marker for the university, and a salute by the Carlisle cannons.

NOTES

CHAPTER ONE

Good Schools Make Good Towns

1 *Phillips' Little Giant Vest Pocket Guide and Business Directory of Arlington, Texas* (Fort Worth: Beaumont and Purdom, Printers, 1894), 3-7; John A. Kooken, *Memoirs: Thirty Friendly Years with Arlington Public Schools* (Arlington: The Citizen, 1941), 21; Carolyn Carney, "Splendid Citizens: Social Values and Population Change in Early Arlington" (Paper presented at the Re-discovering Arlington's Heritage Conference, The University of Texas at Arlington, April 23, 1994), 1-3. The official name of the school is "The University of Texas at Arlington." I have chosen not to capitalize "the" preceding "university" in the text for the sake of readability and style.

2 Clarence P. Denman Collection, Box 1, Files 1-15, Special Collections Division, The University of Texas at Arlington Libraries; Arista Joyner Papers, GA 149, Folder 6, Special Collections Division, The University of Texas at Arlington Libraries.

3 Junia Evans Hudspeth, "A History of North Texas Agricultural College" (Masters thesis, Southern Methodist University, 1935), 6-12; *Arlington Citizen-Journal*, March 12, 1970.

4 At this time in Texas, the typical normal school was part of the primary school system and had the status of a lower vocational school. A teacher's certificate was practically equivalent to a lower secondary school certificate.

5 For biographical information on Hammond, see "L. M. Hammond," vertical file, University Archives, Special Collections Division, The University of Texas at Arlington Libraries; *Fort Worth Star-Telegram*, August 9, 1948; October 30, 1949; November 17, 20, 1959. Biographical information on Trimble can be found in B. B. Paddock, *History of Central and Western Texas* (Chicago: Lewis Publishing Company, 1911), 1:295-296; "William M. Trimble," vertical file, University Archives, Special Collections Division, The University of Texas at Arlington Libraries; *Fort Worth Star-Telegram*, January 23, 1922.

6 "L. M. Hammond," vertical file.

7 *Fort Worth Star-Telegram*, November 20, 1959; Arlington College class photographs in The University of Texas at Arlington Photograph Collection, University Archives, Special Collections Division, The University of Texas at Arlington Libraries. *Arlington Journal*, May 1898, photocopy of clipping, in Denman Collection, Oversize Box 125-14.

8 For the text of the rhyme, see Louise M. Natt Hardin to Arista Joyner, February 12, 1965, Arista Joyner Papers, GA 145, Folder 25. For other references used in the paragraph, see Hudspeth, "A History of North Texas Agricultural College," 15-16; Clarence P. Denman, "History of the University of Texas at Arlington, 1895-1917 (typescript), 4-7, in Denman Collection, Box 1, Folder 1; "L. M. Hammond," vertical file. By the time Hammond sold his interest in the college, he had married Lillie Ann McKinley, the daughter of the family with whom he had boarded in Arlington and a former student. They had three children: a daughter, Mae, who married Lester R. Hooker of Fort Worth, and two sons, William Knox Hammond and John Hayes Hammond, both of whom resided in Fort Worth. After leaving Arlington, Hammond held a number of positions in education, including that of a chemistry teacher in Fort Worth; school superintendent for Tarrant County; principal at Sam Houston School Number 6; teacher at Lindale, Texas; and principal at the Carroll M. Peak School in Fort Worth. Hammond retired in 1935 and lived the rest of his life in Fort Worth. He died on February 10, 1962.

Trimble left Arlington and became superintendent of the public schools of North Fort Worth, at that time a separate municipality which had grown up around the stockyards. He also returned to college, attending North Texas Normal School in Denton, Texas, where he graduated in 1901. Shortly after 1901, Trimble began preparing himself to enter the medical profession, studying medicine at the now defunct Fort Worth University and eventually graduating from Baylor University Medical School with his M.D. in 1908. After graduation, Trimble was appointed city physician of "Greater Fort Worth," and he established a private practice on Main Street. He and his wife, Susie Borah Trimble, had five children: Green B. Jr., Terrell, Willie Louise, Walter Lee, and J. B. William M. Trimble died in Fort Worth on January 22, 1922.

9 The stockholders included: M. J. Brinson, M. H. Cravens, R. W. Collins, A. W. Collins, A. M. Coble, J. D. Cooper, J. W. Ditto, W. M. Dugan, J. H. Elliott, Joseph P. Finger, C. D. King, Cyrus Lowe, R. W. McKnight, J. S. McKinley, D. R. Martin, W. P. Miller, Will Robinson, A. J. Rogers, Ed Rudd, S. W. Rudd, Thomas Spruance, B. F. Sawyers, S. H. Thompson, W. C. Weeks, and John Watson. See *The Arlington College Exponent*, January 1901, 8.

10 *Arlington Journal*, June 6, 1901. The school trustees at the time were J. I. Carter, J. H. Watson, and T. B. Collins.

11 Ibid., August 15, 22, 29, 1901. The teachers hired for the public school were W. W. Witt, superintendent; Cora Pilant, fifth and sixth grades; Mary McInnes, third and fourth grades; Eliza Hayter, first and second grades; and J. E. Rogers, principal of the high school.

12 Ibid., August 29, 1901; March 6, 1902.

[13] Ibid., April 10, 17, 1902. The election results were 201 votes for creating the independent school district, 84 against. See also *The Laws of Texas, Supplement Volume to the Original Ten Volumes, 1822-1897* (Austin: Gammel's Inc., 1904), 12: 102-103; *Arlington Journal*, June 12, 1902. The bond election discussed in this paragraph was eventually nullified because of a technicality. It was not until the summer of 1903 that a $15,000 bond election was approved by the voters and was allowed to stand. See *Arlington Journal*, August 6, 1903.

[14] Denman, "The History of the University of Texas at Arlington, 1895-1917," 8-9.

CHAPTER TWO

A High-Grade Preparatory School for Manly Boys

[1] *Arlington Citizen-Journal*, March 12, 1970, Special Events Section, "University of Texas at Arlington, Seventy-fifth Anniversary, 1895-1970," 14-15.

[2] Lee Wayne White, "Popular Education and the State Superintendent of Public Instruction in Texas, 1860-1899" (Ph.D. dissertation, The University of Texas at Austin, 1974), 180-183; L. E. Daniell, *Personnel of the Texas State Government* (San Antonio: Maverick Printing House, 1892), 590-594; "James M. Carlisle," vertical file, University Archives, Special Collections Division, The University of Texas at Arlington Libraries.

[3] Denman, "The History of the University of Texas at Arlington, 1895-1917," 11-12; *Arlington Journal*, January 12, 1905.

[4] Denman, "The History of the University of Texas at Arlington, 1895-1917," 16-17.

[5] *Carlisle Military Academy Fifth Annual Announcement, 1904-1905*, 34-35.

[6] Ibid., 49-53; *Carlisle Military Academy Seventh Annual Announcement, 1907-1908*, 33-37; and *Carlisle Military Academy Tenth Annual Announcement, 1911-1912*, 29-34.

[7] *Carlisle Military Academy Fifth Annual Announcement*, 33, 38, 42; *Arlington Journal*, September 10, 1903.

[8] Denman, "The History of the University of Texas at Arlington, 1895-1917," 16, 20, 22, 28, 31, 37, 44.

[9] *Arlington Journal*, January 12, May 18, August 24, September 5, 1905.

[10] Denman, "The History of the University of Texas at Arlington, 1895-1917," 19-22, 28-29; *Arlington Journal*, August 11, 1904. For the school's land transactions, see Deed Record, County Clerk's Office, Tarrant County, 261: 618; 236: 69; 206: 425; 285: 517; 309: 105; 292: 192; 269: 366; 261: 249.

[11] *Arlington Journal*, January 30, April 30, June 11, December 17, 1903; March 17, April 7, 14, 21, 28, May 12, 26, September 29, 1904; March 2, 23, April 6, 1905; January 24, May 16, 1907. For the quotation at the end of the paragraph, see "The Early Years and the Making of a School" (Unpublished typescript produced by The University of Texas at Arlington's Military Science Department, ca.1993), 5-6.

[12] Ibid., May 12, 1904; Denman, "The History of the University of Texas at Arlington, 1895-1917," 35.

[13] *Arlington Journal*, May 9, August 29, 1907; April 16, 1909.

[14] Ibid., October 26, 1905; Denman, "The History of the University of Texas at Arlington, 1895-1917," 33-38.

[15] *Arlington Journal*, November 27, 1908; February 19, 1909. Organized football returned to the school the following year in 1909.

[16] Ibid., May 19, 1911; *J. M. Thompson vs. Carlisle Military Academy*, Case No. 31222, "Order on Application of Plff. [sic] for Rec. Granted 13th day of May, 1911," Minutes of the District Court, 17th Judicial District, Tarrant County, April Term, 1911, 359-360.

[17] *J. M. Thompson vs. Carlisle Military Academy*, Case No. 31222, 359-360.

[18] *J. M. Thompson vs. Carlisle Military Academy*, Case No. [left blank], "Order to sell property, October 14th, 1911," Minutes of the District Court, 17th Judicial District, Tarrant County, October Term, 1911, 503-504.

[19] *J. M. Thompson vs. Carlisle Military Academy*, Case No. 31222, "Final Judgment, August 16, 1913," Minutes of the District Court, 17th Judicial District, Tarrant County, July Term, 1913, 420-424.

[20] *J. M. Thompson vs. Carlisle Military Academy*, Case No. 31222, "Plaintiff's First Supplement, Petition and Application for Receivership," Filed May 13, 1911, 1-2, in Case Papers File, 17th Judicial District, Tarrant County; *Arlington Journal*, May 23, 1913.

[21] Carlisle left Whitewright, Texas, in 1917 to become superintendent of schools in Rock Springs, located in Edwards County in West Texas. Shortly before his death, he returned to Arlington. He died on July 21, 1922. Upon his death, Carlisle was eulogized as one of the state's outstanding educators and the flag at the state capitol was placed at half staff. Throughout his career in Texas, Carlisle advocated and worked for a uniform textbook law for the state and a program where the state would furnish books for public school students. Both of these measures became a reality in his lifetime. *Arlington Citizen-Journal*, March 12, 1970, Special Events Section, 15; "James M. Carlisle," vertical file.

CHAPTER THREE

One of the Best and Safest Places in Texas for Boys

1 *Arlington Journal*, May 16, 23, August 1, 1913; *Arlington Training School Catalog, 1913-1914*, 1-4. More biographical information can be found in Taylor's obituary, see *Dallas Times Herald*, January 23, 1934.

2 [Agreement Made and Entered into Between Thomas Spruance, A. W. Collins, M. H. Cravens, W. M. Dugan, W. C. Weeks, J. H. Watson, W. B. Fitzhugh, Frank McKnight and J. W. Burney, with H. K. Taylor and J. J. Godbey, dated May 1, 1913, and signed on August 4, 1913.] Photocopy, University Archives, Special Collections Division, The University of Texas at Arlington Libraries.

3 *Arlington Journal*, August 1, 1913.

4 Ibid., September 26, 1913; *Arlington Training School Catalog, 1913-1914*, "Superintendent's Preface," n.p., 45.

5 Ibid., 45-49.

6 Ibid., 49.

7 Ibid., 11.

8 Denman, "History of the University of Texas at Arlington, 1895-1917," 51-52.

9 *Arlington Training School Catalog, 1913-1914*, 50.

10 *Arlington Journal*, October 31, 1913; Denman, "The History of the University of Texas at Arlington, 1895-1917," 53-55.

11 Denman, "The History of the University of Texas at Arlington, 1895-1917," 55-56. The board of advisors included W. M. Dugan, A. W. Collins, W. B. Fitzhugh, W. C. Weeks, Joe W. Burney, Thomas Spruance, J. H. Watson, M. H. Cravens, and Frank McKnight.

12 *Arlington Training School Catalog, 1914-1915*, 1-6.

13 Arlington Training School, Senior Class, *The Blue Bonnet*, 1915, n.p.

14 Denman, "The History of the University of Texas at Arlington, 1895-1917," 58-59; *Arlington Journal*, March 19, 1915.

15 *Arlington Journal*, April 2, 1915.

16 Ibid., April 9, 16, 1915.

17 Contract Entered into Between the Board of Directors of the Arlington Training School, of the First Part, and H. K. Taylor, of the Second Part. Photocopy, University Archives, Special Collections Division, The University of Texas at Arlington Libraries.

18 Denman, "The History of the University of Texas at Arlington, 1895-1917," 61.

19 Ibid., 61-65.

20 See *Arlington Training School vs. H. K. Taylor*, Case No. 41556, in Case Papers File, 17th Judicial District, Tarrant County.

21 For the final verdict, see *Arlington Training School vs. H. K. Taylor*, Case No. 41556, Minutes of the District Court, 17th Judicial District, Tarrant County, January Term, 1917, 194-195.

22 Denman, "The History of the University of Texas at Arlington, 1895-1917," 66, note 3.

23 *Arlington Journal*, July 7, December 29, 1916.

24 Ibid., July 14, 1916.

25 Ibid., September 29, November 24, December 8, 15, 29, 1916; January 12, 1917.

26 Ibid., September 29, 1916; February 9, 1917.

CHAPTER FOUR

A Hard Road to Travel

1 *Arlington Journal*, February 3, 10, 1911; March 23, 1917.

2 Ibid., March 23, 1917; *Houston Post*, January 23, 26, 1907; *Fort Worth Star-Telegram*, January 25, February 3, 11, 1907.

3 "V. W. Grubbs," vertical file, University Archives, Special Collections Division, The University of Texas at Arlington Libraries; Texas Legislature, *Journal of the House of Representatives, 1917* (Austin: Von Boeckmann-Jones Co., 1917), 1258, 1113, 64; *Arlington Journal*, April 13, 1917; The Kaufman County Historical Commission, *A History of Kaufman County* (Dallas: Taylor Publishing Company, 1978), 90-91.

4 *Farmers' Fireside Bulletin*, April 11, 1917.

5 V. W. Grubbs, "The Establishment of the Grubbs Vocational College and its Clandestine Organization" (Unpublished

typescript), 1-3, in Grubbs Family Papers, University Archives, Special Collections Division, The University of Texas at Arlington Libraries.

[6] Ibid., 3-5; *Arlington Journal*, April 6, 13, 1917.

[7] Ibid.

[8] Texas Legislature, *Journal of the Senate of Texas, 1917* (Austin: State Printers, 1917), 1637-1639.

[9] *Arlington Journal*, April 13, 1917; Grubbs, "Establishment of the Grubbs Vocational College," 5-6.

[10] *Arlington Journal*, May 18, June 22, 1917; Grubbs, "Establishment of the Grubbs Vocational College," 6; *Grubbs Vocational College, Preliminary Announcements, Session 1917-18* (Arlington, Texas), 3.

[11] *Arlington Journal*, September 7, 1917; Grubbs, "Establishment of the Grubbs Vocational College," 6.

[12] "Myron Lawson Williams," vertical file, University Archives, Special Collections Division, The University of Texas at Arlington Libraries.

[13] *Bulletin of the Grubbs Vocational College, First Biennial Report* (March 1, 1919), 8.

[14] Ibid., 8-10.

[15] Ibid., 10; *Arlington Journal*, September 7, 1917.

[16] *Bulletin of the Grubbs Vocational College, First Annual Catalogue, Announcements for 1917-18* (September 1, 1917), 13-22.

[17] Ibid., 20-24. Some of the "short courses" offered at Grubbs were soil and fertilizers, seed selection, cropping systems, stock judging, breeds and types of farm animals, poultry, hogs, dairying, animal breeding, advanced milk testing, and care and management of animals. For this list see *Bulletin of the Grubbs Vocational College, Second Annual Session for September 18, 1918 to May 27, 1919* (June 1, 1918), 31-33.

[18] *Bulletin of the Grubbs Vocational College* (March 1, 1919), 12.

[19] *Reports of Subcommittees of The Central Investigating Committees of the House and Senate, Third Called Session of the Thirty-fifth Legislature of Texas, Including Audits* (Austin, Texas: Von Boeckmann-Jones Co., Printers, 1919), 798-837. For the quotation, see 837.

[20] Kenneth Whitt, "A Brief Biography of M. L. Williams" (Unpublished typescript), 22-24, in "Myron Lawson Williams," vertical file; *Arlington Journal*, February 15, 1919.

[21] *Bulletin of the Grubbs Vocational College* (March 1, 1919), 8-9, 12-13; ibid. (March 1, 1918), 11, for quote.

[22] Ibid., 13; *The Shorthorn*, June 1919, 29, for quote; *Arlington Journal*, January 18, 1918.

[23] *Bulletin of the Grubbs Vocational College* (March 1, 1919), 9-10. The *Bulletin* incorrectly labels the structure as the "New Agricultural Building." See also *The Shorthorn*, June 1919, 43.

[24] *Bulletin of the Grubbs Vocational College* (March 1, 1919), 13-14.

[25] For the enrollment figures, see *Bulletin of the Grubbs Vocational College, Third Annual Report for September 1, 1919 to August 31, 1920* (November 1, 1920), 9; *Bulletin of the Grubbs Vocational College, Annual Report of the Grubbs Vocational College for the Fiscal Year 1921-1922* (November 15, 1922), 3-4.

[26] *Bulletin of the Grubbs Vocational College* (November 1, 1920), 1-9.

[27] *Bulletin of the Grubbs Vocational College* (March 1, 1919), 15; ibid. (March 1, 1923), 11; ibid. (July 1, 1920), 29-30.

[28] Ibid. (July 1, 1921), 22-25; *The Shorthorn*, October 1919, 27.

[29] *The Shorthorn*, April, 1919; May 6, 1994; *The Grubbonian*, vol. 1, no. 1.

[30] *Bulletin of the Grubbs Vocational College* (November 1, 1920), 6; ibid. (July 1, 1920), 20-25; ibid. (July 1, 1921), 22; *The Shorthorn*, April 1919, 36-37.

[31] *Bulletin of the Grubbs Vocational College* (July 1, 1921), 21-23.

[32] For the quote about women's uniforms, see ibid., 23-24; for the quote by Rosemary Ribbon, see *The Shorthorn*, November 1919, 18.

[33] *Bulletin of the Grubbs Vocational College* (July 1, 1921), 24-25; for dormitory information see *Bulletin of the Grubbs Vocational College* (November 15, 1922), 11-12.

[34] *The Shorthorn*, April 1919, 22-23; ibid., May 1919, n.p., Whitt, "A Brief Biography of M. L. Williams," 26.

[35] Hudspeth, "A History of North Texas Agricultural College," 31.

[36] Ibid., 67-68.

[37] Index to California Death Records (microfilm), 4285, Genealogy Department, Central Dallas Public Library, Dallas, Texas.

[1] E. E. Davis, "Report on General Conditions as of April 30, 1945" (unpublished typescript), 1, in "History of North Texas Agricultural College," vertical file, University Archives, Special Collections Division, The University of Texas at Arlington Libraries; C. D. Richards, interview by Duncan Robinson, February 26, 1974, 14, University Archives, Special Collections Division, The University of Texas at Arlington Libraries.

[2] B. C. Barnes, interview by Duncan Robinson, January 29, 1974, 4, University Archives, Special Collections Division, The University of Texas at Arlington Libraries; Davis to Will H. Mayes, May 12, 1939, in "Dean E. E. Davis," vertical file, University Archives, Special Collections Division, The University of Texas at Arlington Libraries.

[3] "Dean E. E. Davis," vertical file.

[4] Hudspeth, "A History of North Texas Agricultural College," 85.

[5] Ibid.; H. A. D. Dunsworth, interview by Duncan Robinson, September 26, 1973, 24-25, University Archives, Special Collections Division, The University of Texas at Arlington Libraries. For the block quote, see E. E. Davis to Jack Danciger, April 3, 1941, in Office of the Presidents Records, Special Collections Division, The University of Texas at Arlington Libraries, Box 2, Folder 14.

[6] For Davis' quote, see *Annual Report of the North Texas Agricultural College, 1929-30* (Arlington, Texas), 5. For an example of Davis' requests, see *Bulletin of the North Texas Agricultural College* (September 1, 1928), 8-9.

[7] [Mailing to Students and Ex-students of NTAC], June 30, 1928, Office of the Presidents Records, Box 1, Folder 20; *The Shorthorn*, October 9, 1928.

[8] *Annual Report of the North Texas Agricultural College, 1928-1929* (Arlington, Texas), 47; ibid., for 1925-26, 41. For the quote concerning high school students, see *Bulletin of the North Texas Agricultural College* (September 1, 1930), 2; "Aims and Objectives of the North Texas Agricultural College," Office of the Presidents Records, Box 22, Folder 11.

[9] *Bulletin of the North Texas Agricultural College* (September 1, 1926), 1-25; see also pamphlets bound with above: ibid. (December 1, 1926), "Special Announcement for Second Semester"; ibid. (March 15, 1927), "Summer Announcements"; Cothburn O'Neal, interview by Duncan Robinson, March 14, 1975, 17, University Archives, Special Collections Division, The University of Texas at Arlington Libraries; *The Shorthorn*, May 10, 1927; May 1, 1928; October 2, 1928; January 21, 1930.

[10] *North Texas Agricultural College, Tenth Annual Catalog* (July 1, 1926), 39-42.

[11] "N.T.A.C. Enrollment During Dean Davis' Administration, 1925-26 Through 1946-47," Office of the Presidents Records, Box 31, Folder 23; *Bulletin of the North Texas Agricultural College*, (September 1, 1928), 10.

[12] Ibid., 9-12.

[13] "N.T.A.C. Enrollment During Dean Davis' Administration"; *Bulletin of the North Texas Agricultural College* (September 1, 1932), 6-9; Davis, "Report on General Conditions," 1.

[14] *Bulletin of the North Texas Agricultural College* (September 1, 1932), 6; ibid. (September 1, 1933), 5-6.

[15] Ibid.

[16] The Joint Legislative Committee on Organization and Economy and Griffenhagen and Associates, *Part XI—Education; the Agricultural and Mechanical College of Texas and its Affiliates* (December 31, 1932).

[17] Ibid., 218-219, 251-252; Zelda Ramsey, interview by Susan Smith, April 14, 1994, 6, University Archives, Special Collections Division, The University of Texas at Arlington Libraries.

[18] Griffenhagen and Associates, *Part XI—Education*, 214-256.

[19] Davis, "Report on General Conditions," 1.

[20] North Texas Agricultural College, "Enrollment," [1935-1945], n.p., Office of the Presidents Records, Box 31, Folder 21; see also Roy M. Burdett, interview by Elton Smith, June 1975, 9, University Archives, Special Collections Division, The University of Texas at Arlington Libraries.

[21] "Facts About N.T.A.C.," n.d., Office of the Presidents Records, Box 8, Folder 18.

[22] *North Texas Agricultural College, 21st Annual Catalog* (June 1937), 40-42; Alvin Betzel, interview by Duncan Robinson, September 9, 1975, 15, University Archives, Special Collections Division, The University of Texas at Arlington Libraries.

[23] Office of the Presidents Records, Box 3, Folders 7-8; *The Shorthorn*, January 30, 1934; December 17, 1935; April 28, 1936; April 1938, Special Issue; November 5, 1940.

[24] Davis, "Report on General Conditions," 1-27; E. E. Davis, "Our College and the War," 1,3, Office of the Presidents Records, Box 24, File 3A; E. E. Davis, "To All Male Members of the Faculty," April 13, 1942, ibid., Box 21, Folder 16; Senate Bill No. 38, "Oath Bill," to become effective October 2, 1941, ibid., Box 18, Folder 2.

25 E. E. Davis to T. U. Walton, April 7, 1943, Office of the Presidents Records, Box 25, Folder 13; Davis, "Report on General Conditions," 7; *The Shorthorn*, March 31, 1942; January 19, 1943.

26 Davis, "Report on General Conditions," 1-8.

27 Davis to Gibb Gilchrist, May 9, 1945; May 24, 1945, Office of the Presidents Records, Box 28, Folder 4; "N.T.A.C. Enrollment During Dean Davis' Administration, 1925-26 Through 1946-47," ibid.

28 "History of North Texas Agricultural College," vertical file; "E. H. Hereford," vertical file, University Archives, Special Collections Division, The University of Texas at Arlington Libraries; *The Shorthorn*, October 26, 1948.

29 Barnes interview, 9; Richards interview, 44; O'Neal interview, 20-21.

30 Office of the Presidents Records, Box 38, File 7.

31 For information on the impact of returning GIs, see Office of the Presidents Records, Box 31, File 1; Box 32, Files 23-25; Box 40, Files 12-15; Box 43, Files 6, 12-13. For budget information, see Keith Kelly to E. H. Hereford, June 29, 1949, ibid., Box 41, File 16.

32 Davis to the President of the A&M College and Its Board of Directors, October 7, 1938, ibid., Box 12, File 8.

33 "Reasons Why North Texas Agricultural College Should Be Raised to an Institution of Higher Rank," n.d., ibid., Box 12, File 8.

34 Frank Smith, interview by Duncan Robinson, November 20, 1975, 10, University Archives, Special Collections Division, The University of Texas at Arlington Libraries; Tom Vandergriff, interview by Dan Griffith, April 21, 1994, 14-17, University Archives, Special Collections Division, The University of Texas at Arlington Libraries.

35 Senate Bill No. 93, photocopy, Office of the Presidents Records, Box 42, File 19; see also "Report on General Conditions at NTAC as of April 30, 1948," ibid., Box 37, File 24.

36 *The Shorthorn*, 1923-1949; *Junior Aggie*, 1923-1949.

37 Information on the ROTC can be found in every *Junior Aggie*, including rosters and photographs of each company. For information on Davis' attempts to end hazing, see Office of the Presidents Records, Box 31, Folder 7; George E. Watkins, interview by Duncan Robinson, February 14, 1977, 1-18, University Archives, Special Collections Division, The University of Texas at Arlington Libraries; *Fort Worth Star-Telegram*, April 11, 1945; "Good Will," a poem written by "a student in mind only," Office of the Presidents Records, Box 28, Folder 6; William Bardin, interview by Jerry Stafford, April 7, 1994, 6, 13, University Archives, Special Collections Division, The University of Texas at Arlington Libraries.

38 *Junior Aggie*, 1933, 13, in "The Junior Aggie Buzzer" located in the back of the book.

39 Ibid., 1924, n.p., "The Students' Council"; Marcella Wilemon, interview by Diana Mays, April 6, 1994, 11-14, 18, University Archives, Special Collections Division, The University of Texas at Arlington Libraries; Martha Hughes and W. L. Hughes, interview by Duncan Robinson, January 31, 1974, 15-17, University Archives, Special Collections Division, The University of Texas at Arlington Libraries.

40 E. E. Davis to Wayne Gard, January 16, 1936, Office of the Presidents Records, Box 3, Folder 3.

41 The *Junior Aggie* reports the scores on every game of the year, as well as including photographs of many of the games and all of the players. See *Junior Aggie*, 1923-1949. For information on the JTAC bonfire incident, see Frank Yates, interview by Duncan Robinson, February 28, 1973, 13, University Archives, Special Collections Division, The University of Texas at Arlington Libraries; Wilemon interview, 9-10.

42 *Junior Aggie*, 1926, 26.

43 Ibid., 1927, 86; ibid., 1933, 64-72.

44 "The Report of the Committee on Elections of Student Faculty Committee," 1941, Office of the Presidents Records, Box 19, Folder 1; "Minutes of the Meeting of the Faculty Cabinet," September 6, 1945, ibid., Box 30, Folder 24.

45 "Students Handbook: Instructions to Students," ca. 1936-1937, ibid., Box 6, Folder 16.

46 Wilemon interview, 5-15.

CHAPTER SIX

We Are at the Crossroads

1 Arlington State College, *The Arlington State College Self-Study* (Arlington, Texas, 1963), 5-6.

2 Ibid.

3 *Arlington State College, 35th Annual Catalogue* (January 1953), 1-36; "Military-ROTC," vertical file, University Archives, Special Collections Division, The University of Texas at Arlington Libraries.

4 Office of the Presidents Records, Box 44, Folders 18-19; Box 45, Folder 19; Box 48, Folders 7-8, 11; Box 50, Folder 14; Box 51, Folders 1, 15; Box 52, Folder 19. Also see "Report of the Highlights during the Fiscal Year 1949-1950 at

Arlington State College," in "History-Arlington State College," vertical file, University Archives, Special Collections Division, The University of Texas at Arlington Libraries. Once the new science building was opened in 1950, the building formerly used for science was renamed Preston Hall, in honor of Joe B. Preston, who came to the school in 1927 as a history instructor and later served as registrar.

5 *The Shorthorn*, April 1, 1958; *Fort Worth Star-Telegram*, June 1, 1960.

6 *Fort Worth Star-Telegram*, November 13, 1960.

7 "Arlington State College, General Information," in Don Kennard Papers, Box 12, Folder 13, Special Collections Division, The University of Texas at Arlington Libraries; "History-Arlington State College," vertical file; *The Texas A&M University System, Annual Report of the Chancellor, 1963-1964*, n.p. Until its transfer from the A&M system, ASC received building funds from the A&M board, which was authorized to allocate them from the Available Fund of the Permanent University Fund. These funded the Engineering Building, library, Science Building, and a central heating and cooling plant. In addition, the college sold bonds to build dormitories and other facilities, and the fees for use of these buildings were used to amortize the cost of the facilities. Lipscomb Hall and Trinity House were financed in this way. ASC also used federal matching loans, allocated by the Texas Commission on Higher Education and later the Coordinating Board, for constructing academic and general use buildings. Under Woolf's leadership, ASC received the second highest amount of these federal funds after the University of Houston. When ASC joined the UT system in 1965, the Texas legislature authorized a constitutional amendment which, after it was approved by the voters, added the college to the ad valorem tax source and increased the tax from $.05 to $.10 for every $100 of valuation. The college used ad valorem taxes to finance new construction until 1979, the year the legislature eliminated the tax. Chapter 7 discusses the end of the tax.

8 "Report of Arlington State College," 6-8, in "History-Arlington State College," vertical file; *The Dallas Morning News*, July 9, 1966; *Arlington Journal*, October 6, 1966. In 1965, ASC operated with educational and general space of approximately 60 square feet per full-time equivalent student; the average square footage for Texas colleges at the time was more than 100 square feet for every student.

9 *Arlington Journal*, October 6, 1966. Former president Jack Woolf told the author that he recommended to the UT regents that pedestrian bridges be built over Cooper Street to facilitate student movement east-west on campus. The regents decided not to allocate the money for the bridges, believing the money could be better spent elsewhere.

10 *Fort Worth Star-Telegram*, November 24, 1958; June 30, 1959; February 21, 1960; *The Shorthorn*, July 30, 1958; February 28, 1960.

11 Ibid., February 28, 1960.

12 [Record of bills introduced in the Texas legislature to make ASC a four-year school], Kennard Papers, Box 11, Folder 13; *The Shorthorn*, November 16, 1954; October 23, 1956; January 17, 1957; M. T. Harrington to Robert W. Baker, March 3, 1955, Western Union Telegram, in "Four-Year Status," vertical file, University Archives, Special Collections Division, The University of Texas at Arlington Libraries; *Fort Worth Star-Telegram*, March 3, 1955.

13 *The Shorthorn*, February 26, March 5, 1957; Robert L. Montgomery, Jr., "Are Money and Planning Enough?", *The Texas Observer* (January 8, 1965), 1-2.

14 Ibid., March 5, 12, April 16, 1957; *The Dallas Morning News*, February 26, March 1, April 18, 1957; *Dallas Times Herald*, April 8, 1957.

15 *The Shorthorn*, April 16, 1957; December 9, 1958.

16 [Report of the Texas Commission for Higher Education], December 15, 1958, 2-13; for the quote see ibid., 11-12. Report found in Jack Royce Woolf Papers, Box 30, Folder 6, University Archives, Special Collections Division, The University of Texas at Arlington Libraries. See also *The Shorthorn*, December 16, 1958.

17 *The Shorthorn*, December 16, 1958; January 6, February 10, 1959; *The Dallas Morning News*, December 21, 22, 23, 1958; Vandergriff interview, April 21, 1994, 13-17.

18 *The Shorthorn*, February 10, 17, 24, 1959.

19 Ibid., April 7, 21, 28, 1959; *Arlington Citizen-Journal*, April 20, 23, 1959; *Fort Worth Star-Telegram*, April 28, 1959; *The Dallas Morning News*, April 10, 1959.

20 *The Shorthorn*, April 28, 1959; *Fort Worth Star-Telegram*, April 28, 1959.

21 *The Shorthorn*, May 5, 1959. For the text of the bill, see *Vernon's Annotated Revised Civil Statutes of the State of Texas* (Kansas City, Missouri: Vernon Law Book Company, 1963), 8: 57, pocket supplement; *Dallas Times Herald*, May 5, 1959.

22 Almetris Marsh Duren, *Overcoming: A History of Black Integration at the University of Texas at Austin* (Austin: University of Texas Press, 1979), 1-4; "Sweatt v. Painter," Walter Prescott Webb, et al., *The Handbook of Texas* (Austin: Texas State Historical Association, 1952-1976), 2: 942-943.

23 *The Shorthorn*, February 28, 1956; Jack W. Burke, IV, "Arlington State College's Unsuccessful Successful Integration" (typescript dated May 1994), 1-3; *Fort Worth Star-Telegram*, October 8, 1994.

24 Burke, "Arlington State College's Unsuccessful Successful Integration," 2-3; Jack Woolf, interview by Lynn Swann Davis, 1975, 18-19, University Archives, Special Collections Division, The University of Texas at Arlington Libraries; Jack Woolf, interview by Neil Simmons, March 29, 1994, 17-18, University Archives, Special Collections Division, The University of Texas at Arlington Libraries. In October 1994, the university recognized Jesse Oliver, one of the school's first African-American students, as an outstanding alumnus. After helping to break the color barrier at ASC, Oliver graduated from Dallas Baptist University with a B.A. in management in 1976 and earned a law degree from UT-Austin in 1981. Oliver has held a number of elected and appointed positions in Austin and Dallas. See *Fort Worth Star-Telegram*, October 8, 1994.

25 Harrington to Members of the Board of Directors, July 11,1962, Woolf Papers, Box 9, File 6.

26 *Arlington Daily News Texan*, July 11, September 13-14, 1962; Woolf to George Hawkes, July 16, 1962; Arthur F. Stovall to Woolf, July 25, 1962; Mrs. F. G. Ogden to Woolf, undated; Carey Daniel to Woolf, July 13, 1962, Woolf Papers, Box 4, File 10.

27 Burke, "Arlington State College's Unsuccessful Successful Integration," 17-22.

28 Ibid., 22-25; *Reveille 1966*, 166.

29 Charles T. McDowell, "1958-1968: A Decade of Change," January 3, 1969, 1-2. For the admission standards, see Arlington State College Faculty Newsletter, December 16, 1964, 1-2.

30 McDowell, "1958-1968: A Decade of Change," 2-4; "Arlington State College, General Information," Kennard Papers, Box 12, Folder 13.

31 "Arlington State College, General Information," Kennard Papers, Box 12, Folder 13; *The Dallas Morning News*, February 3, 1963.

32 For the statistics in the table, see McDowell, "1958-1968: A Decade of Change," 4; *The Shorthorn*, September 22, 1959; Arlington State College Faculty Newsletter, March 3, 1965; *The Texas A&M University System, Annual Report of the Chancellor, 1963-64*, n.p.

33 *The Texas A&M University System, Annual Report of the Chancellor, 1963-64*, n.p.; *The Dallas Morning News*, February 3, 1963; Woolf interview, March 29, 1994, 9-10; "Report of Arlington State College," 3, in "History-Arlington State College," vertical file.

34 *Arlington State College Self-Study*, 97-99, 149-150.

35 "Report of Arlington State College," 1, in "History-Arlington State College," vertical file.

36 Ibid., 7-8.

37 Frank Harrison, interview by Gerald Saxon, December 12, 1991, 11-12, University Archives, Special Collections Division, The University of Texas at Arlington Libraries; Samuel B. Hamlett, interview by June Dalrymple, March 31, 1994, 25-30, University Archives, Special Collections Division, The University of Texas at Arlington Libraries; Woolf interview, March 29, 1994, 11-12.

38 "Preliminary Comparison of Texas A&M University and Arlington State College," n.d., 1, Kennard Papers, Box 23, Folder 9.

39 For the Woolf quote, see Woolf interview, March 29, 1994, 12; for the Nichols quote, see Marvin C. Nichols to J. B. Thomas, December 31, 1964, Kennard Papers, Box 23, Folder 9.

40 *Arlington News Texan*, December 15, 17, 19, 20, 1964; James A. Cribbs to "Fellow Ex," December 28, 1964, Kennard Papers, Box 23, Folder 9.

41 Nichols to Thomas, December 31, 1964, Kennard Papers, Box 23, Folder 9; see also an undated memorandum in ibid., Box 23, Folder 8.

42 For the Vandergriff quote, see Vandergriff interview, April 21, 1994, 20-21; the Woolf quote can be found in Woolf interview, March 29, 1994, 11. When Harrington stepped down as chancellor of the A&M system, the title of the executive officer of the system was changed to president and Rudder became both "President of The Texas A&M University System and President of Texas A&M University." Even before Harrington retired, the board looked to Rudder for guidance, not Harrington. Rudder officially assumed his new title on September 1, 1965. See *The Texas A&M University System, Annual Report of the Chancellor, 1964-1965*, 6.

43 *Arlington News Texan*, January 6, 7, 1965; Jenkins Garrett to Gerald Saxon, April 18, 1995, The University of Texas at Arlington Centennial History Collection, Special Collections Division, The University of Texas at Arlington Libraries.

44 *The Dallas Morning News*, January 8, 1965; *Arlington Citizen Journal*, January 11, 1965; *Dallas Times Herald*, January 27, 1965.

45 *Arlington News Texan*, January 10, 1965; Jenkins Garrett, interview by Gerald Saxon, December 11, 1990, 207-213, University Archives, Special Collections Division, The University of Texas at Arlington Libraries.

46 Hamlett interview, March 31, 1994, 27-28; Emory D. Estes, interview by Mike Brown, April 19, 1994, 5-9, University Archives, Special Collections Division, The University of Texas at Arlington Libraries.

47 *Arlington News Texan*, March 13, 17, April 4, 9, 21, 23, 24, 26, 1965; *Arlington Citizen Journal*, April 26, 1965.

48 *Arlington News Texan*, April 24, 25, 1965.

49 Wendell Nedderman, interview by Duncan Robinson, April 18, 27, May 29, 1977, 37, University Archives, Special Collections Division, The University of Texas at Arlington Libraries.

50 *Arlington State College Self-Study*, 215-219; Arlington State College Faculty Newsletter, December 27, 1964.

51 Harrison interview, December 12, 1991, 5.

52 Ibid., 7; University of Texas at Arlington, *Reveille 1967*, 277; Frank Harrison, interview by Lynn Swann Davis, February 25, 1976, 5-8, University Archives, Special Collections Division, The University of Texas at Arlington Libraries; "Report of Arlington State College," 9-10, in "History-Arlington State College," vertical file.

53 *Arlington Journal*, March 9, 1967; *The Shorthorn*, March 3, 10, 17, 1967.

54 In 1965, there was an unsuccessful attempt to have the radical Student Non-violent Coordinating Committee (SNCC) on campus and, in 1967, a group of students tried, but failed, to have the Students for a Democratic Society (SDS) approved as a campus organization; see Rusty Russell Papers, Box 1, Folder 2, University Archives, Special Collections Division, The University of Texas at Arlington Libraries.

55 McDowell, "1958-1968: A Decade of Change," section entitled Student Organizations, n.p.; see also *Reveille 1967*, 50-182; *Reveille 1965*, 292-298.

56 McDowell, "1958-1968: A Decade of Change," section entitled Student Services, 3-4; *Reveille 1965*, 26-34.

57 The eighteen committees on which students served in the late sixties were: Advisory Committee on Student Life and Activities; Alumni Relations; Athletic Council; Catalogue and Official Publications; Committee on Student Organizations; Discipline Panel; Football Entertainment Committee; Registration, Calendar, and Scheduling Committee; Safety and Sanitation Committee; Scholarship, Loans, and Awards Committee; Speakers Policy Committee; Student Activities Board; Student Center Advisory Committee; Student Congress; Student Judicial Board; Student Publications Board; Student Rewards Committee; and U. T. Arlington Goals Committee. See McDowell, "1958-1968: A Decade of Change," section entitled Student Participation in University Affairs, n.p.

58 *Arlington Journal*, December 6, 10, 13, 17, 1956; Arlington State College, *Reveille 1957*, 146, 178-180; Claude R. "Chena" Gilstrap, interview by Rebekah Bandy, April 10, 1994, 20-21, University Archives, Special Collections Division, The University of Texas at Arlington Libraries.

59 Coach Gilstrap was first named Texas junior college coach of the year in 1948, when he coached for Paris Junior College, and again in 1953 after ASC won the Pioneer Conference; see *Reveille 1957*, 149. For other sources cited in the paragraph, see *Arlington Journal*, December 13, 17, 1956; *The Shorthorn*, January 8, 1957; Thomas J. Tinker, interview by Eric Oglesby, March 16, 1994, 18, University Archives, Special Collections Division, The University of Texas at Arlington Libraries; Hamlett interview, March 31, 1994, 21-22.

60 *The Shorthorn*, December 10, 17, 1957; *Arlington Journal*, December 5, 17, 19, 1957; Gilstrap interview, April 10, 1994, 14.

61 Gilstrap interview, April 10, 1994, 16-17; Rusty Russell, interview by Richard Culbertson, March 19, 1994, 4-6, University Archives, Special Collections Division, The University of Texas at Arlington Libraries; Woolf interview, March 29, 1994, 28. In 1966 and 1967, the school won back-to-back Southland Conference championships in football. In fact, in 1967 its team defeated North Dakota State in the Pecan Bowl by a score of 13-0.

62 Tinker interview, March 16, 1994, 23; *Reveille 1957*, 145-180; *Reveille 1965*, 213-255; *Reveille 1967*, 184-231; Gilstrap interview, April 10, 1994, 10-12.

CHAPTER SEVEN

A Positive Slope Institution

1 *The Shorthorn*, September 22, 1967; for the Woolf quote, see "Prepared Speech [rough draft], March 15, 1967," in "Dr. J. R. Woolf-Office of the President," vertical file, University Archives, Special Collections Division, The University of Texas at Arlington Libraries.

2 *The Shorthorn*, April 26, May 3, 1968.

3 Ibid.; Alan Schup, "Dr. Jack Woolf: A Guiding Influence," *The Engineering Perspective* (Spring 1983), 28.

4 *Dallas Times Herald*, June 29, 1969; *Fort Worth Star-Telegram*, June 29, 1969; The University of Texas at Arlington, [Newsletter], July 1969.

5 "Frank Harrison," vertical file, University Archives, Special Collections Division, The University of Texas at Arlington Libraries; Frank Harrison, interview by Lynn Swann Davis, February 25, 1976, 1-12; *Dallas Times Herald*, June 29, 1969; *The Dallas Morning News*, June 29, 1969. Harrison told the author that he was the third Frank Harrison to arrive on the Arlington campus. His father attended Carlisle Military Academy and his son was a student at Arlington State College.

[6] "Wendell H. Nedderman," vertical file, University Archives, Special Collections Division, The University of Texas at Arlington Libraries; *The Shorthorn*, March 21, April 25, 1969; Office of the Vice President for Academic Affairs Records, Box 3, Folder 7, University Archives, Special Collections Division, The University of Texas at Arlington Libraries; *Fort Worth Star-Telegram*, January 8, 1969; University of Texas at Arlington, [Newsletter], July 1969.

[7] Office of the Vice President for Academic Affairs Records, Box 3, Folders 6-7.

[8] Harrison, interview by Lynn Swann Davis, February 25, 1976, 3-15; "Resolution," in "Frank Harrison," vertical file. For the quote, see Harrison, interview by Gerald Saxon, December 12, 1991, 12-13. During President Woolf's administration, there was an elected Faculty Advisory Committee, which met with him and had an unlimited scope.

[9] University of Texas at Arlington News and Information Office Records, Box 4, Folder 11; *The Dallas Morning News*, January 3, 6, 1969.

[10] Ibid.; see also Tom Vandergriff, interview by Dan Griffith, 23-25.

[11] *Fort Worth Star-Telegram*, May 31, June 13, 1969.

[12] Memorandum to Elwood J. Preiss, February 14, 1975, "Fast Facts," vertical file, University Archives, Special Collections Division, The University of Texas at Arlington Libraries; Head Count of University Enrollment for Previous Five Years by Level and by College, Appendix I, in Self Study, 1971-1974, n.p.

[13] The University of Texas at Arlington, Self-Study, Existing Facilities, [August 31, 1972], 1-4, in University of Texas at Arlington Self-Study Collection, Box 1, Folder 18, University Archives, Special Collections Division, The University of Texas at Arlington Libraries; *The Shorthorn*, January 12, May 10, December 12, 1968; July 4, August 1, December 12, 1969; March 10, 1972; see also Minutes of the President's Advisory Committee, February 2, 1972, in Frank Harrison Papers, Box 2, Folder 13, University Archives, Special Collections Division, The University of Texas at Arlington Libraries. The buildings listed in this paragraph as completed during Harrison's presidency were authorized and planned while Woolf was president.

[14] Jim McClellan, *Old Times There Are Not Forgotten* (October 1968), n.p., in Rebel Theme Controversy Collection, Box 1, Folder 2, University Archives, Special Collections Division, The University of Texas at Arlington Libraries. See also "Chronological History and Events Affecting the School Theme at UT Arlington," in ibid., Box 1, Folder 6; *The Shorthorn*, September 18, 1951.

[15] McClellan, *Old Times There Are Not Forgotten*, n.p.

[16] *The Shorthorn*, April 9, October 29, 1965; March 20, 1970; Rebel Theme Controversy Collection, Box 1, Folders 1-4.

[17] James Frank Wyman, "The Old Fires," *Arlington Review* (Fall 1967), 57-59.

[18] *The Shorthorn*, May 3, 1968; March 20, 1970; McClellan, *Old Times There Are Not Forgotten*, n.p.; *Wall Street Journal*, May 22, 1968.

[19] Rebel Theme Controversy Collection, Box 1, Folders 3-6; Thurman Jasper, interview by Jan Hart, 1976, 19-22, University Archives, Special Collections Division, The University of Texas at Arlington Libraries. *Austin American-Statesman*, December 1, 1968; *San Antonio Express*, November 26, 1968; *Fort Worth Star-Telegram*, November 23, 1968.

[20] UTA News and Information Office Records, Box 15, Folder 19; Rebel Theme Controversy Collection, Box 1, Folder 3; *Reveille 1969*, n.p.

[21] *The Shorthorn*, October 24, 1969; March 20, 1970; Donna Darovich, interview by Don Mitchell, March 24, 1994, 6-7, University Archives, Special Collections Division, The University of Texas at Arlington Libraries.

[22] Frank Harrison Papers, Box 2, Folder 5; *The Shorthorn*, October 24, November 14, 1969; January 9, 1970; "Chronological History and Events Affecting the School Theme at UT Arlington," Rebel Theme Controversy Collection, Box 1, Folder 6.

[23] Rebel Theme Controversy Collection, Box 1, Folders 2, 4.

[24] Ibid., Box 1, Folder 1.

[25] *The Arlington Urbanite*, January 31, 1971; *The Shorthorn*, February 5, 1971; *Arlington Citizen-Journal*, November 5, 1970. For Harrison's quote, see Frank Harrison, interview by Lynn Swan Davis, February 25, 1976, 13.

[26] Rebel Theme Controversy Collection, Box 1, Folders 5-6; "Name Changes," vertical file, University Archives, Special Collections Division, The University of Texas at Arlington Libraries; Donna Darovich, interview by Don Mitchell, 17-18. The Maverick to whom UTA's theme refers is Samuel Augustus Maverick. He came to Texas from South Carolina in 1835 and fought in the Texas Revolution, served as a delegate to the convention held at Washington-on-the-Brazos where Texas independence was declared in 1836, and was a signer of the Texas Declaration of Independence. After the revolution, Maverick, an attorney, invested in Texas land and cattle. He was twice elected mayor of San Antonio, chief justice of Bexar County during the Civil War, and served in the Texas House of Representatives and Senate. His practice of letting his cattle run about unbranded gave the English language the word "maverick," meaning an independent person as well as an unbranded animal. The UTA Maverick symbol implies independence, non-conformity, and a can-do spirit, just like the attributes displayed by Sam Maverick. "Maverick Theme Controversy," vertical file, University Archives, Special Collections Division, The University of Texas at Arlington Libraries; *The Shorthorn*, July 28, 1994.

27 Office of the Vice President for Academic Affairs Records, Box 2, Folder 6.

28 *The Shorthorn*, March 3, September 8, 1972. For the Cary quote, see ibid., November 3, 1972.

29 Ibid., September 8, 1972; "Blacks at UTA," vertical file, University Archives, Special Collections Division, The University of Texas at Arlington Libraries.

30 Frank Harrison, interview by Gerald Saxon, December 12, 1991, 33-34.

31 Ibid., 21; "Wendell H. Nedderman," vertical file.

32 *Fort Worth Star-Telegram*, October 12, 1980; April 30, 1987.

33 Wendell H. Nedderman, interview by Gerald Saxon, October 4, 1991, 3; "Wendell H. Nedderman," vertical file.

34 Office of Institutional Research and Planning, "Ethnic Distribution of Enrollment," unpublished typescript, December 1993; "W. H. Nedderman," vita, found in "Wendell H. Nedderman," vertical file.

35 Donna Darovich, "Nedderman to Retire after 19 Years as UTA President," *Presence* (July 1991), 10. The degree programs added during President Nedderman's administration were as follows. The doctoral programs: mathematical sciences, 1973; biomedical engineering, 1974; administration (business, social work, and urban studies), 1974; humanities, 1974; aerospace engineering, 1982; computer science, 1982; electrical engineering, 1982; materials science, 1982; mechanical engineering, 1982; civil engineering, 1982; computer science and engineering, 1982; industrial engineering, 1982; applied chemistry, 1982; applied physics, 1984; social work, 1984; business administration, 1990; quantitative biology, 1990; and urban and public administration, 1990. With the addition of the doctoral programs in social work, business administration, and urban and public administration, the joint Ph.D. in administration listed above was dropped. The new master's programs included: architecture, 1973; sociology, 1973; computer science, 1973; biomedical engineering (jointly with University of Texas Southwestern Medical Center), 1974; humanities (jointly with University of Texas at Dallas), 1974; masters of arts in teaching, humanities (jointly with UTD), 1974; city and regional planning, 1975; M.A. in interdisciplinary studies, 1975; M.S. in interdisciplinary studies, 1975; aerospace, civil, electrical, industrial, and mechanical engineering, 1977; nursing, 1977; landscape architecture, 1978; criminal justice, 1979; M.S. in computer science engineering, 1982; M. Engr. in computer science and engineering, 1982; taxation, 1983; accounting, 1983; personnel and human resources management, 1985; real estate, 1985; information systems, 1988; teaching, 1988; marketing research, 1988; public administration, 1989; and international studies option (M.A. in political science), 1990. The bachelor's degrees added during Nedderman's tenure include: chemistry, geology, and physics, 1973; economics, 1973; biochemistry, 1973; communication, 1973; nursing, 1976; drama, 1977; computer science and engineering, 1978; microbiology, 1978; social work, 1979; general studies, 1980; applied aeronautics (later dropped), 1981; studio art, 1982; art history, 1982; anthropology, 1982; interior design, 1982; landscape architecture, 1982; computer science, 1982; information systems, 1985; art, 1989; and classical studies, 1989. For these lists see "Wendell H. Nedderman," vertical file.

36 W. A. Baker, interview by Chris Ohan, December 14, 1994, 3-6, University Archives, Special Collections Division, The University of Texas at Arlington Libraries.

37 Ibid., 22-24.

38 Darovich, "Nedderman to Retire after 19 Years as UTA President," 10. The major construction projects completed while Nedderman was president were: Fine Arts Building, 1975; Tennis Center and Creek Beautification, 1975; Activities Building, 1976; utilities expansion, 1977; Business Administration Building, 1977; University Center addition, 1978; University Bookstore, 1978; Maverick Stadium, 1980; Nursing-Math Building, 1982; University Village, 1982; General Services Building, 1983; Engineering Annex, 1983; Thermal Energy Building, 1987; Architecture Building, 1986; University Center addition and renovation, 1987; Engineering Complex, 1987-1988; Advanced Robotics Institute (in Fort Worth), 1987; Cooper Street depression, 1990; Parking Garage, 1986; Science Building addition, 1991; Day Care Center, 1991; and tunnel renovation, 1991. See "The University of Texas at Arlington, Physical Plant Expansion, 1973-1990 [sic]," in "Wendell H. Nedderman," vertical file.

39 Faculty Senate Minutes, May 4, 1977; March 1, 1978; February 3, September 29, 1982; *Arlington Daily News*, February 22, 1981; University of Texas at Arlington News Service Records, Box 16, Folder 5, University Archives, Special Collections Division, The University of Texas at Arlington Libraries.

40 The amendment proposed to bring all UT and A&M system components under PUF for bond proceeds purposes only. Nedderman explained at the time that that meant bonds would have to be issued against PUF and then the proceeds used for construction, renovation, or land acquisition. The repayment of the bonds would come from the income on the principal, which is the available funding. The amendment also raised the ceiling on bonded indebtedness from 20 to 30 percent of the cash value of the endowment at any one given time. This was done to provide more flexibility to accommodate the new institutions brought under PUF. Faculty Senate Minutes, February 1, 1985. See also *Arlington Daily News*, September 2, October 2, 1984; *The Shorthorn*, October 18, 1984. The amendment passed by a 70 to 30 percent margin. See *The Shorthorn*, November 7, 1984.

41 Donna Davorich, "Nedderman, Leader in Dynamic Decade," *The Magazine of UTA* (March 1983), 10.

42 *The Dallas Morning News*, February 20, April 4, 1985; *Fort Worth Star-Telegram*, April 30, 1987.

[43] *The Dallas Morning News*, February 20, 1985; see also "Colleges and Universities, UT-Arlington," clipping file, Texas/Dallas History Division, Central Dallas Public Library, Dallas, Texas.

[44] *The Dallas Morning News*, April 4, 1985; *The Shorthorn*, April 23, 1985.

[45] *The Dallas Morning News*, November 26, 1985. Former UTA president Frank Harrison told this author on March 6, 1995, that he seriously considered ending football in the early seventies because the program was running a deficit of $300,000 a year. He decided not to cancel football for fear of alienating the school's alumni.

[46] "Football Program Demise," vertical file, University Archives, Special Collections Division, The University of Texas at Arlington Libraries; Faculty Senate Minutes, November 27, 1985; *The Shorthorn*, November 14, 26, 1985.

[47] Ibid.

[48] *Arlington Citizen-Journal*, January 1, 1986; "Football Program Demise," vertical file.

[49] Ibid., Wendell Nedderman, interview by Gerald Saxon, 52-54; Wayne Duke, interview by Chris Ohan, December 15, 1994, 10-11, University Archives, Special Collections Division, The University of Texas at Arlington Libraries. Football, of course, was not the first sport to be dropped at UTA. In 1979, the university abolished its swimming team, claiming that it was too costly at a time when the federal government was mandating equity between women and men's sports through Title IX. See *The Shorthorn*, June 6, 1979.

[50] *The Dallas Morning News*, November 25, 1990.

[51] *Fort Worth Star-Telegram*, April 30, 1987; Faculty Senate Minutes, January 28, 1987.

[52] *The Shorthorn*, January 27-30, February 4, 6, 10, 12, 1987.

[53] Ibid., February 19, 1987. Later, when the Select Committee submitted its report to the legislature, the section originally intended to delineate role and scope statements for state universities was omitted. Moreover, in the late 1980s, additional doctoral programs were approved for UTA, bringing the total to eighteen. According to President Nedderman, this established UTA as one of seven universities in the state that could claim to be comprehensive multi-doctoral universities.

[54] Darovich, "Nedderman Leader in Dynamic Decade," 7; *The Dallas Morning News*, December 12, 1970.

[55] *The Shorthorn*, March 27, November 14, 1979; February 14, 19, 1980. For the McDowell quote, see Charles T. McDowell, interview by Woodley Oren Truitt III, April 7, 1994, 17, University Archives, Special Collections Division, The University of Texas at Arlington Libraries.

[56] UTA News and Information Office Records, Box 14, Folders 3-4; UTA News Service Records, Box 21, Folder 2; *Reveille 1976*, 28.

[57] Wendell Nedderman Papers, Box 22, Folder 14, University Archives, Special Collections Division, The University of Texas at Arlington Libraries; Office of the Vice President for Academic Affairs Records, Box 2, Folder 4; UTA News and Information Office Records, Box 14, Folder 3.

[58] Mark Permenter, "Movin Mavs Dazzle Home Crowd with Fourth Straight National Title," *Presence* (Vol. XVI, No. 3), 10-11; Jim Hayes, "Disabled, Handicapped or Neither?", ibid., 8-9; Wayne Duke, interview by Chris Ohan, 4-5, 24.

[59] *The University of Texas at Arlington Fact Book, 1993-1994*, 19; "Wendell H. Nedderman," vertical file.

[60] *The University of Texas at Arlington Fact Book, 1993-1994*, 4, 24; Office of Institutional Research and Planning, "Ethnic Distribution of Enrollment," 93/12, n.p. See also a memo from Linda S. Moxley to Administrative Council Members, Academic Advisors, and Self-Study Steering Committee Members and Chairs, July 14, 1994, 4.

[61] Darovich, "Nedderman to Retire after 19 Years as UTA President," 14.

[62] "Commentary-W. H. Nedderman," in "Wendell H. Nedderman," vertical file.

[63] Wendell Nedderman, interview by Gerald Saxon, 2-3.

[64] Darovich, "Nedderman to Retire after 19 Years as UTA President," 14; W. A. Baker, interview by Chris Ohan, 22-24; Wayne Duke, interview by Chris Ohan, 17. Upon Nedderman's retirement, the board of regents and the Arlington City Council, in recognition of his long service to UTA and the UT system, changed the names of Campus Drive to South Nedderman Drive and Monroe Street to West Nedderman Drive. In addition, the regents changed the name of the Engineering II Building, completed in 1988, to Nedderman Hall.

[65] Wendell Nedderman, interview by Gerald Saxon, 60-61; Darovich, "Nedderman Leader in Dynamic Decade," 10.

CHAPTER EIGHT

Change Is Hard

[1] *The Shorthorn*, April 14, 1992.

[2] Ibid.; *The Dallas Morning News*, July 12, 1992.

[3] Ibid.

[4] Ibid.; "Ryan C. Amacher," vertical file, University Archives, Special Collections Division, The University of Texas at Arlington Libraries.

[5] *The Dallas Morning News*, July 12, 1992.

[6] *Fort Worth Star-Telegram*, September 2, 1992; September 15, 1994; *The Shorthorn*, September 1, October 6, 1992; January 20, February 17, 1993; September 1, October 5, 1994; Faculty Senate Minutes, February 6, 1991, October 30, 1992.

[7] *The Shorthorn*, January 20, 1993; August 30, 1993; Dalmas Taylor, interview by Gerald Saxon, January 4, 1995, 1-12.

[8] *The Dallas Morning News*, February 11, August 27, October 15, 1994; *Fort Worth Star-Telegram*, October 2, 1994; *The Shorthorn*, October 25, 1994; *Communiqué*, December 1994, 1.

[9] Faculty Senate Minutes, April 24, 1985; *The Shorthorn*, October 13, 1993; *The Dallas Morning News*, September 27, 1994; *Fort Worth Star-Telegram*, August 29, 1994.

[10] *The Dallas Morning News*, March 12, 1994; *The Shorthorn*, September 21, 1994.

[11] *Fort Worth Star-Telegram*, March 27, 1994; Ryan C. Amacher, interview by Gerald Saxon, January 3, 1995, 14, University Archives, Special Collections Division, The University of Texas at Arlington Libraries; *Communiqué*, December 1994, [3].

[12] *Fort Worth Star-Telegram*, March 7, 1995; *The Dallas Morning News*, March 7, 1995.

[13] Rebecca Sherman, "Fast Times at UTA," *Dallas Observer*, January 12-18, 1995, 14-29; *Fort Worth Star-Telegram*, January 26, 27, 1995; *The Dallas Morning News*, January 27, 1995.

[14] *The Shorthorn*, February 2, 1995; *Fort Worth Star-Telegram*, February 2, 1995.

[15] The Faculty Senate was following the university system's "Handbook of Operating Procedures," which outlined the process for a vote of confidence in the president. The handbook specified that those faculty members eligible to vote included "instructors with two consecutive years of full-time service, assistant professors, associate professors, and professors." In 1995 the "voting faculty" eligible numbered 578. *Fort Worth Star-Telegram*, February 2, 17, 18, March 3, 28, 1995; *The Shorthorn*, February 17, March 28, 1995.

[16] *Fort Worth Star-Telegram*, March 7, 12, 15, 1995; *The Shorthorn*, March 7, 8, 1995; *Dallas Observer*, March 16-22, 1995, 7, 9.

[17] For the questions asked the provost and his answers, see *Fort Worth Star-Telegram*, March 27, 1995. For information about the meeting, see *The Shorthorn*, March 9, 1995. For the Rosen quote, see *Dallas Observer*, March 16-22, 1995, 9.

[18] *The Shorthorn*, March 28, 1995; *The Dallas Morning News*, March 28, 1995; *Fort Worth Star-Telegram*, March 28, 1995.

[19] *The Dallas Morning News*, March 25, 1995; *Fort Worth Star-Telegram*, March 25, 26, 1995; *The Shorthorn*, March 28, 1995.

[20] Ibid.

[21] Ibid.

[22] *The Dallas Morning News*, May 23, 1995; *Fort Worth Star-Telegram*, May 23, 1995; *The Shorthorn*, June 6, 1995. The audit findings can be found in: The University of Texas System Audit Office, "The University of Texas at Arlington 1995 Management Control Audit" (Austin, n.d.). For the audit's conclusion, see 1, 25-26.

[23] *Communiqué*, November 1994, [1-2]; Faculty Senate Minutes, October 29, 1993.

[24] *Inside UTA*, May 1994, 1, 3; *Fort Worth Star-Telegram*, April 26, 1994; *The University of Texas at Arlington Graduate School News*, December 1994.

BIBLIOGRAPHY

Unless otherwise indicated, the sources listed in the bibliography can be found in the Special Collections Division of The University of Texas at Arlington Libraries. Since the late 1960s, Special Collections has served as the official archives of the university.

Manuscript and Archival Sources

Arlington Citizen-Journal Negative Collection.
Armstrong, Andrew T. Papers.
Cantwell, Donald W. Papers.
Carlisle, James M. Papers.
Carlisle Military Academy Annual Announcements Collection.
Chandler, Pierce. Papers.
Clark, Lloyd. Papers.
Contract Entered into Between the Board of Directors of the Arlington Training School, of the First Part, and H. K. Taylor, of the Second Part. Photocopy.
Denman, Clarence P. Collection.
Dunlop, J. W. Photograph Collection. In Mr. Dunlop's possession, Arlington, Texas.
Dunsworth, H. A. D. Papers.
Ex-Students Association of North Texas Agricultural College Records.
Ex-Students Association Records.
Faculty Senate Minutes, 1975-1995.
Fort Worth Star-Telegram Collection.
Fort Worth, Texas. Tarrant County Courthouse. County Clerk's Office. Deed Record.
Fort Worth, Texas. Tarrant County Courthouse. 17th District Court. Case Papers File.
Fort Worth, Texas. Tarrant County Courthouse. 17th District Court. Minutes of the District Court.
Frazar, Morris. Collection.
Grubbs Family Papers.
Harrison, Frank. Papers.
Index to California Death Records. Microfilm. Genealogy Department, Central Dallas Public Library, Dallas, Texas.
Irons, Colonel Earl D. Papers.
Joyner, Arista. Papers.
Joyner, Howard and Arista. Collection.
Kennard, Don. Papers.
Meier, L. G. Papers.
Nedderman, Wendell. Papers.
Office of the Vice President for Academic Affairs Records.
President's Advisory Committee, Minutes, 1972.
Ransom, W. A. Grade Books.
Rebel Theme Controversy Collection.
Robinson, Duncan. Papers.
Russell, Rusty. Papers.
Smith, W. D. Photograph Collection.
Terrill, James M. and Amelia H. Collection.
University of Texas at Arlington Alumni Association Newspaper Collection.
University of Texas at Arlington Campus Scenes Slide Collection.
University of Texas at Arlington Centennial History Collection.
University of Texas at Arlington Liberal Arts Constituent Council Records.
University of Texas at Arlington Library. Administrative Office Records.
University of Texas at Arlington Library Records.
University of Texas at Arlington News and Information Office Records.
University of Texas at Arlington News Service Photograph Collection.
University of Texas at Arlington News Service Records.
University of Texas at Arlington Office of the Dean of Liberal Arts Records.

University of Texas at Arlington Office of the Presidents Records.
University of Texas at Arlington Office of the Vice President for Academic Affairs (W. A. Baker) Records.
University of Texas at Arlington Photograph Collection.
University of Texas at Arlington Reserve Officers' Training Corps Scrapbook Collection.
University of Texas at Arlington Self-Study Collection.
University of Texas at Arlington Underground Newspapers Collection.
University of Texas at Arlington Women's Center Records.
Whitt, Kenneth L. Papers.
Williamson, Robert L. Papers.
Wilson, Glenn O. Collection.
Woolf, Jack Royce. Papers.

INTERVIEWS

Amacher, Ryan C. Interviews by Gerald Saxon, January 3, April 18, 1995.
Baker, W. A. Interview by Chris Ohan, December 13, 1994.
Bardin, William. Interview by Jerry Stafford, April 7, 1994.
Barksdale, E. C. Interview by Duncan Robinson, March 18, 1974.
Barnes, B. C. Interviews by Duncan Robinson, January 29, February 28, 1974.
Bearden, Burley. Interview by Duncan Robinson, August 17, 1978.
Betzel, Alvin. Interview by Duncan Robinson, September 9, 1975.
Boon, J. D. Interview by Duncan Robinson, February 8, 1977.
Burdett, Roy M. Interview by Elton Smith, June 1975.
Burkholder, Daniel. Interview by Chandler Jackson, April 10, 1994.
Darovich, Donna. Interview by Don Mitchell, March 24, 1994.
Duke, Wayne. Interview by Chris Ohan, December 15, 1994.
Dunsworth, H. A. D. Interview by Duncan Robinson, September 26, 1973.
Dycus, John W. Interview by Bobbye Wade, June 10, 1994.
Estes, Dorothy. Interview by Bobbye Wade, April 11, 1994.
Estes, Emory D. Interview by Mike Brown, April 19, 1994.
Estes, Emory; Swadley, Don; Blakney, Paul; Sutherland, Tom. Group interview by Duncan Robinson, March 2, 1973.
Ford, Jeanne. Interview by Allen Langford, April 8, 1994.
Garrett, Jenkins. Interviews by Gerald Saxon, August 28, September 11, 27, October 25, November 1, 13, December 11, 1990.
Gilstrap, Claude R. "Chena." Interview by Duncan Robinson, July 10, 1978.
Gilstrap, Claude R. "Chena." Interview by Rebekah Bandy, April 10, 1994.
Hamlett, Samuel B. Interview by June Dalrymple, March 31, 1994.
Hammack, Melba. Interview by Duncan Robinson, November 18, 1975.
Harrington, Alberta. Interview by Duncan Robinson, July 30, 1973.
Harrison, Frank. Interview by Gerald Saxon, December 12, 1991.
Harrison, Frank. Interview by Lynn Swann Davis, February 25, 1976.
Hughes, Martha. Interview by Mike Cochran, 1970.
Hughes, Martha and W. L. Hughes. Interview by Duncan Robinson, January 31, 1974.
Irons, Mrs. Earl D. Interview by Duncan Robinson, October 22, 1974.
Jasper, Thurman. Interview by Jan Hart, 1976.
Joyner, Howard. Interview by John Konzal, March 25, 1994.
Joyner, Howard and Arista. Interview by Duncan Robinson, March 25, 1974.
Keltner, Colonel Edgar. Interview by Duncan Robinson, November 14, 1973.
Killough, M. N. Interview by Kenneth Whitt, July 9, 1969.
McDowell, Charles T. Interview by Woodley Oren Truitt III, April 7, 1994.
Meier, L. G. Interview by Duncan Robinson, December 14, 1977.
Nedderman, Wendell. Interviews by Duncan Robinson, April 18, 27, May 29, 1977.
Nedderman, Wendell. Interview by Gerald Saxon, October 14, 1991.
O'Neal, Cothburn. Interviews by Duncan Robinson, March 14, 21, 1975.
Preiss, Elwood. Interview by Chris Ohan, December 20, 1994.

Ramsey, Zelda. Interview by Duncan Robinson, March 28, 1974.

Ramsey, Zelda. Interview by Susan Smith, April 14, 1994.

Richards, C. D. Interview by Duncan Robinson, February 26, 1974.

Russell, Rusty. Interview by Richard Culbertson, March 19, 1994.

Saxe, Allan. Interview by Wayne Nichols, April 4. 1994.

Shupee, George. Interview by Duncan Robinson, February 17, 1977.

Slaughter, Richard L. Interviews by Duncan Robinson, November 8, 27, 1973.

Smith, Frank. Interview by Duncan Robinson, November 20, 1975.

Smith, G. Elton. Interviews by Duncan Robinson, June 25, July 30, 1974.

Springer, Lloyd Randolph. Interview by Duncan Robinson. April 18, 1973.

Taylor, Dalmas. Interview by Gerald Saxon, January 4, 1995.

Tinker, Thomas J. Interview by J. Eric Oglesby, March 16, 1994.

Vandergriff, Tom. Interview by Dan Griffith, April 21, 1994.

Vickery, Ione. Interview by Duncan Robinson, September 16, 1977.

Vincent, Ella V. Interview by Duncan Robinson, December 14, 1977.

Watkins, George E. Interview by Duncan Robinson, February 14, 1977.

Wetsel, Dudley. Interview by Chris Ohan, December 19, 1994.

Wilemon, Marcella. Interview by Diana Mays, April 6, 1994.

Witt, Robert E. Interview by Gerald Saxon, April 28, 1995.

Woolf, Jack. Interview by Lynn Swann Davis, 1975.

Woolf, Jack. Interview by Neil Simmons, March 29, 1994.

Wyatt, James L. Interview by Duncan Robinson, July 2, 1974.

Yates, Frank. Interview by Duncan Robinson, February 28, 1973.

PUBLISHED PRIMARY SOURCES

Annual Report of the North Texas Agricultural College, 1923-1949.

The Arlington College Exponent, January 1901.

Arlington Review, 1962-1973.

Arlington State College. *The Arlington State College Self-Study*. Arlington, Texas, 1963.

Arlington State College, Annual Catalogue, 1950-1967.

Arlington State College Faculty Newsletter, 1963-1966.

Arlington Training School Catalog, 1913-1915.

Arlington Training School. Senior Class. *The Blue Bonnet*. 1915.

Bulletin of the Grubbs Vocational College, 1917-1922.

Bulletin of the North Texas Agricultural College, 1923-1949.

Carlisle Military Academy Annual Announcements, 1904-1912.

Gammel, H. P. N. *The Laws of Texas, 1822-1897*. 10 vols. Austin: The Gammel Book Co., 1898.

Gammel, H. P. N. *The Laws of Texas, Supplement Volume to the Original Ten Volumes, 1822-1897*. 22 vols. Austin The Gammel Book Co., 1902-1927.

Grubbs Vocational College, Preliminary Announcements, Session 1917-18. Arlington, Texas.

Joint Legislative Committee on Organization and Economy and Griffenhagen and Associates. *Part XI—Education: The Agricultural and Mechanical College of Texas and its Affiliates*. December 31, 1932.

Junior Aggie, 1923-1950.

Kooken, John A. *Memoirs: Thirty Friendly Years with Arlington Public Schools*. Arlington: The Citizen, 1941.

McDowell, Charles T. "1958-1968: A Decade of Change." Typescript, January 3, 1969.

Phillips' Little Giant Vest Pocket Guide and Business Directory of Arlington, Texas. Fort Worth: Beaumont and Purdom, Printers, 1894.

Prism, 1970-1971.

Reveille, 1950-1980.

Sam Street's Map of Tarrant County Texas. Fort Worth: Texas Map Publishing Company, 1895.

The Texas A&M University System, Annual Report of the Chancellor, 1963-1965.

Texas Legislature. *Journal of the House of Representatives*. Austin: Von Boeckmann-Jones, 1895-1995.

Texas Legislature. *Journal of the Senate of Texas*. Austin: State Printers, 1895-1994.

University of Texas at Arlington. *Fact Book, 1993-1994.* Typescript, 1994.

University of Texas System Audit Office. "The University of Texas at Arlington 1995 Management Control Audit." Austin, n.d.

Vernon's Annotated Revised Civil Statutes of the State of Texas. Kansas City, Missouri: Vernon Law Book Company, 1949-c.

NEWSPAPERS, NEWSLETTERS, AND MAGAZINES

Arlington Citizen, 1937-1969.
Arlington Citizen-Journal, 1973-1993.
Arlington Daily News, 1966-1980.
Arlington Daily News Texan, 1958-1959.
Arlington Journal, 1895-1969.
The Arlington Urbanite, 1970-1971.
Austin American-Statesman, 1965-1972.
Communiqué, 1994-1995.
The Dallas Morning News, 1895-1995.
Dallas Observer, 1994-1995.
Dallas Times Herald, 1917-1990.
Farmers' Fireside Bulletin, April 11, 1917.
Fort Worth Star-Telegram, 1917-1995.
Houston Post, 1900-1924.
Inside UTA, Faculty/Staff Newsletter, 1986-1994.
Presence, 1988-1994.
San Antonio Express, 1965-1972.
The Shorthorn, 1919-1995.
The University of Texas at Arlington Graduate School News, 1994-1995.
The University of Texas at Arlington, [Newsletter], 1969-1980.
UTA Magazine, 1994-1995.
UTA: The Magazine of The University of Texas at Arlington, 1978-1987.

SECONDARY SOURCES

"Amacher, Ryan C." Vertical file.

"Blacks at UTA." Vertical file.

Burke, Jack W., IV. "Arlington State College's Unsuccessful, Successful Integration." Unpublished paper, May 1994.

"Carlisle, James M." Vertical file.

Carney, Carolyn. "Splendid Citizens: Social Values and Population Change in Early Arlington." Paper presented at the Re-discovering Arlington's Heritage Conference, The University of Texas at Arlington, April 23, 1994.

Daniell, L. E. *Personnel of the Texas State Government.* San Antonio: Maverick Printing House, 1892.

"Davis, Dean E. E." Vertical file.

"Dr. J. R. Woolf—Office of the President." Vertical file.

Duren, Almetris Marsh. *Overcoming: A History of Black Integration at the University of Texas at Austin.* Austin: University of Texas Press, 1979.

"The Early Years and the Making of a School." Unpublished typescript produced by The University of Texas at Arlington's Military Science Department, ca.1993.

"Fast Facts." Vertical file.

"Football Program Demise." Vertical file.

"Four-Year Status." Vertical file.

"Grubbs, V. W." Vertical file.

"Hammond, L. M." Vertical file.

"Harrison, Frank." Vertical file.

"Hereford, E. H." Vertical file.

"History of North Texas Agricultural College." Vertical file.

Hudspeth, Junia Evans. "A History of North Texas Agricultural College." Masters thesis, Southern Methodist University, 1935.

Kaufman County Historical Commission. *A History of Kaufman County*. Dallas: Taylor Publishing Company, 1978.

"Maverick Theme Controversy." Vertical file.

"Military-ROTC." Vertical file.

Montgomery, Robert L. "Are Money and Planning Enough?" *The Texas Observer* (January 8, 1965):1-5.

"Name Changes." Vertical file.

"Nedderman, Wendell H." Vertical file.

Office of Institutional Research and Planning. "Ethnic Distribution of Enrollment." Unpublished typescript, December 1993.

Paddock, B. B. *History of Central and Western Texas*. 2 vols. Chicago: Lewis Publishing Company, 1911.

Reports of Subcommittees of the Central Investigating Committees of the House and Senate, Third Called Session of the Thirty-fifth Legislature of Texas, Including Audits. Austin: Von Boeckmann-Jones Co., Printers, 1919.

Schup, Alan. "Dr. Jack Woolf: A Guiding Influence." *The Engineering Perspective* (Spring 1983): 28.

"Trimble, William M." Vertical file.

Wall Street Journal, 1968.

Webb, Walter Prescott, et. al. *The Handbook of Texas*. 3 vols. Austin, Texas: Texas State Historical Association, 1952-1976.

White, Lee Wayne. "Popular Education and the State Superintendent of Public Instruction in Texas, 1860-1899." Ph.D. dissertation, The University of Texas at Austin, 1974.

Whitt, Kenneth. "A Brief Biography of M. L. Williams." Unpublished typescript, in "Myron Lawson Williams," Vertical file.

Whitt, Kenneth. "The Shorthorn, 1919-1969: A History of a Student Newspaper." Masters thesis, The University of Texas at Arlington, 1970.

"Williams, Myron Lawson." Vertical file.

ILLUSTRATION CREDITS

1.1 *Sam Street's Map of Tarrant County Texas* (Fort Worth: Texas Map Publishing Co., 1895); Howard and Arista Joyner Collection, AR195-OS123-1; Clarence P. Denman Collection, AR199-OS125-25.

1.2 J. W. Dunlop Photograph Collection.

1.3 Dunlop Collection.

1.4 Howard and Arista Joyner Collection, AR195-OS123-1.

1.5 University of Texas at Arlington Photograph Collection (hereafter referred to as UTAPC), AR324-1-4.

1.6 UTAPC, AR324-1-9.

1.7 UTAPC, AR324-1-1.

1.8 Denman Collection, AR199-OS125-25.

1.9 Denman Collection, AR199-OS126-p4.

1.10 Denman Collection, AR199-OS125-12.

2.1 Dunlop Collection.

2.2 Denman Collection, AR199-OS126-p1.

2.3 Carlisle Military Academy, *The Tenth Annual Announcement 1911-1912*, found in Denman Collection, AR199-OS125-6.

2.4 Denman Collection, AR199-OS126-p31; quote from *The Fourth Annual Announcement 1906-1907*, found in Denman Collection, AR199-OS125-4.

2.5 Denman Collection, AR199-OS126-p21.

2.6 Denman Collection, AR199-OS126-p3.

2.7 Dunlop Collection.

2.8 UTAPC, AR324-1-25; quote from *The Tenth Annual Announcement 1911-1912*, found in Denman Collection, AR199-OS125-6.

2.9 Illustration and quote from *The Tenth Annual Announcement 1911-1912*, found in Denman Collection, AR199-OS125-6.

2.10 Dunlop Collection; UTA Artifact 62.

2.11 Denman Collection, AR199-OS126-p15.

2.12 *The Tenth Annual Announcement 1911-1912*, found in Denman Collection, AR199-OS125-6.

2.13 Morris Frazar Collection, GA149.

2.14 *The Tenth Annual Announcement 1911-1912*, found in Denman Collection, AR199-OS125-6.

3.1 Lloyd Clark Papers, AR352-25-14; quote from Arlington Training School, *Announcements 1915-16,* found in Denman Collection, AR199-OS125-17.

3.2 Denman Collection, AR199-OS125-25.

3.3 *Announcements 1915-16*, found in Denman Collection, AR199-OS125-17.

3.4 *Announcements 1915-16,* found in Denman Collection, AR199-OS125-17.

3.5 Photograph and quote from *Announcements 1915-16*, found in Denman Collection, AR199-OS125-17.

3.6 Dunlop Collection; citation from Arlington Training School, *The Blue Bonnet,* found in Denman Collection, AR199-OS125-18.

3.7 Photograph and quote from *Announcements 1915-16*, found in Denman Collection, AR199-OS125-17.

3.8 *Announcements 1915-16*, found in Denman Collection, AR199-OS125-17.

3.9 Photograph and quote from *Announcements 1915-16*, found in Denman Collection, AR199-OS125-17.

3.10 *Announcements 1915-16*, found in Denman Collection, AR199-OS125-17.

3.11 Denman Collection, AR199-OS125-25.

3.12 UTAPC, AR324-1-24.

3.13 Denman Collection, AR199-OS125-15.

4.1 UTAPC, AR324-OS180-8.

4.2 UTAPC, AR324-OS181-1.

4.3 UTAPC, AR324-OS180-1.

4.4 UTAPC, AR324-OS180-5.

4.5 UTAPC, AR324-OS181-3.

4.6 UTAPC, AR324-OS181-2.

4.7 *Junior Aggie*, 1924.

4.8 UTAPC, AR324-OS180-1.

4.9 UTAPC, AR324-OS180-7.

4.10 UTAPC, AR324-OS181-10.

4.11 UTAPC, AR324-OS180-5; quote from *Bulletin of the Grubbs Vocational College*, Vol. IV, No. 4, Arlington, Texas, July 1921.

4.12 UTAPC, AR324-OS180-5; quote from *Bulletin of the Grubbs Vocational College*, Vol. IV, No. 4, Arlington, Texas, July 1921.

4.13 UTAPC, AR324-OS181-8.

4.14 UTAPC, AR324-OS180-4.

4.15 UTAPC, AR324-OS180-5.

4.16 James M. and Amelia H. Terrill Collection, AR212-1-2.

4.17 UTAPC, AR324-OS180-5.

4.18 UTAPC, AR324-OS180-3.

4.19 UTA Artifact 40.

4.20 UTA Artifact 63.

4.21 UTAPC, AR324-OS181-4.

4.22 UTAPC, AR324-OS181-5; citation from *Bulletin of the Grubbs Vocational College*, Vol. VI, No. 4, Arlington, Texas, June 1923.

5.1 UTAPC, AR324-2-15.

5.2 Gordon Smith, student 1945-1946, W. D. Smith Inc., Commercial Photography, Fort Worth, Texas.

5.3 Denman Collection, AR199-OS126-1.

5.4 UTAPC, AR324-2-8.

5.5 UTAPC, AR324-2-8.

5.6 UTAPC, AR324-2-10.

5.7 UTAPC, AR324-2-20, envelope 8, no. 6.

5.8 UTAPC, AR324-3-5.

5.9 *Junior Aggie*, 1935.

5.10 UTAPC, AR324-2-20, envelope 8, no. 6.

5.11 *Fort Worth Star-Telegram* Collection, folder "Arlington State College, 1949-1967"; quote from *Junior Aggie*, 1937.

5.12 *Junior Aggie,* 1929.

5.13 *Bulletin of the North Texas Agricultural College,* Fall 1942.

5.14 *Junior Aggie*, 1944; UTAPC, AR324-2-20, envelope 8, no. 36.

5.15 *Junior Aggie*, 1949.

5.16 Howard and Arista Joyner Collection, AR195-OS123-10.

5.17 *Junior Aggie*, 1941.

5.18 *Junior Aggie*, 1943.

5.19 Quote and photograph from *Junior Aggie*, 1938.

5.20 *Junior Aggie*, 1941.

5.21 Ex-Students Association Records, AR216-1-11.

5.22 UTAPC, AR324-2-13.

5.23 UTAPC, AR324-3-1, envelope 10, no. 15; quote from *Bulletin of the North Texas Agricultural College*, Summer and Fall, 1943.

5.24 UTA Artifact 46.

5.25 UTAPC, AR324-2-14; NTAC window sticker courtesy of Virginia Stanford (Deis).

5.26 Photograph and quote from *Bulletin of the North Texas Agricultural College*, August 1942.

6.1 "Junior Rose Bowl," Vertical File, Special Collections Divison, The University of Texas at Arlington Libraries.

6.2 The University of Texas at Arlington News Service Photograph Collection (hereafter referred to as UTANS).

6.3 UTAPC, AR324-3-15.

6.4 UTAPC, AR324-3-13.

6.5 *Reveille*, 1953.

6.6 UTAPC, AR324-4-29.

6.7 UTANS.

6.8 *Reveille*, 1962.

6.9 UTANS.

6.10 Photograph and quote from *Reveille*, 1963.

6.11 UTAPC, AR324-5-17.

6.12 *Reveille*, 1953.

6.13 *Reveille*, 1960.

6.14 UTAPC, AR324-OS181-14; quote from Elwood Preiss as stated to the author.

6.15 *Reveille,* 1963.

6.16 UTAPC, AR324-4-24.

6.17 *Reveille*, 1963.

6.18 UTAPC, AR324-5-14.

6.19 UTANS.

6.20 UTANS.

6.21 UTANS.

6.22 UTAPC, AR324-3-10.

6.23 *Reveille*, 1962.

6.24 *Reveille*, 1958.

6.25 UTAPC, 324-3-17.

6.26 University of Texas at Arlington Athletic Department; flag courtesy Bobby Lane.

6.27 *Reveille*, 1957.

6.28 *Reveille*, 1956; *Reveille*, 1955.

6.29 *Reveille*, 1961.

7.1 UTANS.

7.2 *Reveille*, 1971.

7.3 *Reveille*, 1969.

7.4 *Reveille*, 1969.

7.5 UTAPC, AR324-5-20.

7.6 UTANS.

7.7 Rebel Theme Controversy Collection, AR232-1-7.

7.8 Rebel Theme Controversy Collection, AR232-1-7.

7.9 Rebel Theme Controversy Collection, AR232-1-7.

7.10 UTANS.

7.11 UTANS.

7.12 UTANS.

7.13 *Reveille*, 1975.

7.14 *Reveille*, 1977.

7.15 Courtesy Dudley Wetsel.

7.16 *Reveille*, 1981.

7.17 UTANS.

7.18 UTANS.

7.19 UTANS.

7.20 UTANS.

7.21 UTANS.

7.22 Slide Collection, Special Collections Division, The University of Texas at Arlington Libraries.

7.23 *Reveille*, 1974.

7.24 *Reveille*, 1971.

7.25 *Reveille*, 1980.

7.26 *Reveille*, 1980.

7.27 *Arlington Citizen-Journal* Negative Collection, 92-47, September 24, 26, 28, 1975, Special Collections Division, The University of Texas at Arlington Libraries.

7.28 UTANS.

7.29 UTANS.

7.30 UTANS.

7.31 UTANS.

7.32 UTANS.

7.33 UTANS.

8.1 UTANS.

8.2 UTANS.

8.3 UTANS.

8.4 UTANS.

8.5 *The Shorthorn*.

8.6 UTANS.

8.7 *The Shorthorn,* illustration: Dale Taylor.

8.8 *The Shorthorn*.

8.9 *The Shorthorn*.

8.10 *The Shorthorn*; Office for Students with Disabilities.

8.11 *Fort Worth Star-Telegram,* photograph: Bruce Maxwell.

8.12 *Fort Worth Star-Telegram*.

8.13 *The Shorthorn*.

8.14 *The Shorthorn*.

8.15 UTAPC 324-1-14; Glenn Patterson, Sky Cam Aerial and Commercial Photography, Krum, Texas.

8.16 UTANS.

8.17 *The Shorthorn*.

INDEX

N

Nacogdoches, Texas, 36, 54
Nader, Ralph, 130
National Association for the Advancement of Colored
    People (NAACP), 87, 88, 146
National Defense Program, 63
National Guard, 18
National Hockey League, 143
National Inter-Collegiate ROTC Match, 46
Native Americans, 119
Navy, 64
NCAA Division I, 131
Nedderman, Betty, 120
Nedderman Drive, 172n.64
Nedderman, Wendell, 90, 109, 119-121, 122, 123, 124, 125,
    126, 127, 128, 129, 130, 132-134, 140, 142, 143,
    172n.64
Nelson, Wallace B., 91
Nelson, Willie, 130
Netherby, James H., 24
Newton, John, 92
Nichols, Marvin C., 93, 95
Nitty Gritty Dirt Band, 130
North Fort Worth, Texas, 3
North Texas Agricultural College, 48, 53, 54, 73, 74;
    athletics at, 70-72; curriculum at, 55, 56; depression's
    impact on, 57-58; enrollment, 57, 58, 61, 63, 64, 65;
    faculty, 54-55, 58; fees at, 56-57, 66; first president of,
    65; gateway, 55; move to change name, 68; physical
    plant, 54-55; push for four-year status, 66-67; student
    behavior, 72-73, 74; student life, 68-70; threats to the
    school, 58-61; World War II impact on, 62-64
North Texas State College, 65, 85, 94, 96, 127
"Northaggieland," 53, 71
Northwest State Teachers' College, 21
Northwestern University, 108
nursing, 78
Nursing-Math Building, 171n.38

O

O'Neal, Cothburn, 56, 65
Oak Cliff College, 28
Oak Cliff, Texas, 28
Oenaville, Texas, 38
Office for Students with Disabilities, 131
Ogden, Mrs. F. G., 88
Ohan, Chris, 152
Olympics, 109
Okinawa, 120
Oklahoma State University, 91
Old South Days, 84, 113, 136
Oliver, Jesse, 168n.24
Orange, Texas, 123

orchestra, 44
Organization of Arab Students, 129
Owen, Ruth Bryan, 70
Owsley, Clarence, 26

P

Pachl, Delmar, 79, 80
Pachl Hall, 78-79, 80
Palley, Nevin, 83
Palmer, Stanley, 127
Panic of 1907, 14
parade grounds, 33
parades, 78, 101
Paris Junior College, 70
Park Row, 65, 79
Parkhouse, George, 85
parking fees, 80
Parking Garage, 171n.38
parking lots, 80
Pasadena, California, 101, 102
Paschal High School, 74
Paul Helms Trophy, 102
Paxton, Orsen, 65
Peacock Military Academy of Dallas, 70
Pearl Harbor, 62
Pearl, Minnie, 69
Pecan Bowl, 169n.61
"pecan specialist," 39
penmanship, 10
Pennsylvania State University, 148
pep rallies, 101
Pepper, Lieutenant Kelton L., 14
Perkins, Frances, 70
Permanent University Fund (PUF), 79, 123, 124, 171n.40
Peterson, L. F., 92
petroleum engineering, 61, 78
Peveto, Wayne, 123
Phi Kappa Theta, 69
Philippines, 120
Phillips, Lou Diamond, 133
philosophy, 90
physical education, 23, 39, 40, 51, 78, 84, 90
Physical Education Building, 79, 80
physics, 11, 23, 38, 39, 63, 84, 90, 99
physiology, 23
Pi Mu Club, 69
Pickard Hall, 113
picnics, 47
Pilant, Cora, 161n.11
pilot training program, 63
Pioneer Conference, 101, 103
Planetarium, 104
police, 104
political economy, 11

X

Y

Z